RETHINKING RESIDENTIAL CHILD CARE

Positive perspectives

Mark Smith

This edition published in Great Britain in 2009 by

The Policy Press
University of Bristol
Fourth Floor
Beacon House
Queen's Road
Bristol BS8 1QU
UK

Tel +44 (0)117 331 4054
Fax +44 (0)117 331 4093
e-mail tpp-info@bristol.ac.uk
www.policypress.org.uk

North American office:
The Policy Press
c/o International Specialized Books Services (ISBS)
920 NE 58th Avenue, Suite 300
Portland, OR 97213-3786, USA
Tel +1 503 287 3093
Fax +1 503 280 8832
e-mail info@isbs.com

© The Policy Press 2009

British Library Cataloguing in Publication Data
A catalogue record for this book is available from the British Library.

Library of Congress Cataloging-in-Publication Data
A catalog record for this book has been requested.

ISBN 978 1 86134 908 8 paperback
ISBN 978 1 86134 909 5 hardcover

Cover design by Qube Design Associates, Bristol.
Front cover: image kindly supplied by www.alamy.com
Printed and bound in Great Britain by TJ International, Padstow.

This book is dedicated to the De La Salle Brothers, my first and best teachers in residential child care, and to Onanda Randall, a much loved colleague and friend, who died too soon. She said she would like to write a book. It wouldn't have been dull....

Contents

Foreword

It is ironic that as the first decade of the 21st century is nearing its end, we are encouraged to rethink residential child care. The irony is not because of any dramatic changes in residential child care per se but because of the discourses that have attempted to rid child welfare services of residential child care. Some have argued that all residential or institutional services are oppressive and should no longer be included among the variety of service options available to families or to health, education and welfare professionals. Such arguments are commonly put forward by so-called scholars who have never, ever worked with troubled or troublesome children and young people in residential child care. Theirs is an opinion allegedly informed through research about residential child care, not through practice research located from within the worlds where looked-after children and young people live. Theirs is a language filled with a discourse on outcomes and graphic claims offered by the disaffected. Rarely have they listened to life stories told by those who found respite, solace, opportunities and emotional commitment through relationships offered through positive residential child care experiences.

For all of these reasons it is timely for an intellectual stocktake and an opportunity to rethink residential child care. In the first place, residential care and education are among the oldest forms of human service ever to have been established. The first social work training dates from the late 19th century when the National Children's Home introduced in-service training for its carers. Residential child care is also the most internationally used of all health, education and welfare services with residential provisions of various sizes – from smaller, localised facilities to large-scale villages – located throughout the world, in so-called developed countries as well as in those others described as developing. Residential child care caters for the nation's most vulnerable or challenging children and young people, who are still most commonly looked after by that nation's least formally qualified people. There remains a strongly held view that real care cannot be taught and that the best carers are those who are 'born' with innate capacities and abilities to provide nurturing care. It is timely that all of these assumptions should be subjected to a systematic rethink.

Those who argue against the use of residential child care frequently omit residential schools from the list of services they would target for closure. Here one is not only referring to residential schools for troubled and troublesome children or young people but also residential schools favoured by the economic elite who for generations have sought an exclusive education for their children. Private, public and independent sectors have all become blurred in recent times, even as the characteristics of living and learning environments such as these remain the same: shared living and learning within groups where the organisational characteristics of service delivery revolve around social interactions within a 168-hour week (24 hours a day × 7 days per week) over the course of academic terms, school years and school careers.

Considerable debate has prevailed around residential child care since the 1970s, centred primarily on political ideologies of caring, and it can be seen how various social policy imperatives have impacted on residential child care. Such imperatives have been largely derived from six ideological tenets – *normalisation, de-institutionalisation, mainstreaming, minimal intervention, diversion* and *use of the least restrictive environment* – and each of these ideologies has had a major impact on residential child care during the past quarter-century. Normalisation promoted culturally normative services where participation in atypical, segregated or specialised environments with other *socially devalued persons* was considered detrimental to personal development. De-institutionalisation was aligned closely with normalisation fuelling efforts to close residential services in favour of community-based alternatives. Mainstreaming challenging young people within normative learning environments and in the least restrictive environments offered politically correct opportunities for policy makers. However, all too often the performance of these young people contributed to an ongoing litany of failure, not because these children failed but because the system found it impossible to address their particular and specialised needs. Diversion of young people away from 'the system' and minimal intervention all too often simply delayed the inevitable. Far too many of these young people have ended up contributing to significant increases in young offender populations in prisons. Ideological correctness simply reinforced new forms of Social Darwinism, where failure of the care system gets blamed on individuals who do not take advantage of the freedom and opportunities given to them.

At the core of all this has been the argument that residential child care is too costly, and that more cost-efficient approaches should be used. Still others have argued that the very notion of 'care' is oppressive, favouring the introduction of a new language of corporate parenting and looked-after status rather than focusing on kinship care or out-of-home placements. It is certainly the case that younger children, those under the age of 12, are much less likely to be placed in residential child care than ever before. More often younger looked-after children are placed in foster care, where there are far more opportunities than previously for carefully monitored and supervised foster care placements. Most young people placed in residential child care are aged between 12 and 18 years. This begs the question as to why we continue to use the language of 'residential child care' and not 'residential child and youth care'. These issues, too, are worthy of a rethink, since developmental and educational issues for young people present their own specialised arguments and discourse.

Mark Smith is ideally situated to facilitate this rethink of residential child care. As a parent with an extensive professional career as a residential child care worker and manager, Mark has lived experience of working alongside countless children and young people who have taught him important lessons that are rarely learned through reading books or analysing data. As a researcher of residential child care practice, Mark brings a particular awareness of the issues involved in daily caring for looked-after children and young people. Having worked with the more challenging of characters, Mark also knows what is required to get alongside these characters and to influence such young people towards new pathways and careers. As a teacher and educator of residential child care workers and managers, Mark has engaged with those who are seeking to make a difference in this challenging sector of the human services. His commitment to an examination of philosophies of caring as well as concerns about the pragmatics of caring provide a unique perspective that is rarely found in the contemporary residential child care literature.

The rethink that Mark encourages in what follows is located in the real world of residential child care. It is a bold undertaking and one that Mark takes on with determination and sensitivity. Those whose minds are already made up about the future of residential child care will have to step back and reconsider the substantive arguments found in this volume. Those seeking reaffirmation will find much to admire in the clarity and sensitivity of Mark's writing. But most of all, looked-after and accommodated children and young people – those living in out-of-home care – are likely to be the major beneficiaries of this rethink. The policy agenda is set out in the Scottish Government's *We Can and Must Do Better*, and elsewhere in the UK in *Every Child Matters*. *Rethinking residential child care* goes a long way towards putting flesh around the bones of these distinctive policy agendas and will be a must-read for policy makers, managers and practitioners alike. I recommend this volume without reservation.

Leon C. Fulcher, MSW, PhD
International Child and Youth Care Consultant
September 2008

Introduction

Back in 1981, having just graduated, I was whiling away my time working in a bar. I had an idea that I wanted to teach, but at that time history teachers were ten-a-penny. My mum was more concerned than I was that I should get a real job and spotted an ad in the local evening newspaper for a temporary residential social worker in what was then called a 'List D' school, the successors in Scotland to approved schools. So I applied, was offered a one-year contract and, as often happens in such cases, I stayed.

I was one of those characters who by today's standards should not have got anywhere near residential child care. I was 22, with a degree in modern history and absolutely no relevant experience. I had spent my spare time at university playing football rather than engaging in the kind of voluntary work that might have indicated some predisposition towards a career in social work. In fact I had little idea what social work was.

As soon as I walked through the gates of St Joseph's, however, I picked up a strong sense that this was for me. This was confirmed by the interview itself, which, contrary to assumptions of recruitment in days gone by as being perfunctory and nepotistic, was professional and thorough, involving a range of internal and external representatives. One of the questions I was asked was whether I had ever been sent off playing football, which I hadn't. In these days of heightened scrutiny for prospective residential workers I can't help but think that questions such as this are every bit as likely to provide relevant insights into an individual's qualities as the barrage of psychometric tests that are increasingly utilised.

I have a lingering suspicion, in fact, that one of the reasons I was appointed to the post was due to my interest in football. The school football team, captained by the head of education, was in need of a 'youth policy'. Looking back I would confidently justify appointments on such grounds. As I discuss later in this book, the football team can be the most powerful intervention in the life of any residential school. It is an interesting reflection on how residential child care is perceived that recruitment processes often target individuals who want to counsel children around their difficulties, rather than run around a park with them. Again, I will elaborate on this point as the book progresses.

Like everyone else, I was thrown in at the deep end of residential care. Two of us, along with a housemother, were responsible for the running of a 'cottage' housing 20 boys. The dining hall where the whole school came together for lunch involved two members of staff patrolling 60 boys. I started off with the naive belief that if I was reasonable with the boys, firm but fair, I would get their respect. This is a conceit shared by many who have never worked in residential child care. Irrespective of how reasonable or fair you might be, this doesn't absolve you from gratuitous insult, inviting you to prove your mettle, indeed, demanding that you do so. There were times when I questioned if I would ever get to the stage that more experienced staff had reached, where boys seemed to go along with their requests. Despite the bad days, though, I always felt that this was for me. I felt what might be thought of as an old-fashioned sense of vocation; residential child care became part of who I was. Leanne-Rose Sladde, a Canadian child care worker, states 'I am a child and youth care worker'. Not, 'I work in child and youth care', or 'I do it for a living' but 'I am'.

Anyway, over the years, I settled in to my role, gained the kind of authority and confidence with boys that I had doubted I ever would and after four years on the job went back to university to do social work training. I had little inclination to do what was then called 'field social work', something that training did nothing to alter. So I returned to my old school for another couple of years.

I moved on to an assistant head's post in another List D school, where the culture was quite different. The first school I worked in was run by a teaching order, the De La Salle Brothers. There was little sense of hierarchy or positional authority, but the Brothers inspired an intense loyalty and followership. Their leadership was rooted in values of human dignity and respect, of discipline but also of forgiveness.

The school I moved to placed a greater emphasis on systems and procedures. I was initially impressed by the sense of order that seemed to prevail. However, I soon became aware that attempts to ensure control through systems and procedures were not as effective as I had at first thought. One procedure invariably conflicted with another and staff got themselves tied in knots over what were ultimately trivial matters. Moreover, I became aware that, for some staff, procedures could be used as a substitute for building close and authoritative personal relationships with the boys. And much of the apparent sense of order was in fact on the surface. When things went wrong, there was not the same strength or quality of relationship between boys and staff to bring it back round. Establishments might have i's dotted and t's crossed, but they also need 'soul'.

These experiences were formative in terms of the way I thought about residential child care. I became aware of the importance of organisational culture, especially as it related to human services. I developed a belief that first and foremost residential child care was about living out particular values. After a couple of years in this second school I was asked to take over another establishment. From that point onwards I ran my own units, ending up as a principal for secure accommodation. I never lost my enthusiasm for or belief in what I was doing with the children and staff groups I worked with. And wherever I worked I came across some incredibly committed and talented individuals who I learned much from. However, I found it increasingly difficult to operate in the organisational climate that came to dominate social work over the course of the 1990s. Ideas of vocation became suspect, as did personal relationships, which were subsumed beneath a range of short-term technical rational interventions, manifest in a proliferation of risk assessments and social skills programmes.

Since moving to a university environment in 2000, my views have formed around this essential dissonance between the residential child care I came into and what it has become. What troubles me is the way in which the shift is postulated to represent improvement, modernisation and progress. To justify the shiny happy new world of residential child care requires that what went before is rubbished. My persistent unease is that this is not the true picture; we have lost much along the way and many of the assumptions that frame modern-day residential child care do not bear scrutiny in respect of asserting any wider developmental or indeed moral purpose for children. This book is in many respects an exploration of this dissonance. It is not a policy guide, nor does it pretend to be a good practice manual; it is essentially a book about ideas on residential child care, about challenging some of those I believe hold the sector back and about offering others that might chime better with the task of caring for children.

The book proceeds from a premise that residential child care does not exist as hermetically sealed in its present time and place. Any proper understanding requires an awareness of how micro- and macro-systemic influences interact to determine how services are conceptualised and delivered, how biography and context intersect. Chapter One is an attempt to set that wider context, identifying particular historical, cultural, political and professional trends that have shaped and continue to shape residential child care. Workers on the ground might question the relevance of the Enlightenment project to their immediate difficulties when confronting an angry child, but failure to understand what is going on for this child against the backdrop of wider social forces affords little purchase on what might cause things to go wrong. Very often what causes things to go wrong lies at levels far beyond the immediate influence of the individual child or worker. The current context in which care is provided is, I argue, not necessarily conducive to its optimum delivery.

To make any sense of how and why residential child care exists as it does today we need to understand its history. Chapter Two outlines some of that history. As a resource for needy children this history is a chequered one; arguably its present is equally chequered. Indeed the more recent history of residential care is one that is defined by scandal, as revelations of abuse have rocked residential care services across the developed world. Chapter Three takes a critical look at some of these scandals, the responses to them and the impact this has had on the delivery of care. Chapter Four outlines some current trends to present a picture of how residential child care is currently constituted. A perennial difficulty for residential workers is how to use theory to justify how they look after children. To date most of that theory has come from broadly psychological traditions. Chapter Five identifies some theoretical insights that workers might find helpful in illuminating practice. It concludes by questioning the dominance of psychological theory in residential care and suggests that the discipline needs to cast its net more widely in seeking to articulate an appropriate theory base.

The following two chapters, Six and Seven respectively, discuss some of the determinants of culture in residential units and key processes of assessment, care planning and programming. Chapter Eight identifies the centrality of the personal relationship in working with children, highlighting sensitive areas of practice where the 'selves' of the carer and the cared-for intersect. This leads into a discussion of personal and professional boundaries and an argument that appropriate boundaries derive, not from codes or procedures, but from the moral stance adopted by individual carers. Chapter Nine takes the task of the residential worker beyond the homes they work in, stressing the need for residential child care to be considered within the wider context of family and community. Chapter Ten widens the lens still further by considering how other countries and traditions deliver residential care services, asking what we might learn from them.

All of this builds towards the concluding chapter, which calls for a fundamental reappraisal of how we think about residential child care. I argue that discourses of care and upbringing need to take precedence over those of protection and rights, both of which contribute to the soulless state of much residential care. Care is argued, ultimately, to be a moral and political endeavour (Moss and Petrie, 2002) rather than the instrumental one it has become. Inevitably, in attempting to address such a broad sweep of historical, conceptual and practical subject matter, I leave much, some of which will be considered contentious, underdeveloped. If what I write provokes contention it can only be for the good. One of my concerns over recent years is a tendency to deny the messy bits and the areas of inevitable value conflict in residential child care and to act as though the task can be readily condensed into a series of quality standards or 'best practice' guides. The book takes as a premise that attempts to impose 'best practice' are elusive at best and potentially dangerous in their need to expunge ambiguity from practice that is irredeemably ambiguous; as such they ultimately get in the way of the human and moral dimensions of caring.

In coming to the conclusions I do, I draw more widely than from the standard sources on residential child care in the UK, little of which in the past couple of decades has been written from a practice base. Much of my thinking reflects perspectives drawn from child and youth care, the approach that frames practice in much of North America, and on European models of social pedagogy. Both traditions are discussed in Chapter Ten. I am indebted to the work done by academics at the Thomas Coram Research Unit at the University of London (Moss and Petrie, 2002, and subsequent work from the same stable) for introducing me to wider ideas around care and to theorists such as Tronto, Bauman and Levinas, whose influence threads through the book. Much of my thinking has been developed and affirmed over recent years through interaction with students and former colleagues on the MSc in Advanced Residential Child Care at the University of Strathclyde/Glasgow School of Social Work.

My entire career has been spent in Scotland. As a result, examples used (and perhaps assumptions made) reflect that Scottish dimension. And while residential care takes place in a range of different settings, my own background in residential schools is inevitably reflected in what I write. I hope and suspect that the broad trends I identify and address will, nevertheless, have a resonance across different settings and across the different countries of the UK and indeed further afield.

Questions of terminology in writing about children can elicit different views. Thomas (2005), for instance, argues that teenagers do not like to be called children and hence uses the term 'young people'. Milligan and Stevens (2006) use the word 'children', as this is consistent with legislation and with the United Nations Convention on the Rights of the Child (UNCRC). Arguments can be made for either approach. I use the term 'children', not just because it reflects the legal position but also because I dislike the term 'young people'. Some of the reasons for this might become apparent as readers make their way through the book. Essentially, I suspect that 'young people' derives from the rights and consumerist discourses which I subject to criticism.

One final word on terminology: I use the term 'discourse' fairly regularly throughout the book. Parton (2002, p 241) describes discourse as 'structures of knowledge, claims and practices through which we understand, explain and decide things'. Discourse 'makes some actions possible while precluding others'. It imposes limits on what we can say and, more obviously, what we are not allowed to say. For example, it can become very difficult to question child protection discourses in a climate where 'protecting children' is such a political and media hot potato. The concept of discourse, through exposing the ideologies and power structures that underlie actions, reflects, I think, the complexity of how things happen in the social world. It asks us to consider which voices speak the loudest on a particular subject, generally those of the powerful, including the professionally powerful. However, Dahlberg and Moss advise of the need to make loud voices stutter, to 'make the familiar seem strange, make visible invisible assumptions and values ... question truth claims based on expertise, technology and management that seek to impose consensus and to close down the contestability of subjects, often expressed as "quality", "excellence", "best practice"' (2005, p 139). In rethinking residential child care I seek to make the familiar strange and to question the truth claims of those whose voices have held sway over the discipline in recent decades.

It seems to be customary at this point to thank significant others for their unstinting support in writing this book. Unfortunately my wife and children do not do unstinting support as far as my writing is concerned. Nevertheless, I would like to thank Maura, Niamh, Ruairidh and Aidan, for ensuring that life went on as near to normal as possible and that I did not get carried away with becoming an author.

ONE

The context of care

Introduction

After many years as a neglected area of social welfare, residential child care has experienced a resurgence of interest in recent years, but often for the wrong reasons. The picture painted within the literature is generally bleak, depicting episodes of abuse, poor outcomes for children across a range of measures and low levels of qualifications and morale among staff.

Since the election of the New Labour government in 1997 looked-after children have featured prominently in policy agendas. The extent to which the experiences of children in care have actually improved is questionable, however. Political initiatives betray a particular view of care. They are positioned around concepts of children's rights, corporate parenting, increased choice and a language of outcomes. Such concepts can be contested, however; they are the products of particular political and professional ideologies, ideologies that might be argued to contribute to the current difficulties faced by residential child care.

Residential child care exists within particular historical, cultural, political and professional contexts. An understanding of these wider macro-systemic influences is vital to any understanding of the ways in which care is currently conceived and practised. In this chapter I seek to identify some of these trends and influences and to provide examples of how they impact on everyday practice. I conclude that the ecology within which residential child care currently exists is not always conducive to effective or ethical practice. Maximising what residential child care might offer to children requires a more fundamental rethink. This in turn requires that those who assert a positive role for residential child care engage in moral and political debate about the possibilities for the sector rather than becoming caught up in the search for ever more prescriptive technical and administrative fixes.

Strange though it may seem, any exploration of the wider context of residential child care maybe needs to go back 300 years or so, to the start of what is thought of as the modern period of history. Many commentators argue that modernity has run its course. Increasingly the social work literature reflects what has been termed a post-modern turn. Journal articles and texts confront readers with a language that reflects such an orientation and it is appropriate to consider residential child care within some of these wider ideas from social theory. To make sense of concepts of post-modernity requires some prior understanding of features of modernity.

Modernity

The modern period is associated with the Enlightenment, an upsurge in scientific and philosophical advance that swept across Europe from the late 17th and early 18th centuries. People in medieval and early modern times relied on a belief in the supernatural and on tradition to explain the world around them. The Enlightenment, by contrast, asserted a faith in human reason and in the possibilities held out by scientific advance. Modernity is characterised by a belief in human progress through mastery over the physical, natural and social worlds, fuelled by science and an increasingly secular humanist rationality. The core premise of the Enlightenment, that of human progress, is reflected in particular 'meta-narratives' or 'big stories'; these are often referred to as the 'isms': socialism, capitalism and feminism being common examples. Such meta-narratives provide their adherents with articles of faith through which to interpret the world.

Social work is a child of modernity adhering to a unifying logic of human progress through the advance of science and reason:

> Born within the period of modernity ... social work began to take on the omniscient voice of science.... It is within this culture of cure and control that the discipline has seen its most pronounced development ... Given its birth during the period of modernity with its emphasis on reductionist, logical positivist rationality ... social work took on this dominant discourse in the pursuit of status and professionalism. To this end we have seen codified systems of ethics, the move towards greater standardisation and competencies development ... systems of accreditation, a proliferation of managerial and market discourses in welfare ... and an increase in the development and use of professional jargon. (Sewpal, 2005, p 211)

The modern project has undoubtedly witnessed significant scientific and social progress. In social terms the development of welfare states to provide baseline standards across society to counter accidents of birth is perhaps its high point.

Modernity may have a downside, however. Critics of the modern project (for example, Bauman, 1993) suggest that its unremitting pursuit of progress and its faith in scientific rationality are implicated in some of the less savoury episodes in recent history such as the Holocaust and in the increasing fragmentation and social polarisation of a globalised economy (Bauman, 1993, 1998). Modernity's quest for rationality and its recourse to bureaucracy to achieve its aims has implications for relational conceptions of care, a point I return to in the final chapter.

Irrespective of one's take on modernity its foundations have been rendered rather less secure in recent decades. Belief in continual progress and of controlling the natural and social worlds has been shaken by natural disasters and by events such as 9/11 and the spectre of global terrorism. Belief in the ability of science to provide categorical answers to the major questions of the day is similarly less sure and more contingent than it was once imagined to be. Examples from the field of child welfare, for instance, where ostensibly scientific theories around shaken babies and around labels such as Munchausen's syndrome by proxy have been shown to lack the kind of scientific status once claimed for them, illustrate this point.

Despite, or perhaps because of, increasing uncertainty, some very current themes in social welfare reflect core beliefs of the modern project. These centre around ostensibly scientific ways of understanding and intervening in social problems, around the push towards identifying measurable outcomes and around seemingly objective and rational views of human relationships and of how organisations work. The push in social work towards evidence-based practice might be thought of as an attempt to impose certainty and rationality on an increasingly uncertain and complex world.

The Enlightenment was also concerned with ethical thought. The work of the Prussian philosopher Immanuel Kant emerged as the dominant ethics of the modern project. The central premise of Kantian ethics is encapsulated in his categorical imperative: 'Act only on that maxim through which you can at the same time will that it should become a universal law' (Kant, 1979, 1779). Ethics assumed a universal dimension; what was right in one situation ought to be right in every situation. Kantian ethics also valorise the place of the rational, autonomous individual, bound by duty to help others. Care is thus conceived of as rational rather than primarily relational.

Kantian ethics have become the dominant ethical framework in social work (Wilks, 2005). Their legacy is evident in rule-bound and procedural approaches to practice and to recourse to codes of conduct to regulate behaviours. Increasingly, social work literature is beginning to question the appropriateness of Kantian ethics (for example, McBeath and Webb, 2002; Wilks, 2005; Clark, 2006). Social work practice is considered too complex, diverse and contingent to lend itself to the application of the prescriptive and universal 'best practice' approaches beloved by politicians and managers. A number of authors (for example, Meagher and Parton, 2004) are turning to other ethical traditions and particularly perhaps to the literature around an ethic of care as offering a more authentic and ethical base for social work. Care ethics are discussed in more detail in the final chapter.

Post-modernity

Given the difficulties of sustaining erstwhile beliefs of steady human progress amidst growing uncertainty, questions are raised as to whether modernity has run its course and we are now living in a post-modern world. Post-modernity is described in simple terms as an incredulity towards meta-narratives (Lyotard, 1984). Other commentators describe the period we live in, variously, as 'high' modernity (Giddens, 1991), reflexive modernity (Beck, 1992) or liquid modernity (Bauman, 2000a). In each conceptualisation the old certainties of the modern period can no longer be taken for granted. We have not yet, however, reached the stage where we can embrace the uncertainties of a post-modern world. We hearken back and cling to what we knew from the past. Late modernity is unsure, tentative and fearful; it has become obsessed with notions of risk (Beck, 1992), increasingly equated with danger, and with devising ever more elaborate systems through which risk might be assessed and managed. According to Parton (1999) risk has become a collective state of mind rather than an objective reality. The teminology of risk, epitomised in the refrain that will be so common to social workers or residential workers, 'Have you done a risk assessment?', is symptomatic of this collective, essentially fearful, state of mind, and can only be made sense of within these wider social trends and attitudes towards risk.

Neoliberalism

Another set of ideas, which resonate with individualistic ways of thinking about relationships and which impact fundamentally on how we consider and provide welfare, is the growth since the 1970s of neoliberal economic and social thinking. Such ideas are dominant in the US and UK and influential across the developed world and, by virtue of increasing globalisation, on the developing world. Neoliberal thinking is intrinsically individualistic, epitomised in Margaret Thatcher's pronouncement that 'there is no such thing as society. There are individual men and women, and there are families' (interview with *Women's Own* magazine, 31 October 1987).

Harvey describes neoliberalism as:

> ... a theory of political economic practices that proposes that human well-being can best be advanced by liberating individual entrepreneurial freedoms and skills within an institutional framework characterised by strong property rights, free markets and free trade. (2005, p 2)

Neoliberal philosophies have implications for care. Services are to be 'personalised' towards the individual rather than aiming to address wider social welfare agendas. A market philosophy is evident in the introduction of purchaser–provider splits and the proliferation of private residential child care agencies. In relation to nursing care, which is further along the road that children's services are headed, Scourfield (2007) identifies residential care as a commodity 'to be traded and exploited for its surplus value, like any other commodity' (2007, p 162). He concludes that 'business values, reductions in costs and income generation have been prioritized above the quality of care' (2007, p 170). Marketisation has also brought about a more fluid and transient workforce with ever more use of agency staff, fundamentally shifting caring from vocation to commodity, something to be contracted to, a hotelling service, right down to its en suite bathrooms.

Conceptualising care along economic lines might on the surface point to a laissez-faire approach to child care whereby responsibility is vested in parents. Caring for children outside of their families becomes a residual obligation calculated to provide a safety net rather than a universal welfare service, as remains the situation in most European countries. Residual approaches to welfare lead to widening gulfs between the 'haves' and 'have-nots' in society, creating 'them and us' divides (Boddy et al, 2006).

Things are not quite that simple, however. Neoliberalism is shot through with contradictions. While propounding small government it is, at the same time, obsessed with knowledge accumulation and this leads to increasingly interventionist policies with children and families. Children have become political hot potatoes, partly because they are perceived as an investment for the future, a future that is conceived of as uncertain, but based largely around economic enterprise and technology. The idea of the 'social investment state' emerged in the UK as an element within Giddens' 'Third Way', the path to be trodden between old-style socialism and capitalism. This has involved reconfiguring the welfare state around principles of economic opportunity and prosperity through the redistribution of opportunities rather than income (Lister, 2003). Within such a mindset children become future units of production to be invested in. This investment also needs to be protected and politicians are desperate to be seen to be protecting children. While once they plied their trade kissing babies, a practice likely to land them in hot water in the present climate, they now have to be seen to be protecting children, a stance that has been responsible for the proliferation of legislation bringing the state and the law into what previously might be thought to be the private domain of the family or, by extension, of substitute care provision. Fulcher and Ainsworth (2006) note that the extension of a legal dimension into practice renders residential staff particularly vulnerable to litigation or other legal action.

Consumerism

Neoliberalism valorises the free market and its offshoot of choice, manifest in the capacity to consume. Choice and the proposed rights of consumers to exercise choices have replaced the principles of the welfare state, which is denigrated for fostering dependency. Any concept of the collective is surrendered to the primacy of individual identity. The language of consumer choice percolates social work. *Changing lives: 21st century social work review* in Scotland claims that, 'As demanding consumers of goods and services, users of social work services will increasingly expect the same variety, choice and flexibility that they expect from the business sector' (Scottish Executive, 2006, p 20).

Residential child care has become subject to the rhetoric of choice; menus are to demonstrate that they provide children with choice, children are to have a choice of what clothes they wear and, as discerning consumers of goods, they are to have a right to complain when their choices are not met. Of course, good care includes elements of choice, but not necessarily as absolutes; sometimes it is a carer's job to expect that a child eats their greens or to refuse them the latest designer jeans or training shoes. There are limits on choice, which we very often fail to help children appreciate in a society that is driven by consumerist imperatives.

Despite the rhetoric we cannot all be consumers. The poor are still with us but their poverty in neoliberal discourse is not a result of structural disadvantage but because they are 'flawed consumers' (Bauman, 1998). The poor, too, are increasingly identified as a threat and their behaviours cast into the realms of criminality through a proliferation of new laws. Criminalising the poor identifies them as the authors of their own misfortune; by committing criminal acts they place themselves beyond the pale of decent society. This absolves a comfortable but anxious populace of any moral responsibility towards them: 'linking poverty to criminality helps to banish the poor from the realms of ordinary moral obligation' (Bauman, 1998, p 77). Certain classified groups, the poor, the asylum seeker, the child abuser, the anti-social youth or neighbour, the sexually aggressive youth, are identified as a threat, criminalised and removed from the sphere of moral concern. We can perhaps only understand the demonisation of children and youth, and of those caring for them, against these wider social and ideological developments.

Managerialism

The doctrine of managerialism is a by-product of neoliberalism. Managerial principles were introduced to the public services by Margaret Thatcher's 'New Right'. Essentially, New Right social theorists believed that public services were inefficient and self-serving and that the introduction of private sector management regimes were required to inject some much needed rigour (Clarke and Newman, 1997). Managerialism has been described as 'a set of beliefs and practices at the core of which burns the seldom tested assumption that better management will prove an effective solvent for a wide range of economic and social ills' (Pollitt, 1990, p 1). More and better management was deemed to be the means to bring about public sector reform. The watchwords of managerialism were the three Es: economy, efficiency and effectiveness.

Managers within a managerial model had to have the right to manage: it is a command and control model. Management was considered to be a generalist task, requiring skills in areas such as target setting, measuring outcomes and budgetary and personnel management rather than discipline-specific practice knowledge. Managerialism has led to a reduction in the level of professionalism and autonomy previously enjoyed in the day-to-day practice of social work. It has become a business (Harris, 2002).

Without necessarily knowing about managerial ideas, practitioners in residential child care will recognise its manifestations in their daily practice. It is evident in the terminology used (for example, the use of 'unit manager' in residential child care rather than terms such as 'auntie' and 'uncle' which were used under the old family group home system, or 'housemaster' and 'housemother', used in residential schools). The authority of heads of home has been eroded and increasingly located in external managers, often with little experience or understanding of residential child care. The infrastructure of local authority bureaucracies also stakes a claim on residential care; personnel, health and safety and even catering can all seem to have more say in the day-to-day running of a home than those who work in them. The growth of personnel or human resources (HR) sections in bureaucracies has played a major part in disciplining the social care workforce, which in turn has implications for the way that care is conceptualised and practised.

At a practice level care homes are under increased pressure to identify 'what works', to set targets and demonstrate measurable outcomes from their interventions. Just caring for children is no longer enough. Homes need to prove how they are caring for them and how effective they are in this. And of course they need to evidence this. Staff will be familiar with the refrain from inspectors and others, that 'If it isn't written down it hasn't happened!', an injunction that can lead to workers spending more of their time writing things down than they do working with children.

The principles of managerialism can be seductive nevertheless – in many respects they appeal to a common-sense view of how the world should operate. And of course, it is right to be concerned with good management. However, good management and managerialism are not necessarily synonymous. There are a number of problems with managerial models.

The first of these is that there is little evidence that they work; they have failed to produce promised improvements in practice, partly because they are based on a linear and predictable view of human nature and organisational processes. Inappropriate or externally imposed target setting for instance can lead to workers exerting most of their energies meeting targets, irrespective of whether these actually add anything to caring for children. A focus on bottom-line efficiency can actually impede more effective or ethical service delivery (NEF, 2007). Moreover, managerial approaches fail to acknowledge the complexity and ambiguity of residential child care. Attempts to apply bureaucratic solutions to situation that are invariably nuanced, fragile, and very often emotionally laden are likely either to cause more harm than they profess to address, or to become ensnared in the complexity and grind to a halt.

At a conceptual level, in assuming that all problems can be managed, managerialism proceeds from a premise of these being technical problems to which technical solutions can be applied. The proliferation of what Webb (2006) calls technologies of care, manifest in residential care settings in a variety of assessment and risk assessment frameworks and programmed interventions are features of residential practice nowadays. This kind of technical/rational approach becomes problematic in the public services and especially perhaps in social services where most of the problems workers face are not technical, but involve an inevitable moral dimension and more than likely a moral conflict or tension. Such problems require a different approach, an adaptive one (Heifetz, 1994), where managers and practitioners are called to negotiate a range of moral dilemmas to which there are no clear-cut answers. The skills required in such instances are of a different nature to managerial skills; they are softer, more intuitive and more ethically based.

The election of the New Labour government in 1997 heralded a change in tone. Management was to become more 'modern'. Modernisation became the watchword for public services. It involved a spirit of relentless change: 'indeed obsessive and compulsive change (variously called "modernising", "progress", "improvement", "development", "updating") [which] is the hard core of the modern way of being' (Blackshaw, 2005, p 39). Again, this spirit of relentless change, manifest in rafts of new policy or practice initiatives or seemingly perpetual agency reorganisation, is something practitioners will recognise.

For all its talk of modernising (and, by implication, more efficient and streamlined ways of delivering public services), obvious contradictions emerge. New Labour has also presided over a massive increase in regulatory regimes (Humphrey, 2003), which, through their focus on information gathering and target setting, entrenched managerial and bureaucratic ways of working, reinforced through the regulation of care legislation. The requirements to feed the resultant bureaucratic beast often detract from direct care practice.

The legacy of managerial and regulatory approaches to residential child care in the early years of the 21st century is exemplified in a feature comparing children's homes in England and Germany. The head of the English home claimed that: 'Many senior managers in this field are now more interested in reports, statistics and numbers than the individual needs of the child.' He adds: 'Sometimes we get so caught up with procedures, we lose sight of the child' (*Sunday Times* magazine, 18 March 2007).

These wider social and political trends are manifest in the discourses that have come to dominate practice in child welfare generally and residential child care in particular. Foremost among these are ideas of children's rights and child protection. While these can be presented in warmly persuasive terms – few are going to say they are against them – neither concept is unproblematic when it comes to caring for children.

Children's rights

Children's rights perspectives can be postulated to be emancipatory and progressive developments in residential child care (for example, Frost et al, 1999). Utting (1997) identifies children's rights services as one of the most beneficial developments of the last decade. Many practitioners, however, have never bought into the rights agenda, remaining at best agnostic. This is not necessarily because they have anything to hide or because they want to maintain adult power over children. It is because the whole concept of rights is, in conceptual and practical terms, neither neutral nor unproblematic (Dahlberg and Moss, 2005). This section will address some of the tensions that arise in relation to children's rights and suggest the need for broader and more sophisticated approaches that locate rights within wider ethical and relational frames.

The United Nations Convention on the Rights of the Child (UNCRC) came into force in the UK in 1992. The increasing prominence given to children's rights perspectives is reflected legislatively in the 1989 Children Act and the 1995 Children (Scotland) Act. These embrace the provisions of Article 12, which states that a child's views should be taken into account in any decisions affecting them. The source documents for the Convention, however, draw on interpretations of rights that go beyond the civil and individual and encompass social rights to food, clothing and education, either from their parents or the public purse. Jackson (2004) highlights the importance of children's social and cultural rights, their access, if you like, to a concept of the good life. In this sense rights perspectives should be central to thinking on residential child care. However, notions of children's rights also need to be set against the wider backdrop of Kantian ethics and neoliberal capitalism discussed above. Parton (1991) argues that political interest in children's rights has to be understood within the new politics of welfare which speaks a language of consumer choice rather than political or civil rights. Rights perspectives can conceive of us going about our daily business as autonomous individuals bound to one another only through a series of contractual rights and duties. In this sense they become an instrument of a neoliberal state apparatus. Dahlberg and Moss note that:

> ... (it is no coincidence that the prominence given to rights coincides with the dominance of advanced liberalism and increasing recourse to law as a means of mediating relationships) and premised on particular values and a particular understanding of the subject as a rational, autonomous individual. (2005, p 30)

A view of rights as existing within a consumerist framework of legal relationships is institutionalised in residential care. Children are increasingly presented with 'statements of rights (and entitlements) and ... told of a complaints procedure should they feel they are being mistreated by programme staff' (Fulcher and Ainsworth, 2006, p 291). Statements of rights are often more about protecting agencies from liability than they are meaningful affirmations of their hopes for children. Such interpretations of children's rights can actually get in the way of healthy and just ways of negotiating differences and resolving conflicts, which should happen within the context of daily living and caring relationships. They act to build barriers between children and those who care for them. Heron and Chakrabarti argue that 'the superficiality of the rights agenda has added to the complexities and tensions permeating residential provision' and has 'undermined practitioner morale in the process' (2002, p 356).

In residential child care the rights agenda coincided with various abuse scandals coming to light (see Chapter Three). Children's rights were seen as an important tool to help children express their views and to bring any abuse to the attention of outside adults. Advocacy bodies, such as A National Voice in England, Who Cares? Scotland and Voices from Care in Wales became important in forwarding a children's rights agenda. Such bodies have developed largely under the tutelage of, or with the financial backing of local authorities. Local authorities also co-opted the rights agenda by appointing or commissioning their own children's rights officers. These have operated primarily to detect instances of alleged abuse rather than to address wider issues of structural or systemic disadvantage or to argue for children's access to social and cultural rights. Against this backdrop rights have too often become trivialised, bogged down in questions of bedtime, pocket money or petty gripes about daily living.

Another problem with the rights agenda in a neoliberal state is that with rights come responsibilities. And while it is central to any idea of upbringing that children are encouraged to be responsible, they can, in the current political climate, be inappropriately 'adulterised' and 'responsibilised' (Goldson, 2002). Too great a focus on responsibility can assume that access to rights is somehow contingent on meeting responsibilities. A consequence of this is that children are held to account when they make mistakes and the only right then accorded them is a right to due process as more and more of them are subject to an increasing array of correctional interventions. Rights sit quite comfortably within a justice orientation to dealing with children. Problems, whether of care and protection or of juvenile delinquency, which are predominantly social in nature and ought to elicit a social response, become conceptualised and responded to within a justice framework. It is legitimate to question why, over the period since we have become more concerned about children's rights, we have also seen a steady and alarming rise in the numbers of young people deprived of their liberty.

The way that rights have been applied as a rubric within which to care for children is increasingly recognised as problematic. Rights can only be meaningfully realised within the framework of the ties that bind us to one another and to wider society. Barnes argues that 'a care perspective alerts us to the inadequacy of notions of social justice located solely in appeals to individual rights' (2006, p ix). Dahlberg and Moss (2005) elaborate, claiming that rights:

> ... entail a contractual and finite exchange between calculating and independent individuals; care and encounter foreground inter-dependence, infinite responsibility and the impossibility of being free from obligation. Rights are one example of universal codes set up to govern actions; care and encounter pay more attention to the need to make ethical choices in relation to particular contexts and conditions. (2005, p 31)

The rights we should be pursuing for children would enable them to enter into relationships with caring adults that are mutually respectful. This requires a culture of respect for human rights, including those of adult carers. Rethinking residential child care requires a move beyond current rights discourses. These 'may be seen as a product of a society that seeks to measure and monitor that which is intrinsically qualitative in nature: love, respect, security, trust, reliability and responsiveness' (Emond, 2007, p 193). It means that adults need to start enjoying and celebrating children rather than fearing and seeking to control them within a rubric of contractual obligations, rules and technologies of care.

Child protection

Butler and Drakeford (2005) claim that the rights agenda in relation to children has been hijacked by 'the far less emancipatory paradigm of child protection' (2005, p 218). Child protection is another one of these terms that it can be difficult to argue against without leaving oneself open to accusations of not wanting to protect children. And of course there are children who need to be protected from individuals or situations that threaten their development. However, child protection has moved beyond responding to these situations where social workers have an undoubted role to play. It is both a response to and it feeds a state of moral panic around children and childhood. It has taken on a life of its own to become a bureaucratic and process-driven beast, which oftentimes has lost touch with its original purpose to protect and nurture children. It is an essentially conservative and fearful construct, which, as Butler and Drakeford (2005) suggest, can act against children's proper emancipation and which casts a veil of suspicion over adult–child relationships.

The concept of child protection was employed in the mid-1980s by the then Conservative government to shift the focus of work with children and families away from universal family support towards identifying and targeting problem families (Parton, 1985). As it has developed, child protection identifies social work concerns with individual pathology and does little to challenge the causes of children's maltreatment and exploitation. Yet Hacking (1992) observes that, in the wider scheme of things, old-fashioned, unremitting poverty affects more children than individual instances of physical or sexual abuse. Jackson (Jackson, S., 2006) claims that the dominance of a child protection agenda in recent decades has distorted the nature of children's services placing an emphasis on investigation and procedure at the expense of prevention and support.

Nonetheless, child protection is a powerful social discourse in an uncertain world; it holds out some hope of giving children a security that adults do not feel they have. To be seen to be protecting children avoids adults having to confront their more visceral fears about their own insecurities. Yet, as a grand narrative within which to respond to children in society, child protection is partial at best. Protection does little to address children's need for care. Indeed, Tronto suggests that:

> ... protection involves a very different conception of the relationship between an individual or group, and others than does care. Caring seems to involve taking the concerns and needs of the other as the basis for action. Protection presumes the bad intentions and harm that the other is likely to bring to bear against the self or group and to require a response to that potential harm. Protection can also become self-serving, turning into what Judith Hicks Stein calls 'the protection racket' in which the need for protection reinforces itself. (1994, pp 104–5)

A further problem with the application of child protection perspectives is that they have become a tool in the managerial armoury, drawn on to maintain particular discourses around children and the organisational infrastructures erected to support these. The claim by authorities to be acting in a child protection capacity authorises the external control of care. From an education perspective, but one equally applicable to residential care, Dean (1999) argues that:

> Child Protection policies, both in their form and content, act as regulatory frameworks which constrain and proscribe teachers' practices and ... emphasize a 'safe' and 'risk averse' form of practice. They can also be seen as technologies of performance because they presuppose a culture of mistrust in professions. (quoted in Sachs and Mellor, 2005, p 149)

In residential child care the various reports and inquiries into child abuse have contributed to the removal of the locus of authority for the management of homes to external bureaucracies. Maier (1985) identifies inherent tensions in such attempts to provide primary care in secondary settings. The imperatives of a wider organisation, largely around self-preservation, are often not always congruent with those of direct caregiving.

A lack of trust

Constructions of children's rights and child protection locate caring for children within a framework of legal and contractual duties and, as such, seek to impose certainty and order on acts and relationships that are irredeemably uncertain and ambiguous and rarely amenable to clear-cut interpretation. The fear engendered in workers by the sense that there are unequivocally right ways and wrong ways to care and that there are consequences for the slightest breach is echoed in the various discourses of late modernity, from the economic reductionism and litigiousness of neoliberalism to the bureaucracy of managerialism. These impose blaming cultures. According to McLaughlin, current 'social work debate is influenced by a negative, atavistic view of humanity' (2007, p 1266). Butler and Drakeford (2005) identify what they call a 'special pessimism' in relation to residential child care.

Within such climates, adults have become fearful of children or fearful for them. Our fear *of* children is manifest in a raft of legislation to tackle what is labelled as anti-social behaviour. Increasing numbers are locked up; others are subject to a range of surveillance measures, including electronic tagging to monitor their whereabouts, all done under the guise of offering them intensive support. Our fears *for* children are evident in the range of initiatives to protect them. These are often as oppressive as those measures targeting their anti-social behaviour. Within a protectionist discourse children are denied agency in their lives, relying on adults to protect them from 'threats' that range from internet paedophiles through abusing parents or indeed care workers to fatty food and insufficient exercise.

Implications for care

We are, then, witnessing a curious amalgam of underpinning philosophies towards children and child care. They reflect a general sense of children as objects of public concern about whose protection we should be concerned, but often the attitudes that underpin current discourses do not seem to convey much sense of children being particularly real or, perhaps of more concern, of being liked.

The upshot of all this is that the wider conditions for caring for children are not conducive. A cult of the individual subsumes any wider concern with community and responsibility for others within this. Under capitalism and especially resurgent neoliberalism the trend is to see care instrumentally and contractually, to do the least required to fulfil any legal or contractual duty to care, in effect to limit our liability to care. Individualism and consumerism do not provide fertile ground for bringing up children. Against such dominant ideologies ideas of vocation and of group living can seem strangely old-fashioned, even suspect. Care has become a technical/rational task, one that is reduced to a series of procedures or 'best practice' guides. Targets are set for its provision and instruments employed to gauge whether these have been met. Rational and instrumental views of care have implications for the way that carers, too, are conceptualised. They become technicians, charged to carry through particular tasks to a preordained level of efficiency and effectiveness, a view reinforced by the competency or outcome-based models of training that have come to dominate in recent years.

Within such discourses children themselves can appear as abstract, either demonised, or idealised and cocooned for their status as future adults rather than for what they currently are. The care of these abstract children is undertaken by similarly abstract adults, individuals who tick the right boxes on a list of carer competencies generated by HR personnel. Abstract and autonomous adults and children are bound together only by a series of information booklets and complaints procedures. The complex mix of the challenging, infuriating, lovable and contradictory characteristics of children is airbrushed out of this picture. Similarly carers are not the automatons they can be constructed as in job descriptions; they too are a complex mix of characteristics, some good, some perhaps less good. When we dispense with the complexity of children and the adults caring for them and the ambivalence they generate in one another in an attempt to render the whole endeavour rational, we make the job of caring even more difficult than it inevitably is. The messy and irrational bits are at the heart of caring; in seeking to expunge these the very essence of caring is compromised (Bauman, 2000b).

The result is that children in state care are rarely provided with access to the kind of life and experiences we would wish for our own children. Cameron makes this point, noting that:

> ... the concept of care within public care for children has been rarely seen as visible ... poor outcomes, lack of investment in staff training, increased pressure to marketwise care services have all contributed to a narrowing of what we mean by care, a lowering of expectations of what the state can offer in terms of care. Of particular note is the marked contrast between the potential for care within families as centring on control and love, and the optimum expected from state care which is around safekeeping. Care as used in legislation seems to have been emptied of its potential, a dried up expression for how to manage an underclass of disadvantage. (2003, pp 91-2)

Ironically, while we ought to be in a position to be offering more, given the financial resources ploughed into residential child care in recent decades, we are prevented from doing so by ideologies which, in the name of effecting progress, have often impeded it. The following chapters seek to identify and uncover some of the complexity and ultimately the irrationality of caring for children. Throughout, the conceptualisation of care as a technical/rational task or series of tasks is problematised and a picture of care as ultimately a relational and a moral endeavour is constructed. Other ways of thinking about care are introduced as the book progresses.

TWO

History

Fulcher and Ainsworth (1985) point out that: 'The siting and physical design of a centre may represent in bricks and mortar the ideas of earlier generations of practice' (1985, p 61). This chapter attempts to uncover the ideas of earlier generations of practice and to outline some of the twists and turns of policy, practice and ideology that have contributed to how residential child care is currently constituted. The history of how children were cared for over the centuries is not a story of uninterrupted social progress. Nor is it to be found only in the legal and policy documents that form the 'official' version of events in respect of residential child care; these merely give some pointers to concerns and beliefs extant at any period of time. Policy documents merely reflect wider ideas and ideologies that have determined how the service has developed, ideas and ideologies about children and childhood and how best to provide for them.

What and how we think about children also reflects the power of particular professionals and interest groups. Michel Foucault the French historian and philosopher argues that power in respect of how we care for people has been vested, for most of the 20th century, in the hands of those he calls the psy-professionals, psychiatrists, psychologists and, more recently, social workers, who seek to privilege their own ideas of children and how to care for them. These ideas are based largely around medical or quasi-medical models of diagnosis or assessment and treatment. Dominant professional ideologies can assume a self-evident status, privileging particular ways of thinking and making it difficult to challenge these. This in turn can lead to the adoption of easy but unhelpful value positions, which serve to judge rather than to understand what went on in the past. An example of this might be a tendency to look back in horror at ideas of sending children from residential homes and schools to the colonies. In some situations such policies might resonate with present-day examples of ethnic cleansing, as in the case of government policies in Australia and Canada throughout most of the 20th century, which resulted in a 'stolen generation' of aboriginal children, removed from their homelands and placed in residential schools in order that they might assimilate the dominant culture and be 'civilised'. In the UK assisted passage schemes can be represented rather differently, a point I return to later in this book.

While an appreciation of history is, I argue, essential for any contextual understanding of residential child care, it should also be borne in mind that this history is incomplete. It is remarkable what can be gleaned about policies, practices and beliefs extant at any point of time from the admissions records, punishment books and medical records of an establishment. It is fascinating just how extensive and varied some of their histories were. Understandings of the history of residential child care are at best provisional. In many cases they are partial, seeking, consciously or otherwise, to focus, especially in recent years, on where such provision has gone wrong in order to justify policy preferences intended to limit its use.

The pre-Reformation church and society

The history of care is in many respects a religious one. Traditions of caring for and educating children were evident within the pre-Reformation church, based around monasteries. Early collections of Celtic church law, emanating from religious communities like Iona, included detailed provisions for the care of foundlings and orphans (Furnivall et al, unpublished). After the Reformation parishes assumed responsibility for social welfare provision. In Canada the first examples of residential child care were in institutions run by the Ursiline nuns in the 16th century (Anglin, 2002). Throughout most of the 20th century, even, much care was provided directly by religious orders or religiously motivated charities. The long roots of care in religious service have only been loosened in recent decades.

The Poor Laws and their legacy

The Elizabethan Poor Laws of 1601 located responsibility for social welfare with parishes. Poor relief could be offered as 'outdoor' relief where paupers were given an allowance so that they might be maintained in their own homes or 'indoor' or institutionally based relief based around poor houses. In providing a rudimentary form of social welfare the Poor Laws differentiated between the deserving and the undeserving poor, the former, such as dependent children and people with disabilities, were deemed to be poor on account of circumstances beyond their control, while the latter, the 'able-bodied' poor, were adjudged to be responsible for their own plight on account of moral deficit, essentially a predisposition towards laziness. The Poor Laws thus embedded punitive and negative images of the poor (Jones and Novak, 1999), in which poverty was individualised and considered in isolation of the social context from which it stemmed.

Industrialisation and the need to respond to rising numbers of urban poor led, in England, to the 1834 Poor Law Amendment Act. This introduced the doctrine of 'less eligibility', the idea that life in a state institution should be less desirable (eligible) than that which a person might experience outside of the institution. This was deemed necessary to prevent people wanting access to the workhouses and thereby becoming a financial burden on the authorities. Workhouses, as a consequence, were deliberately austere and unwelcoming places. Whereas recourse to institutional care was integral to the English system, in Scotland the poor were more likely to be maintained in communities rather than in institutions (Abrams, 1998). The hospital or workhouse model was less entrenched, largely due to a tradition of boarding children out to respectable families, an early form of fostering. This contributed to a greater reluctance to use institutional care in Scotland (Triseliotis, 1988).

Poor Law principles have been and arguably remain pervasive within Anglo-American approaches to welfare, having been:

> ... transplanted and adapted to the New World of North America where they continue to shape attitudes and policies towards 'the poor'....They reinforce a belief in self-help and the American Dream, which constitutes poverty as a failure. (cited in Lister, 2004, p 104)

The transplantation of a Poor Law ideology across the Atlantic was influential in shaping the development of social work in the US along individualistic lines. According to Myers (2000), 'the American discourse about poverty has evolved from a belief that it was a symptom of poor character to a belief that poverty is a consequence of psychological or familial dysfunction'. As a result responses to social problems tend to be located at the level of individual and/or family therapies rather than at wider structural or educational levels. This way of thinking made its way back to the UK where the developing social work profession was heavily influenced by North American psycho-social traditions (Higham, 2001) and practice developed along casework, albeit social casework, models. In recent decades case management and deficit-based approaches to social work practice have reinforced the focus on the individual at the expense of broader social and community development-based approaches. Attitudes that individualise poverty and responses to it are far less pronounced in other European countries (see Chapter Ten).

Royal hospitals

In England an institutional response to vagrant children was apparent with the establishment of Royal hospitals, the first of these being Christ's Hospital in London, in 1552. The hospital model spread across England, providing wet-nursing for infants and lodging and education for older children (Corby et al, 2001), thus establishing a residential tradition for the care of children. Many of the original hospitals closed on the grounds of cost, and the focus of residential care shifted as increasing numbers of children were admitted to the workhouses that had been created from the mid-17th century onwards. The London Foundling Hospital, established by Thomas Coram, was an attempt to provide an alternative to the workhouse for illegitimate children. In basing admission criteria around the marital status of a baby's mother, Coram emphasised a persistent theme in care provision based around the stigma of illegitimacy (Oliver, 2003).

'Ragged' schools

The onset of industrialisation in the early part of the 19th century brought about a fragmentation of social structures and of the parish-based welfare infrastructure that had existed in rural communities. Families seeking work made their way to the developing cities, where children were of necessity regarded as economic units, required to contribute to the family income. Ironically, the Factory Acts of the 1830s, which sought to cushion children from the worst excesses of industrialisation, actually forced them to substitute for industrial earnings whatever they could forage on the streets through begging or stealing. When their activities were deemed to constitute deviance, the response was often prison. In the early 1840s Bailie Mack in Edinburgh reported to the Parochial Board that children as young as five were regularly appearing before him charged with stealing. He was reluctant to send them to prison but for the seven-year-old recidivist he felt he had little option but to do so.

Reformers under the auspices of the Philanthropic Society sought to respond to such situations by establishing industrial or 'ragged' schools. In England the ragged schools flourished under the leadership of John Pound. Inspired by Pound, a notable reformer of the period, Mary Carpenter, authored a book, *Reformatory schools* (1851), in which she argued against the imprisonment of children (quoted in Carlebach, 1970).

An early realisation of the ragged school philosophy in Scotland was the opening of the first industrial feeding school in Aberdeen in 1941, under the patronage of Sheriff Watson. The school sought to feed, train in work habits and give basic education to the children who attended (Seed, 1974). Children were first and foremost to be educated for the purpose of ensuring they could earn a living and hence not become a burden on the state, rather than from a belief in any intrinsic worth that education might bring. Again there were differences between Scottish and English incarnations of the ragged schools. Scottish pioneers such as Watson and Dr Thomas Guthrie operated from a belief that there was little to separate the destitute child from the offender; they both had common needs to be cared for, and that care should consider the family as a unit. Scottish ragged schools were generally day schools. English reformers were more predisposed to residential provision and to classify and place children according to whether or not they had offended (Seed, 1974). Legislation in the 1850s confirmed this distinction, establishing industrial schools for children in need of care and protection and reformatories for those who had offended. Both types of provision 'depended on regimes founded on discipline and hard work with "brutal punishments, Spartan diets and austere living conditions"' (Heywood, 1959, p 189, cited in Butler and Drakeford, 2005, p 177).

Rescue period

The second half of the 19th century has become known as the 'reformation-rescue period' in social welfare provision (Grant and Gabor, 2006). The family came to be seen as a contaminating influence from which children needed to be removed and protected. A number of small orphanages generally run by Christian philanthropists sprung up across the country. However, this era is perhaps best characterised as that of the large orphanage such as those established by, for example, Dr Barnado, National Children's Homes (NCH) and William Quarrier. While there was an undoubted altruistic and affective dimension to the drive to provide care during the latter half of the 19th century, it was perhaps primarily motivated by a moral purpose to eradicate vice. Reformers were concerned with poverty and ignorance, less for its own sake and more with the possibility that these social conditions might lead to vice and immorality. These institutions prospered, resonating with a Victorian Puritan ethic. Investing one's energies and resources into caring for children 'provided many with an opportunity to take account of the fate of their own souls as much as those of the children for whom their charitable efforts were ostensibly joined, [and in time] degenerated into mere sentimentality' (Butler and Drakeford, 2005, p 174).

At its most extreme, the 'rescue' philosophy was manifest in the emigration of children to the colonies in pursuit of a better life, a practice that continued from the 1860s until it eventually died out as late as the 1960s. This is a period in welfare history that attracts considerable opprobrium when judged against present-day standards and understandings based around the importance of contact with birth families. However, for the governors of many charities and schools engaged in the practice it represented a genuine attempt to provide a fresh start and the chance of a better life to those children who earned that privilege, for that was how the policy was considered. Assisted passage to the colonies was held out as a goal for the better-behaved and better-performing boys in schools such as Kibble in Paisley. In fact such policies might claim some success as is evident in the establishment of alumni networks of boys from approved schools in the 'New World'. It is only with the benefit of present-day understandings of the importance of children's attachments to their families of origin that they become problematic. Without that perspective, which only became apparent in Bowlby's (1951) work after the Second World War, they are more readily understood.

Theoretical influences

The emergence of the psychoanalytic movement, based around the work of Sigmund Freud in the early 20th century, led to a questioning of traditional and controlling ways of responding to children. This led to some interesting experiments in child rearing and education. Among the best known of these is Summerhill, established by A.S. Neil in the 1920s. These schools known as 'free schools' sought to allow children to choose how they should live their own lives. Neil's views on education and child rearing were set out in a book *Summerhill* (1966) that became a best seller. He believed that the happiness of the child was paramount and that self-respect and respect for others would result. Most children's problems could be attributed to the repressed (particularly sexually repressed) attitudes foisted on them by parents and formal educational systems. Neil's ideas were influential in bringing a progressive edge to many approved schools, and ideas such as the development of house or cottage meetings, to involve children in decisions about everyday life, became fairly common. Present-day ideas about listening to children are not altogether new.

While there were beacons of enlightened practice, most residential care existed untouched by theory, reflecting prevailing beliefs about how to bring up children and in particular poor children. Regimes were often marked by strong discipline and casual cruelty. What care felt like to those brought up there cannot be generalised as universally bad, however. Much would have depended on the characters of those caring. McKenzie (1996), for instance, points to very happy memories of being brought up in an orphanage in the US. It has become fashionable, however, to focus on negative images of care.

Legislation

The UK 1908 Children Act brought together previous legislation relating to children. It remained extant in the Republic of Ireland until the 1991 Child Care Act. In England and Scotland, it was overtaken by legislation in the 1930s, which established separate juvenile courts and introduced a 'welfare' principle, requiring reference to the best interests of the child in any decisions about them. This has been central to subsequent child care philosophy and legislation, although it is increasingly threatened by correctional or 'justice'-based philosophies. The passage of this legislation coincided with the start of the Second World War, which led to the evacuation of children from the cities to the countryside. These years also witnessed a significant increase in the use of approved schools, largely to deal with problems of social disruption. Many of the approved schools were managed by voluntary bodies, a number of them religious orders, catering for the growing Catholic population of Irish descent.

The aftermath of the Second World War and the acknowledgement of the disruption of family life caused by evacuation prompted social reformers to take stock of provision for children. The Curtis Committee and its Scottish counterpart the Clyde Committee, reporting in 1946 in response to concerns about children's welfare, criticised large-scale institutional living and proposed that children should be provided for in smaller units (where smaller was considered to be around 20!), located nearer to centres of population. The child guidance movement, drawing on Freudian psychology and emphasising the importance of working with children in the context of their family relationships, was a powerful influence on the thinking of these committees. Substitute care where it was required was to be modelled on family life and the needs of individual children were to be taken into account. These developments were enacted in the 1948 Children Act, which established local authority children's officers under the tutelage of children's departments. At the height of the welfare consensus ideas of care and welfare converged.

Although implementation of the 1948 Act was patchy it resulted, by the early 1960s, in the development of the family group home, where groups of children were looked after by 'auntie' and 'uncle' figures, ostensibly modelling the experience on family living. Many residential schools moved away from large institutional arrangements at this time to a 'cottage' living model where children were cared for in smaller groups by housemasters and housemothers. These developments, influenced by psychoanalytic thinking but also increasingly by attachment theory (Bowlby, 1951), which accorded a primary importance to the maternal relationship, imposed a gendered imprint on care, locating its day-to-day execution with women while placing men in breadwinner and perhaps disciplinary roles.

Developments elsewhere

Developments in residential homes and schools in the UK, especially in terms of moving towards 'cottage' models, reflected those taking place across the Atlantic. Over the course of the 1960s residential care in the US and Canada moved from a primary role in containment to one of treatment. The locus of this treatment was also shifting. Historically treatment was conceived as being distinct from care, the domain of outside experts such as psychologists or medical social workers. The job of residential workers was to provide daily care, a task with little professional value attached to it.

Pioneers such as Bruno Bettelheim (1950) challenged this separation of treatment from care, arguing that disturbed children needed a round-the-clock psychotherapeutic 'milieu' in which care workers provided the bulk of any therapeutic work with children in the course of their everyday interactions with them. This thinking was developed by Redl and Wineman (1951, 1957) and in the classic text *The other 23 hours* (Trieschman et al, 1969), the title conveying the relative importance of what happened in the hours of the day when children were not engaged in therapy or formal treatment.

The fact that residential workers might provide more than a basic feeding and watering function has had implications for the professionalisation of residential child care. In North America, and Canada in particular, child and youth care has developed into a distinct academic and professional discipline, as discussed in Chapter Ten. In the UK it was subsumed within the emerging social work profession.

Residential child care within social work

Legislation following the Kilbrandon (1964) and Seebohm (1968) reports in Scotland and England respectively located residential child care within the new social work profession. The early years of this arrangement were ones of considerable optimism. Inroads were made to reduce the numbers of children 'lost' in the care system and a greater sense of purpose was introduced to care planning. The 1970s witnessed developments in residential schools in particular in both Scotland and England. In Scotland the development of the List D schools psychological service provided the former approved schools with a body of knowledge around assessment and care planning rooted within models of child development (Martin and Murray, 1976, 1982). In England the period saw a growth in therapeutic communities and a shift in terminology from approved schools to community homes with education (CHE). Social work ideas around treatment began to challenge those of moral guidance and control as the dominant paradigm governing the care of children.

However, all was not well and significant tensions simmered between educationalists and the new social work profession, whose claims to be able to address delinquency without recourse to institutional care were at best untested. Much of the suspicion levelled at social work by educationalists was perhaps understandable. At an ideological level, the emerging social work profession was influenced by the literature of dysfunction (Jones and Fowles, 1984). Bowdlerised versions of Goffman's (1968) total institutions were swallowed whole to stereotype and justify the non-use of residential care. Although of questionable intellectual provenance, suspicion of institutional care is a persistent thread in social work belief systems. A practical outcome of this ideology was the decimation of the approved school system with a massive loss of child care expertise (Kahan, 1995). Ironically these 'institutions' were in time replaced by secure training centres, which arguably come much closer to fitting the bill of a 'total institution'.

Alongside this anti-institutional bias, substitute family care became the placement of choice for children deemed unable to continue to live at home. The developing preference for family care was given a shot in the arm by the publication of the *Children who wait* report (Rowe and Lambert, 1973). This has been particularly influential in the years since its publication, embedding a strong preference for fostering within social policy discourse. Yet significant criticism can be levelled at the report's rigour (Kelly, 1998). Its context was a crisis in adoption in the early 1970s caused by increased contraception and abortion and a greater tolerance of single parenting. Numbers of white babies available for adoption fell by 40%. *Children who wait* claimed that a majority of children in care were expected to stay there throughout childhood and that many of these were deemed to need a permanent family. The report concluded that there were 7,000 children nationwide in this position. These findings resonated with a growing awareness of Bowlby's attachment theory and of the importance of family bonds. The report became associated with the phrase 'Every child has a right to a family of their own'. And of course those children identified as languishing in the care system provided a convenient supply of children to satisfy the demand for children for adoption.

Children who wait saw the beginning of the permanency movement in child care and within this discourse permanence was initially associated with adoption. Early articulations of permanency theory did not envisage that it could be provided in residential care (Milligan, 1998). In the aftermath of this report all local authorities developed policies centred round family placement. This developed to include fostering as well as adoption, a fact not without some irony given the number of foster care breakdowns and placement moves that have resulted from a policy justified on the premise of providing children with permanence.

Reorganisation of local government in the 1970s created the opportunity for councils to reappraise their child care strategies and to reorganise residential care provision along more functional lines. Policy developments shifted in the direction of shorter placements and better defined purposes for residential care, often with a view to preparing children for substitute family care. Residential care was no longer considered a place where children might spend their years until adulthood. The period also saw a push towards what was claimed to be greater professionalism. This saw a shift away from 'live-in' carers operating on a family model towards greater numbers of staff working shift systems. Policy and procedure statements also began to be developed more systematically around areas such as care and control. The 1980s also witnessed the growing secularisation of child care as religious orders or organisations withdrew from provision. The discourse of care became a secular/humanistic one and erstwhile religious motivations were cast at best as old-fashioned and very often as suspect. Large voluntary organisations such as Barnardo's and NCH also began to re-evaluate their functions, moving away from direct service provision to more community-based and advocacy roles.

While the new generically based social work departments might make claims that developments around this period represented the improvement and professionalisation of residential child care, dispensing of old-fashioned and perhaps at times oppressive practices and opening the sector up to new ideas, the overall picture was more mixed. Within the new social work departments, children's services had less of a profile than previously and the demise of the old children's officers led to a significant loss of expertise within child care generally (Jackson, S., 2006). In residential child care a tradition of writing from a practice base (for example, Balbernie, 1966; Dockar-Drysdale, 1990) gradually dissipated.

A further consequence of the move towards ostensible professionalism was the imposition of increasing spatial and emotional distance between carers and those cared for and arguably the depersonalisation of the care task. This was manifest at practical levels in the shift away from live-in staff and the introduction of shift systems. It was also evident at an ideological level, where ideas of intimacy became suspect, either thought to foster dependency or to open the door to abuse. Contemporary writers on residential child care did not see this move towards professionalisation favourably. Douglas and Payne claimed that 'neither staff nor residents have really benefited from the introduction of industrial practices and conditions to human service organisations, like residential units has brought as many, if not more, problems than it was expoected to solve'. They went on to say that 'staff through no fault of their own, have given up trying' (1981, pp 110-11).

The professional preference for family-based care also began to coalesce during the 1980s with demands for public service economy. The role of the state was reconfigured in relation to children and families, away from universal support and welfare, and towards a greater targeting of problem families. The effect of all of this was to further marginalise residential child care, identifying it as a residual and expensive service. Permanency theory, along with other approaches such as normalisation and minimal intervention, became elevated to ideology (Fulcher, 2001). The 1980s witnessed the height of such ideological dogmatism to the point that some local authorities such as Warwickshire and Fife sought to dispense with residential provision altogether. The 1984 Short Report felt the need to bolster the sector by affirming its role as the best option for some children.

Training for residential child care

Following the implementation of the Social Work Acts in the early 1970s the newly established regulatory body for social work, the Central Council for Education and Training in Social Work (CCETSW), set out to review the training of residential workers (CCETSW, 1973). It identified some particular requirements of residential work such as the holistic, spiritual and charismatic nature of practice. It made a rather ambivalent declaration that residential child care was social work and should be subject to an equivalent level of qualification while at the same time instituting a qualification specifically for residential workers, the Certificate of Social Service (CSS), which was not deemed to be pitched at an appropriate standard as to allow its holders to practise in other areas of social work (Smith, 2003). CCETSW, throughout its existence until the early 21st century, maintained this early ambivalence to residential work. It never managed to address the training of workers and presided over a gradual dilution of the standards deemed appropriate for such work, to the point that any aspirations towards a professional workforce were dropped when its replacement bodies, the various care councils, came into being and adopted vocational models of training for workers in residential child care.

Concept of group care

In an attempt to affirm residential care as a specialist area of practice within social work, Ainsworth and Fulcher (1981) adopted the term 'group care' to cover client groups across the lifecourse requiring services delivered on either a residential or day care basis. The defining features of group care provision were that it involved a group of clients being cared for by a staff team within a discrete physical location. CCETSW supported the development of specific group care curricula (Fulcher and Ainsworth, 1983). Ward (1993) sought to further develop the idea of group care. He coined the term 'opportunity-led work' to describe the way in which residential workers exploited daily living opportunities for therapeutic purposes. Despite these attempts to assert a role for residential child care within the social work discourse, the sector on the whole faced overwhelming indifference and occasional hostility from the wider profession. Because of the dominance of what was then called 'field social work' few workers from a residential background taught on social work training courses. When residential child care was taught at all, it was often by staff with no direct practice experience

(Lane, 2001). Standard social work texts throughout the 1990s and into the 2000s rarely even devote chapters to residential care.

Attempts to include residential child care within social work may have been flawed from the outset A tension between residential care and other areas of social work has been highlighted by writers from residential backgrounds (Milligan, 1998; Anglin, 1999; Lane, 2001; Smith, 2003a). A fundamental fault line can be argued to exist between the two domains of practice; a central tenet of social work is the avoidance of residential care, on ideological and increasingly on cost grounds. These trends, together with the crowding out of concepts of care and welfare by child protection and children's rights, raise questions as to whether residential care is best placed or can continue to exist in any meaningful form within the social work profession.

The 1989 Children Act and the 1995 Children (Scotland) Act

The major legislative developments in recent decades have been the 1989 Children Act and the 1995 Children (Scotland) Act. Both sets of provision reflect, among other things, the influence of the UNCRC, emphasising the importance of taking children's views into account in any decisions that affect them. The 1989 Children Act focused on 'children in need', and duties in respect of this group were vested in local authorities through an extension of ideas around corporate parenting. The concept of care, however, is itself marginalised. Children in the care of the local authority, whether living at home under supervision or in residential or foster care, are now deemed to be 'looked after' rather than 'in care'. Those who are in residential resources are described as 'accommodated' by the local authority. This terminology was introduced to try and highlight rights, to reduce stigma and to reconfigure care as a (preferably short-term) service to parents. However, the focus on rights and on an instrumental and consumerist version of care might also be argued to reflect the wider retreat from welfare evident in late modern society, removing any affective conception of care still further from the centre of the policy agenda. Cameron argues that:

> The therapeutic and preventative approaches to child care favoured in the postwar years were seen to be discredited and displaced in favour of a new legalistic approach in which the focus was child protection (rather than care).... Even the terminology of 'care' in conjunction with local authority

parenting was out of favour and considered stigmatising.
(2003, p 89)

McGhee and Waterhouse likewise claim that the Scottish legislation marks a shift in policy away from a welfare base and 'towards a justice-oriented approach in child-care decision-making where legal principles are uppermost' (1998, p 49).

There is a danger that the principles of the Children Acts, with their emphasis on rights and corporate parenting, which of course is intended to stress a wider responsibility for children, might actually inhibit carers from taking direct, personal responsibility for children's day-to-day care. The likelihood of care becoming depersonalised is compounded by increasing reliance on a range of technologies of care (Webb, 2006), from risk assessments to social skills problems, all of which locate care within systems and tools rather than individual relationships.

The 1990s

While the 1980s were dominated by family-oriented ideologies of care, the 1990s saw the social work task with children and families increasingly defined by revelations of abuse, initially within families but subsequently in residential care, as discussed in the following chapter. Largely as a result of the crisis induced by abuse scandals, the 1990s saw an awakening of political interest in the discipline. The upsurge in political interest in residential child care has been a mixed blessing. The discipline has become incredibly sensitive to political gaze, filtered through a lens of child protection. The application of a predominant child protection focus to practice has detracted from the essential developmental task of residential child care, evident in a range of policies and practices around, for instance, physical touch and health and safety. It has also served (as noted in Chapter One) to remove the locus of control of the profession away from those with experience in the field to a series of external managers and HR personnel.

Conclusion

I began this chapter by making the point that the history of residential child care has not been one of steady progress. Rather it has reflected the belief systems dominant at any particular time around children and how to care for them. Anglin (2002) describes a broad shift from custodial ('warehousing') approaches, to those predominantly concerned with care and protection ('greenhousing'), to more recent trends towards intense interventions focused on particular behaviours or areas of concern ('hothousing'). More recently a legalistic conception of rights has become dominant. According to Grant and Gabor (2006), eras are not discrete but 'overlap and interact and, as such, the evolution of new philosophies have not always meant the disappearance of old ones. The philosophies of the early eras still affect programmes today' (2006, p 17). The doctrine of less eligibility, for instance, while no longer evident in a material sense, can still pervade attitudes towards children in care as indeed can desires to 'rescue' children.

It seems to be a feature of our current age (and perhaps any age) to consider that policy preferences can be ascribed an ahistorical status, where the nature of provision is self-evident. We can buy into a conceit that we know what good care looks like and how it might be measured. We call it 'best practice'. By implication what went before was less than best practice. Yet in reality none of these positions is value-neutral; 'best practice' cannot be divorced from dominant ideologies; aspects of today's 'best practice' may well be tomorrow's abuse. Injunctions against physical contact between adults and children may spring to mind as a case in point.

Throughout the history of residential child care particular ideologies have inhibited the care experiences offered to children. Ideologies of treatment, for instance, while they may appear benign and may cater to a desire among workers to assume a therapeutic role, are only one possible way of mediating the care we offer to children. Grant and Gabor (2006) argue that a treatment ideology merely supplants a focus on a child's psyche for that on their soul, as was the concern of previous generations of practice. In both cases residential care is something imposed on children. The children's rights and consumer involvement agendas which have come to the fore in more recent years bring with them their own problems, as discussed at different points throughout this book.

The tendency to look back on seemingly less enlightened times is not necessarily helpful. It can breed a complacency that somehow we have things sorted to the point that we can reify practice in standards and codes. At another level it curtails our capacity to imagine different and possibly better ways of caring for children; it seeks to deny the historically contingent nature of current practice. Practices that really only reflect the preferences of our own time and place assume a 'taken-for-granted' status. It can be taken for granted that foster care is preferable to residential child care despite the fact that most other countries in the world choose to place more children in residential care and with better outcomes than the UK (Cameron, 2004). It can be taken for granted that small units are better than large ones despite the fact that the evidence for this is contradictory at best (Clough et al, 2006); we increasingly take for granted that ever increasing numbers of children need to be deprived of their liberty through the expansion in the use of secure accommodation. History might judge as to whether such assumptions and policies based on them reflect any greater spirit of enlightenment than those of previous generations.

THREE

Inquiries and their impact

From the early 1990s residential child care across much of the world has been engulfed in allegations of historical abuse and has faced an accompanying barrage of inquiries and publicity. Taking children into public care can only be justified on the grounds that to do so will provide them with a better experience than, or at least one as good as, they might otherwise have had. When they are taken into care elements of the duty of care ascribed to parents under common law transfer to the state (Fulcher, 2002). The realisation that children have been abused in public care has confronted residential child care with a crisis of legitimacy. Accordingly, it is right that attention is focused on how to ensure that the experiences of children in public care properly reflect the state's responsibilities towards them. It is right, too, that those whose lives have been blighted by experiences in state care should be offered appropriate support.

Child abuse is considered to fall under physical, sexual and emotional categories, any of which might be manifest in residential care. The literature similarly identifies three categories of institutional abuse; overt or direct abuse perpetrated by an individual adult on a child, programme abuse where theoretical models are misapplied and system abuse where deficits in the wider child care system prevent children from reaching their potential (Sen et al, 2007). Stein (2006) notes that in many cases categories overlap. He also adds organised abuse as a further category of institutional abuse.

Belief in the widespread and endemic nature of institutional abuse can assume a 'taken-for-granted' status. Ferguson asserts that 'it is beyond question that the entire industrial and reformatory regime was an abusive and cruel one' (2007, p 124). A systemic review into historical abuse commissioned by the Scottish Government (Shaw, 2007) recounts views of former residents that are unremittingly bleak. Such negative views have been influential in informing public perception and policy. The whole 20th century can be presented as something of a dark age for residential child care. Indeed, the period from the turn of the 21st century has been represented as one of recovery from the various scandals that came to light in the 1990s (for example, Crimmens and Milligan, 2005; Milligan and Stevens, 2006).

Yet, the increasing public concern for residential child care which emerged over the course of the 1990s is a recent phenomenon. There is little to suggest that the sector was considered to be problematic over the course of the previous century. In the period from the end of the Second World War until the late 1980s Corby et al (2001) identified only six public inquiries into concerns around care establishments. These were viewed as isolated incidents and not considered to reflect any wider malaise in the system. It is largely hindsight that allows current interpretations of historic abuse allegations to emerge. What then is behind this upsurge in public concern about residential child care? This chapter attempts to locate events of the past couple of decades in historical and social context. It considers the findings of some of the main reports and inquiries and then takes an avowedly critical look at the evidence on which such concerns are based and the implications of the resultant inquiry culture for residential child care. I begin with a discussion of the emergence of child abuse into public consciousness.

The social construction of child abuse

There are certain acts, such as systematic beatings or sexual assaults perpetrated by adults against children, that there can be no doubt about: they are wrong, arguably evil. There are other acts that are far less amenable to such clear-cut moral or professional judgement. The term 'child abuse' can be presented in professional and public discourse as though it has some common understanding. It does not; child abuse is 'a "social construction" if ever there was one' (Hacking, 1992, p 192); views on what constitutes child abuse are culturally and historically contingent.

Concern about the treatment of children in public care can only be understood in the context of how society constructs children more generally. From the mid-19th century dominant constructions of children considered that they required physical sustenance, rigid discipline and moral guidance. The emergence of Freudian psychology and growing theoretical awareness of concepts of attachment introduced a greater appreciation of the importance of attending to the emotional needs of children. Nevertheless, approaches to children and childhood continued to mirror wider social norms and parental mores where a 'spare the rod' belief was well entrenched in many sectors of society.

In residential child care, notions of mistreatment have similarly changed over time. As recently as the 1980s a government report into issues of control in residential child care opined that:

> The clout in anger worries us less than formal beatings....
> Distanced, retributive corporal punishment seems to us ...
> less preferable than cuffs delivered during normal social
> interaction. In any case this type of sanction is very difficult
> to prevent as it can arise quite spontaneously. (Millham et
> al, 1981, p 39)

A clear distinction in the thinking of the day emerges between the spontaneous slap delivered in the course of everyday living and an institutionalised and depersonalised conception of corporal punishment. Residential care workers were not to feel guilty over administering such clouts as they could be considered as an expression of care (Millham et al, 1981). In a social climate where the physical chastisement of children by their parents was widely accepted and care staff were deemed to be 'in loco parentis' this view is understandable. And of course the physical punishment of children in school was still legal; corporal punishment was in fact only banned in residential and foster care from the late 1980s. Even when agencies began to train staff in physical restraint in the early 1990s the method used was a Home Office approved model, which relied on pain control. Present-day unease over the physical abuse of children might benefit from greater historical perspective.

Other contextual issues relate to questions of scale and to privacy, both of which determined how adults cared for children. Staffing ratios which had one or two adults responsible for perhaps 20 children demanded more rigid and less personal discipline than might be possible in present-day situations where staffing ratios can be 1:1. Attitudes towards privacy and nudity have also seen a sea-change in recent years. In large residential schools or children's homes, ideas of privacy, which are now taken for granted, were wholly impractical. Sleeping, showering and changing were communal activities, done in the presence of and at times alongside same-sex staff (Burmeister, 1960). Not only was this a practical necessity, it was considered to be good practice in terms of fostering healthy attitudes towards sexuality (Neil, 1966).

The growth of child protection

Improvements in social conditions in the 1950s and 1960s saw people having more time to devote to family life and becoming more aware of childhood as a phase of growth and development to be protected and cherished. Corby et al (2001) chart how this growing concern for children became reflected in a greater awareness of them being abused. The initial manifestation of this emerged in the 1960s based on the work of the North American paediatrician, Henry Kempe, who coined the term 'battered baby'.

The next wave of concern over protecting children came with the 'discovery' of sexual abuse. Given how pervasive accounts of sexual abuse now seem, awareness of it is strangely recent. The UK government first acknowledged its existence (in family settings) in 1986 (Abrams, 1998). The following year a major public controversy ensued (over the removal of children from their family homes and care homes in Cleveland in the North East of England), on the basis of disputed medical evidence. Nevertheless, the spectre of child sex abuse became etched in the public consciousness. This episode, and events in Orkney in 1991 (Clyde, 1992), where 16 children were taken from their homes in connection with allegations of ritual and organised sexual abuse, on the basis of questionable investigation techniques, led to an upsurge in public concern about the precipitous intervention of social workers in family life. Other episodes of alleged satanic ritual abuse involving family members and wider networks erupted in the late 1980s/early 1990s, based on North American ideas around believing children, however bizarre their stories might appear (Summit, 1983). The satanic ritual abuse controversy and the credulity of social workers in becoming caught up in it is a fascinating episode in social work's history. The very existence of satanic ritual abuse and the methods used by police and social workers to investigate such scares were subsequently discredited (La Fontaine, 1994, 1998).

Corby et al (2001) suggest that concerns over the way in which claims of abuse were managed in cases such as Orkney, Cleveland and elsewhere served to refocus attention in child protection cases away from the removal of children and towards family support. But by now a child protection ideology was well entrenched. The effect of redirecting efforts to find abuse away from the family shifted that focus on to residential child care, an area that, partly because of wider social work antipathy towards institutional care, might be thought likely to conceal an underbelly of abuse. The period from the early 1990s onwards has been one of unparalleled scrutiny, witnessing numerous abuse inquiries and several government reports, which, although not responding to particular events, were indicative of a more general concern about residential care. The next section of this chapter identifies some of the more significant of these reports and inquiries.

Wagner

The first major report into residential care (not just child care), the Wagner Report (1988), pre-dated the major scandals that came to engulf the sector. The report's title, *A positive choice*, reflected its intention to create a positive perception of the place of residential care within a continuum of services. It acknowledged that for this to happen the stressful nature of the task needed to be recognised and staff supported to carry it out; accordingly it addressed a range of issues to do with the recruitment, selection, support and training of staff.

Pindown

The first of the major inquiries into residential care concerned the 'Pindown' regime operated in two children's homes in Staffordshire in the English Midlands between 1983 and 1989. 'Pindown' was a system of controlling young people through isolating them and depriving them of a range of rights and liberties. Unlike other abuse scandals there was no attempt to conceal details of the Pindown regime – the logbooks detailing the restrictions of liberty were freely available and the regime had the explicit approval of senior managers in the social work department. The resulting inquiry by Staffordshire County Council (Levy and Kahan, 1991) stated, nonetheless, that the method went beyond what could be conceived to be acceptable professional practice and that it was unethical and unlawful. This was, in many respects, however, a retrospective judgement – for several years Pindown was very much 'business as usual' in residential child care in Staffordshire (Butler and Drakeford, 2005). The inquiry made what were to become customary recommendations in respect of recruitment practices, staff supervision and training, and the respective roles of senior managers and home staff.

Utting and Skinner

Emerging concerns about the state of residential child care, highlighted by the Pindown experience, reflected a more general disquiet about residential child care and led the UK government to commission Sir William Utting to conduct a general review of the sector in England and Wales, published as *Children in the public care* (1991). This made a range of recommendations around staff selection and training and called for improved procedures. Running alongside this, Angus Skinner, the chief social work inspector, was asked to undertake a similar exercise for Scotland, published as *Another kind of home* (1992). This set out a number of principles, providing a general framework for residential child care practice in Scotland.

Warner

Perhaps the most notorious case of abuse in residential care relates to the conviction of Frank Beck for presiding over a regime of physical and sexual abuse under the guise of 'regression therapy' in children's homes in Leicestershire where he had been officer in charge between 1973 and 1986. He was convicted in 1991 of a catalogue of sexual and physical abuse. This led the government to commission a report into selection and recruitment methods. Norman Warner, a former director of social services, was commissioned to undertake this review, resulting in the publication of the report *Choosing with care* (Warner, 1992), which once again covers a broad range of personnel issues, including training and staff support. *Choosing with care* concluded that recruitment practices in residential child care were slack. Many workers, with no qualifications or experience suiting them for the job, had been appointed due to word-of-mouth recommendation, or family connections. This led to a tightening of methods of selection leading among other things to the increasing use of police checks and more systematic recruitment processes.

Over the course of the 1990s reports of abuse (mostly historical) continued to come to light. The UK government once again commissioned Sir William Utting, this time to review the safeguards for children introduced in the 1989 Children Act and to recommend whether these were sufficient and properly enforced. Roger Kent was asked to undertake a similar exercise for Scotland, his report coinciding with the implementation of the 1995 Children (Scotland) Act (implemented in 1997). The Utting Report was published as *People like us* (1997) and the Kent Report as the *Children's safeguards review* in the same year. In England the *Quality Protects* initiative discussed in Chapter Four stemmed from the recommendations of *People like us*. In Scotland, Kent's recommendations led to the establishment in 2000 of the Scottish Institute for Residential Child Care (SIRCC), a consortium of educational bodies and child care agencies with a remit to develop training and consultancy across the range of residential child care provision.

Waterhouse

The most extensive inquiry into abuse in residential child care centred around Bryn Estyn, a former approved school in North Wales. Throughout the 1980s there had been persistent rumours of abuse in children's homes in this area. These were investigated by the police, who found no evidence of systematic abuse. Largely due to the persistence of a 'whistleblower', Alison Taylor, inquiries were reopened and resulted in the prosecution and conviction of a number of staff who had worked in homes in North Wales. The scale of alleged abuse led to the establishment of a Tribunal of Inquiry, the highest form of inquiry available to the state, under Sir Ronald Waterhouse, published in 2000 as *Lost in care*. Waterhouse concluded that there had been widespread abuse in children's homes although found no evidence to support the more sensationalist claims of paedophile rings preying on young people in care. Waterhouse made 72 recommendations from which emerged the establishment of an independent children's commissioner for Wales and improved procedures for whistleblowing and for dealing with complaints. He also recommended an independent regulatory body to inspect child care services.

Questioning dominant accounts

The raft of inquiries and other accounts of abuse in care settings intertwine to construct a picture of endemic abuse and systematic cover-up in residential care. This is a subject, however, that can become shrouded in emotivism, where expressions of attitude, preference or feeling with little rational justification assume a moral force (Macintyre, 1984). Because the impact of abuse inquiries has been so central to subsequent policy in residential care and has had a detrimental effect on motivation and morale, it behoves us to ask what we really know about abuse in care and whether responses to it have been proportionate or appropriate.

Incidence and prevalence of abuse in care

Ascertaining the scale of abuse in care is problematic. Hacking (1992) attests that attempts to quantify child abuse (of all sorts) fail to measure up to philosophical standards of whether a concept is well understood: for a subject to be so it requires that it is amenable to the question 'How many?'. Attempts to quantify child abuse are 'amazingly discrepant' (Hacking, 1992), made more so in cases of historic abuse by the different standards of what was considered acceptable behaviour at different periods of time.

Aside from the various inquiries, the actual evidence of widespread abuse in care settings is not strong. It would appear to be no more likely in residential than in foster care (Kendrick, 1998) or in community settings where adults have access to children (Gallagher, 2000). In Scotland public petitions to the parliament on the subject of historic abuse in care on one occasion contained one signatory, on another four, while the children's advocacy group Who Cares? (Scotland) had to close down a helpline established to advise victims of historical abuse after it received only one call in a three-month period (Scottish Executive, 2005a). Even in the child protection literature there is a shift from accepting more extreme accounts of the extent of abuse to a position that concludes that we do not really know its extent (Corby, 2006; Shaw, 2007).

Role of public inquiries

Public inquiries are the source of most of the information currently available on abuse in care settings. Inquiries, however, are not neutral but involve a range of political and wider social agendas. Butler and Drakeford suggest that there is 'a symbiotic relationship between scandal, the Committee of Inquiry and public policy' (2005, p 4). Inquiries are used to further political agendas, arguably in this case agendas related to a 'rebalancing' of the criminal justice system in favour of victims.

The purpose of inquiries is to establish a 'master narrative', which 'is only one partisan version of many possible accounts' (Butler and Drakeford, 2005, p 235). The master narrative in respect of abuse in care is one of 'sexual terrorists' (Utting, 1997) infiltrating children's homes, weak management and complicit staff groups. Such cultures were ultimately exposed and brought to right by the person of the 'whistleblower'. All of this is overlain with a concern for 'victims' of abuse and their need for 'closure' through the conviction of their abuser (Smith, 2008). It is a scenario replete with the heroes and villains that are the stuff of which scandals are constructed (Butler and Drakeford, 2005). Butler and Drakeford go on to note that 'dissenting and questioning voices are to be discovered, submerged beneath the dominant discourse' (2005, p 137). The submerged narratives in this situation are perhaps those of the staff who worked in such settings. There can be a dissonance between the official version of alleged abuse in residential child care and the views of those who worked in establishments caught up in abuse scandals, as is apparent in evidence to the Waterhouse Inquiry. Dissenting voices are also to be heard from those children brought up in residential child care who tell of very different experiences of care. In Ireland such voices are brought together around an organisation Let Our Voices Emerge (LOVE), which challenges dominant accounts of abuse in care homes. What is becoming increasingly apparent is that the reality of what went on in residential child care historically is much more diffuse and contested than has been claimed and presented in inquiry reports and most professional literature.

The secret of Bryn Estyn *and the witch-hunt metaphor*

Richard Webster's book *The secret of Bryn Estyn* (2005) demands a more fundamental questioning of the basis of how issues of historical abuse in residential child care are considered. Webster's work more generally (available on his website, www.richardwebster.net), provides a compelling challenge to dominant accounts. Webster is clear that abuse occurred in residential child care, noting that:

> It requires only a little knowledge of human nature to recognise that wherever adults and young people are placed together in residential settings – whether in boarding schools, in religious institutions or in families – sexual abuse will sometimes take place. Care homes are no exception to this and some of those who are now in prison are there for no other reason than that they are guilty of the crimes alleged against them. (2005, p 4)

He goes on, however, to systematically deconstruct the 'official' version, of what went on in North Wales as represented in the Waterhouse Report (2000). He exposes fundamental inconsistencies and falsehoods in many of the allegations of abuse made in North Wales (including casting serious doubt on the conviction of one of the main protagonists there), before extending his critique to the way in which belief in widespread institutional abuse spread from North Wales over most of England and Wales. The lure of financial compensation is deemed central in motivating many claims of abuse. He seeks to understand how such a situation could arise and uses the metaphor of the witch-hunt to liken events in North Wales to earlier historical incarnations of panic over children and sex within a persistent strand of the Christian tradition for demonological fantasy. There is an intellectual rigour to Webster's work that should not be ignored. The rationality promised by the Enlightenment project can appear seriously compromised by attitudes and responses to historical abuse, which expose some of the more primordial recesses of the human psyche.

There are of course difficulties in bringing those who abused children in the past to justice in cases where there is generally no evidence other than the word of those making allegations. On the one hand this can leave former residents who were genuinely abused with no recourse and a feeling of not being believed. Arguably, however, the balance has tilted so far that the default position of many in the social work profession, the police and the prosecuting authorities is to react to the horrors of abuse by accepting allegations uncritically and pursuing them too rigorously. This is often undertaken through a process that has become known as 'trawling', whereby the police seek out former residents of care homes in an attempt to collate sufficient accounts of abuse to gain a conviction. The difficulties inherent in practices of investigating historical abuse are acknowledged in a Home Affairs Committee report from 2002 which states that 'trawling' is an:

> ... absolutely unregulated process tailor-made to generate false allegations. There is deep concern over the conduct of police interviews and the integrity of witness testimony. Set in the context of a growing compensation culture the risks of effecting a miscarriage of justice are unusually high. (Home Affairs Committee, 2002)

It goes on to claim, 'It has been suggested, and we believe it to be so, that a new genre of miscarriages of justice has arisen'. Beckett reiterates this view, claiming that:

> ... the methods involved in obtaining evidence for convictions in the UK have, at times, been seriously questionable. They have typically included inviting adult former care residents, many years after the event, to make allegations and there are instances of demonstrably false allegations being made as well as allegations that seem pretty clearly to have been motivated by the possibility of financial compensation.... I believe that it is likely that a significant number of imprisoned former residential workers may have been wrongfully convicted. (2003, p 217)

In whose interests?

The fact that children were abused in residential care is unacceptable. However, those experiences should not be compounded by responses to alleged abuse. Lee and Pithers, albeit from an earlier period of practice, present a message that might have some resonance in this context. They claim that 'we must resist children in care being led to understand the world through fatalistic experiences; of being persuaded that they are always victims' (1980, p 113). This position has shifted. Furedi claims that:

> … contemporary culture provides a powerful incentive to individuals to manipulate their memory and present themselves as traumatised victims. The assertion of trauma as a result of past suffering has become a way of winning public recognition and attention, and of making a claim on resources. (Furedi, 2008)

The resources invested in investigating allegations of past abuse are justified by invoking the interests of the 'victim'. The term 'victim', however, is not neutral; it has emerged from these wider discourses of individualism and consumerism where personal worth is explicitly linked with questions of financial compensation (Spalek, 2006).

It is perhaps timely to ask whether being labelled a victim has actually served the interests of those alleging abuse. This is not to dismiss the experiences of genuine victims of abuse in care but to question whether what is claimed and done in their name is actually in their interests. Investigation and prosecution proceed from an assumption that the disclosure of previous abuse is somehow cathartic and the conviction of an abuser still more so. There is little evidence to support this supposition. Colton et al (2002) describe how the process of having their pasts resurrected and taken through an investigative and legal process can re-traumatise victims of abuse. Hacking (1992) suggests that the symptoms of child abuse may be iatrogenic, induced by the helping professionals involved in such cases. The role of some counsellors, litigation lawyers and the police allied with the level of hype and publicity around abuse in care may construct its own victims replete with their own symptoms. And, thus constructed, 'victims' can become stuck in such a role, unable to tell a different story of their lives.

The regulation of residential child care

The various inquiries, Waterhouse in particular, have been used to legitimise ever more external scrutiny of residential child care through the establishment of a host of new regulatory bodies. These developments are ostensibly linked to improvement and the consumerist imperative to provide a better service to the public. In England the Commission for Social Care Inspection (CSCI), a single, independent inspectorate for all social care services in England, was launched in 2004. In Scotland, the 2001 Regulation of Care (Scotland) Act established the Care Commission, which inspects all residential care homes against sets of care standards. The Care Standards Inspectorate for Wales, the Northern Ireland Social Care Council and the Irish Social Services Inspectorate have similar remits. All these bodies have powers to demand improvements in services and to impose sanctions on organisations that fail to meet minimum standards. There is little evidence that their existence has brought about service improvement, however.

In addition to the inspection of premises against care standards, there have also been developments to regulate the social care workforce. The various care councils have published codes of practice. The regulation of care can be presented as being fundamental to the modernisation and improvement of residential child care (Crimmens and Milligan, 2005). There is little evidence, however, that it has led to improvement of the sector or to better outcomes for those placed there (DfES, 2006; Scottish Government, 2007a). But regulation is not just about improvement. McLaughlin (2007) argues that it is predicated on meta-narratives of abuse, lack of trust and an assumption that social workers require external surveillance to prevent them from abusing those they work with.

Regulation is also selective in its focus on inquiry and report recommendations. Two prominent recommendations reflected across the various reports are the assertion of the potential for residential care to be a positive choice for some young people and the need for staff to be properly qualified and to feel valued and supported. This has not happened. Residential child care has not become a positive choice for children. For the most part it continues as a residual service, a placement of last resort. The casual assumption of its inferiority is evident in *Changing lives* (Scottish Executive, 2006), the review of the future of social work in Scotland, which states that although residential care might be suitable for a few children many more are currently there because of a shortage of foster placements. This assertion is not supported by evidence and ignores the rate of foster care breakdown

(Berridge and Cleaver, 1987) and the fact that many children prefer residential care over foster care (Milligan and Stevens, 2006).

Rarely too do staff feel adequately valued. The vision of a professionally qualified workforce has not come to pass. Targets to achieve this (for example, the Skinner Report [Scottish Office, 1993]) never came close to being met. With the inception of the various care councils the aspiration towards a professionally qualified workforce has been dropped in favour of registration requirements set at Vocational Qualification (VQ) level, a qualification that can be argued to be pedagogically unsuited to the dynamic and relational nature of residential child care (Heron and Chakrabarti, 2002). So, as various inquiries have highlighted the need to improve professional standing and qualification levels, residential care has in fact witnessed an incremental 'dumbing down' of the nature of qualification required to work in the sector, at a time when the demands posed by the shrinking population of residential settings are becoming more acute. Policy trends in relation to the social care workforce have been to lower the levels of qualifications required to do the job, and to police the workforce through a variety of inspectorial and audit functions (Humphrey, 2003).

The effects of regulation

Just before the publication of the Waterhouse Report, Corby (2000) cautioned against an over-procedural response to its recommendations. His note of caution fell on deaf ears. Anxiety to avoid scandal has led to defensive and foreclosing organisational responses, which have skewed the development of the sector. Residential workers are viewed with suspicion, both publicly and in their own agencies, often subject to precipitous, back-covering investigation in the event of any complaint made against them. There are consequences for children when residential care workers are so devalued. Caregivers need to feel safe if they in turn are to value children in their care. Paradoxically, the more confident and empowered adults feel, the better they are able to listen to and respect children and to take their views into account. When adults are insecure, when they know that ultimate authority lies outside of the care relationship and is vested in various codes, procedures and external regulatory bodies, they are tentative, they stop believing that they can effect change. When staff do not feel safe they act in ways that seek to limit the threat; they pull back from situations where their motives or actions might be questioned; they cover their backs; the primary task of caring for children becomes subsumed beneath a concern to ensure their own safety. As Horwath (2000) notes, they attempt to care with gloves on.

In the current climate an understandable concern for personal safety can be packaged as a hallmark of professionalism. McWilliam and Jones (2005) offer an insight into the ways that teachers define what it is to be professional in a risk-averse climate. They do so by keeping themselves safe – by refusing to touch children, by making sure they are not alone with them – in short, by failing to make the kind of connections a good teacher should. Sachs (2003) notes that it is those who work with children that have become risky subjects within a child protection discourse.

Stripping out social context

While the literature identifies abuse as occurring at different individual, programmatic and systemic levels the tendency in practice is to reduce analysis to a simple matter of powerful adults abusing powerless children. The complexity of the problems faced or exhibited by many of those placed in residential care, including their home circumstances, instances of offending and violent behaviour, the need at times for physical restraint or the intimacy, the messiness, ambiguity and complex psychodynamic processes involved in everyday acts of caring, are explained away, the social is expunged. Problems become 'stripped of social context and social consequences. They are understood in terms of an individualized view of the self' (Atkinson, 1997, p 339).

The tendency to locate blame with workers on the ground when things go wrong in residential care is evident in the Pindown case. It was the home manager who was publicly associated with events rather than departmental managers and politicians who were fully aware of and sanctioned the regime there. In cases of physical restraint, guidance acknowledges that 'young people are always restrained within an organisational context, and decisions on when and how to do so are influenced by many different factors, some of which are in the control of managers and not practitioners' (Davidson et al, 2005, p xi). That organisational context includes dimensions of, for instance, staffing levels and qualifications, support systems for staff and admissions policies.

A similar reductionist tendency applies to those claiming abuse in care. An impression is created that subsequent difficulties in life can be attributed to this experience. Prior and subsequent personal problems and structural issues such as poverty and other disadvantage are marginalised. While some former residents have undoubtedly had their lives blighted by their experiences in care others latch on to this for all sorts of reasons, including attempting to identify a cause of the difficulties in their lives, general vexation and, although it is not de rigueur to mention this in polite company, financial compensation.

A fixation with questions of child protection and children's rights within an increasingly litigious culture also skews discussion away from legitimate debate around key practice issues such as care and control. The failure to adequately confront questions of control is increasingly apparent. Rod Morgan, the former chair of the Youth Justice Board in England and Wales, implicates the failure of staff in children's homes to address issues of control appropriately in a rise in the criminalisation of young people:

> In children's care homes what we are finding is that many children who are committing minor acts in residential accommodation, minor acts of criminal damage or have thrown a punch at a fellow child or member of staff – the police are more and more being used as a disciplinary back-up force for ill-supported and ill-trained residential staff. (Morgan, 2006)

The reluctance of staff to confront children's behaviour is hardly surprising in a climate where they live in fear of allegations being made against them and of the possible implications of this.

Rethinking historical abuse

So how might this malleable and changing phenomenon of historical abuse in residential care be understood? The first thing to say is that there were, of course, instances of abuse that were unambiguous. There were still more cases where the experiences of children in care, if not directly abusive, were characterised by a poverty of aspiration, a lack of affection and a failure to appreciate their emotional needs. The assumption of more widespread abuse, however, is likely to be accounted for by changing ways of thinking about children, the exponential widening of the net of what is considered to be child abuse (Furedi, 2005) and the intrusion of legal discourse into ever more areas of human relationships. Hacking suggests that practices considered commonplace in previous decades have been reclassified, retrospectively viewed as abusive although they were 'not directly and consciously experienced as such at the time' (1992, p 229). Nevertheless, much professional assumption and practice proceeds untroubled by historical contingency.

Some creative tension ought to exist between the capacity of individuals to do good and the need for regulation. The balance struck is currently wrong. Parton argues that:

> In trying to resolve these tensions, primarily by increasing our attempts to control, discipline and regulate, we are in great danger of failing to maximise the possibilities for responsible adults and more particularly children and young people themselves to play a central part in realising and creating their own lives. (2006, p 178)

Conclusion

This chapter has outlined the upsurge in concern about the residential care of children that emerged over the course of the 1990s and has considered the implications of this. This is an episode in the history of residential child care which, when placed under critical analysis, becomes decidedly more opaque than is often presented. The emergent concern for children in residential child care was not neutral. It occurred at a time when public service professionals generally were subject to a lack of trust, increased concern about accountability and a corresponding expansion of regulation. Furthermore, the overwhelming focus on residential child care, as opposed to other areas of practice where children are just as likely to be abused, can only be understood in light of wider contextual and ideological factors such as a persistent antipathy towards residential care in social work, which entails that residential care has many detractors and only lukewarm defenders, along with trends in child protection which focused a gaze on residential care.

Whether political or professional responses to revelations of abuse have been either proportionate or functional is questionable. They have arguably created as many problems as they profess to address. Legalistic and regulatory responses have cast a veil of suspicion over the sector and those working in it. At the extreme this is manifest in the investigation and prosecution of scores of former care workers, often on the basis of preconceived assumptions and dubious investigatory techniques. At a practice level it has sanitised the very essence of care, making it increasingly difficult to offer children the kind of affection and control they need. It has also contributed to a trend of locating the locus of knowledge about residential child care in sets of abstract principles and standards and in an array of external managers rather than in the expertise of those who do the job. Time and money that might have been spent improving practice through professional discourse and addressing the recommendations of the various inquiries for a better qualified and supported workforce has been taken up ensuring that the latest administrative requirements are addressed.

This is a watershed issue for residential child care. The persistent belief in endemic abuse and the nature and ramifications of the measures implemented to counter this risk destroying residential child care altogether, not improving it as is claimed. Rather than being a servant towards the greater aim of improved care the regulatory responses introduced have become its master.

FOUR

Trends and policy directions

Introduction

If the early 1990s were dominated by responses to abuse the latter years of the decade witnessed a change of government from Conservative to New Labour in 1997. The new government quickly put children at the top of its policy agenda. For children in care this signalled a shift in emphasis away from a primary focus on protection and towards improving outcomes across a range of measures. In practice, however, anxiety over child protection ensures that it remains a dominant (and arguably the dominant) concern both in residential child care and for children and families services more generally. This chapter identifies some current trends and policy directions in residential child care. It starts by setting out changing patterns of usage before addressing the political focus on outcomes for children in care. Despite the plethora of policy initiatives, few inroads have been made in effecting meaningful change, and possible reasons for this are discussed.

Trends in the usage of residential child care

Although social work discourses around de-institutionalisation and non-intervention sought to limit the use of residential child care, the years following the passage of the Social Work Acts in the late 1960s actually witnessed a high point in the use of such placements, with numbers in England peaking at 96,000 in 1977. At that point there were around twice as many children in residential care as in foster care. Thereafter numbers fell rapidly, to 67,000 in 1986 (Bebbington and Miles, 1989) and have continued to fall since then, although this decline has bottomed out in recent years.

The 1989 Children Act and the 1995 Children (Scotland) Act introduced the 'looked after' terminology to describe children in state care, which includes children maintained at home, those in foster care and in different types of residential care. In England around 60,000 children are looked after (DfES, 2006); in Scotland around 12,000 (Scottish Government, 2007a). Of those placed out of the family home English figures show that only 13% are in residential care, a substantial majority (68%) being in foster care. Others are placed with family members. There are noticeable age variations within this figure, however; almost 30% of looked-after 15-year-olds are placed in residential care, perhaps indicating difficulties in maintaining them within foster care. It may also indicate a preference that many children have for residential care (Milligan and Stevens, 2006), despite policy preferences and assumptions that restrict its use.

The age profile of residential child care which sees higher proportions of older children placed there highlights structural realities in the child care system. The reliance on fostering as the placement of choice for social work professionals brings with it inevitable breakdowns. Some children can experience 20 or 30 moves of placement (Milligan and Stevens, 2006). Residential care often has to pick up the pieces of the disruption caused by such transience. A consequence of the policy preference for fostering has been the residualisation of residential child care, whereby only the most difficult to place young people are admitted. This has obvious implications for practice, and some of these are discussed elsewhere in the book in terms of cultures of care and in specific practices such as physical restraint.

Other trends, identified by Clough et al (2006), include a shift from single- to mixed-sex establishments, an increase in the level of health or behavioural problems faced by children, a greater ethnic mix, shorter stays and a shift from local authorities providing services directly to a position where they increasingly commission them from charities or private providers. There has also been a rise in the use of residential care for children with disabilities, often in the form of short breaks, and increased use of secure and custodial facilities. The size and nature of residential care homes has also changed over time.

Siting and size of homes

A legacy of the rescue philosophy discussed in Chapter Two was a trend to site care homes away from centres of population, either on the outskirts of towns or in rural locations. At one level this was justified in terms of removing children from the perceived contaminating effects of their families and at another it reflected an obsession among the Victorians with fresh air as being desirable for city children. Arguably there was also an 'out of sight, out of mind' motivation behind such policies. Buildings tended to be large, set in their own grounds and involved dormitory sleeping and communal eating and living arrangements.

Adults can make assumptions about what a residential home should be like. Thus, in these days of en suite bathrooms it can be assumed that children in care should be provided with similar facilities. We might imagine too that the privacy of single and en suite bedrooms provides a safety for children who may have painful memories of night-times. Richard McKenzie, a business professor who as a child had been brought up in an orphanage in North Carolina, tells a different story. He recounts how people sympathise with him regarding how awful it must have been to be taken from home and placed in a large institution. His response to this was that as a nine-year-old boy all he could think about when he saw the large dormitory that was to be his home was 'pillow fights!'. Practice experience would also suggest other possible interpretations of our taken-for-granted value positions. Children can become far more distressed in single room accommodation than they might when sharing with others. Having others around them could provide a distraction and a sense of safety, whereas what adults might think of as a safe (solitary) environment actually gives them too much time to dwell on their thoughts. Saying this is not to argue for a return to dormitory living, however, but rather to suggest that many current assumptions regarding what group care facilities should be like are primarily ideological rather than evidence based.

With the move towards smaller units and drawing on ideologies of normalisation and de-institutionalisation, the trend from the 1960s onwards has been to locate homes in local communities. In many cases this involved knocking together a couple of council houses and designating the resultant building a children's home. While the intention behind such trends was understandable, it was not without its difficulties. Homes often failed to become properly integrated into their host communities and in the worst cases became a focus for mutual suspicion and hostility. Moreover, the policy of housing groups of teenagers in what was built as a family home entailed that there was little of the space that adolescents living together need. The presence of two or three 'go-go kids' (Maier, 1979) in a resident group could make for a bumpy ride for staff and other children. One way that staff sought to deal with this was to shift the focus of activity outside the home. This often did not involve staff other than as a source of bus fares and pocket money; it could be justified on the grounds of providing individualised responses for children and as averting institutionalisation. On the other hand it precluded much of the mutual interaction that shared involvement in daily living can bring. In many homes there was and is little sense of group identity or cohesion and increasing problems of control.

The response to difficulties of control has been a persistent demand from practitioners, generally supported by policy makers, for smaller residential units; a taken-for-granted belief has emerged that smaller is better. In fact there is little evidence to support this (Clough et al, 2006). Quite aside from being prohibitively expensive, practice experience would suggest that there are times when more staff on shift can lead to a lack of focus on the needs of the children. Furthermore, if the culture of a home is not a healthy one, staffing levels are unlikely to make much difference to the experience of children. A well-run residential school may well provide a more individualised and appropriate experience than a well-staffed but badly-run small children's home. Clough et al (2006) argue that debates over the size of units are best considered in relation to their aims and purposes. An education and socialisation remit would suggest the need for larger numbers whereas a more individual therapeutic orientation might arguably be better provided in smaller units, although only if there is a clear sense of staff knowing what they mean by therapeutic.

The growth of secure accommodation

One of the most apparent shifts in the configuration of residential child care provision in recent decades has been the massive expansion of secure accommodation. With roots in the approved schools, its origins are within a welfare tradition; it was not primarily conceived as a response to offending. Indeed the introduction of criteria for admission to secure accommodation was prompted by human rights concerns to restrict rather than facilitate usage (Smith and Milligan, 2005).

Since the inception of secure accommodation, there has been a relentless increase in its use. By 1978 Millham et al note that 'each year more children endure a period under lock and key than at any time since they were taken out of prison by the Children's Charter of 1908' (1978, p 1). Since then the number of secure beds doubled over the course of the 1970s, trebled in the 1980s and quadrupled in the 1990s (Smith et al, 2005). The rise in secure accommodation has gone hand-in-hand with a steady reduction in the use of open beds in approved schools. According to Stewart and Tutt (1987), ratios of secure to open beds in the 1960s were 1:68, in the early 1980s, 1:25, and by 1984, 1:10. By 2003, 'the level of child and youth incarceration in England and Wales vis-à-vis the under 18 population as a whole was four times that of France, ten times that of Spain, and one hundred times that of Finland' (Pitts, 2005, p 186). Although direct comparison between different jurisdictions and types of facility are problematic,

Pitts' figures provide a stark picture of the direction residential child care in the UK has taken.

The welfare focus in relation to youth crime, which characterised the early secure units, was disrupted by reaction to the murder of two-year-old Jamie Bulger by two 10-year-olds in Liverpool in 1993. This event coincided with and was used to justify a wider retreat from welfare and a shift in thinking towards justice-oriented solutions to youth crime. A result was the establishment in England of secure training centres. Older offenders, up to the age of 21, are kept in young offender institutions (YOIs) under the auspices of the Youth Justice Board, while children with particular behavioural and emotional problems can be maintained in local authority secure children's homes. Scotland has not gone down the secure training centre route and caters for all children deemed to need secure accommodation in secure units run by a range of voluntary bodies or local authorities.

Kendrick and Fraser point out that 'the demand for security reflects the requirements of inadequate, open institutions and community services rather than the needs of difficult children' (1992, p 105). Children's homes that are badly managed, poorly resourced or inadequately supported are likely to fuel demand to lock up young people. Research into fast-track children's hearings (Hill et al, 2005) indicates that many of those young people labelled 'persistent young offenders' achieve that status while in residential care. Unless and until problems of care and control in children's homes are adequately addressed they will continue to create demand for secure accommodation and may well create a situation where issues of behavioural management are too readily abrogated to secure units (Harris and Timms, 1993). The expansion of secure accommodation is not a simple response to increasing demand. It actually generates that demand and in so doing skews resources towards the wrong end of child care provision, and a particularly expensive end at that.

The use of secure accommodation can be presented as providing children with intensive programmes of treatment and rehabilitation. Secure units within a managerial culture increasingly face demands to address problematic behaviours through the use of a range of programmes, often imported from criminal justice settings. Goldson (2002b), however, found little evidence of rehabilitative approaches in secure units and identified their primary role as one of containment. The wider shift to secure accommodation can best be understood in light of the developments discussed in Chapter One and in particular the new punitiveness associated with neoliberalism.

'Modernising' residential child care

Following the abuse scandals of the 1990s, discussed in the previous chapter, and the resultant scrutiny of residential child care, the focus of political intervention has shifted from seeking to prevent the abuse of children in care to a wider concern to promote their welfare and to address their relative disadvantage compared with other children in the community.

Quality Protects

This has led to a range of policy developments, adumbrated by Utting (1997) and evident in the *Quality Protects* initiative, which ran from 1998 to 2004, the title conveying the sense that protecting children is best addressed through improving their overall quality of care. *Quality Protects* established national objectives for local authorities with built-in accountability mechanisms. Questions of education and health are central to this agenda. The initiative was not wholly successful, however. Jackson (Jackson, S., 2006) argues that it failed to address structural constraints on residential care and that its objectives did not match what a good parent might expect for their child.

Care standards

Some of the issues involved in the development of care standards under the Regulation of Care legislation have been discussed in Chapter Three. The standards themselves are revealing in what they say about care. The Scottish standards identify themes of dignity, privacy, choice, realising potential and equality and diversity. Themes of privacy and choice might be argued to speak to an individualising and consumerist agenda, while those of equality and diversity stem from the identity politics of recent decades. And, of course, all of these terms are contestable: how might privacy be guaranteed in secure accommodation for instance where there are competing demands for safety and regular supervision? And what are the limits of choice? The care standards betray a commodified, instrumental and universalising view of care, airbrushing out complexity and contingency. What is even more revealing is what they do not say. The 2001 Regulation of Care (Scotland) Act gives us a long list of care services that government bodies have a responsibility to provide and of places where care might be offered and the penalties for failing to provide care of an appropriate standard. They conspicuously fail to say what care might be or to locate it in relational rather than legal and instrumental terms.

Every Child Matters *and* Getting it Right for Every Child

Every Child Matters (ECM) (DfES, 2003) reflects a shift from the 1989 Children Act principles, which targeted children in need, towards a more universal policy framework that applies to all children. Children's needs are recognised as multifaceted and not amenable to being split into different component parts such as health and education, each addressed through different systems. This, and its Scottish counterpart, *Getting it Right for Every Child* (Scottish Executive, 2005b), calls for a multi-systemic approach to meeting children's needs. As such it adumbrates a shift towards generic children's services. As with the care standards, the principles of ECM betray a particular view of children and their needs. They are to be healthy, stay safe, engage and achieve, make a positive contribution and achieve economic well-being. While hard to argue with any of these objectives in their own right, together they reflect a view of children as future citizens in whom the government seeks to invest. It is a strand in a wider move towards a social investment state in which themes of early intervention coalesce with increasing control and surveillance of children and childhood (Parton, 2006).

Care Matters *and* We Can and Must Do Better

For all the investment in children and in particular children in care over the previous decade, *Care Matters* (DfES, 2006) and *We Can and Must Do Better* (Scottish Government, 2007a) acknowledge that the gap in achievement between children in care and the wider population is increasing. Some of the prescriptions to deal with this failure seem strangely misconceived. The role of inspection is to be extended and children are to be listened to more. It is almost as if they were saying: 'what we are doing is not working, therefore we need to do more of the same'. There is significant emphasis within these documents on addressing the educational needs of children in care. This concern to address the educational inequalities apparent between residential child care and children in the community permeates policy and guidance in this area (Francis, 2006).

The education of children in care

As the government turned its attention to outcomes in public services it was apparent that there was a marked divergence in the educational outcomes for children in care compared with those in the wider community, starkly apparent in the numbers of qualifications obtained or nor obtained. Children in care are also over-represented in rates of those excluded from school (Brodie, 2001). Professional legacies in the past could result in a failure to give sufficient emphasis to the education of children in care. The focus in social work on children's emotional needs at times had the unintended consequence of underplaying their educational needs. A culture emerged in some settings based around an assumption that children's emotional needs were so acute that they were not in a position to avail of education, thus underplaying the important role that school and education can have in supporting children.

A successful educational experience is implicated in future life chances across a range of measures (Jackson, S., 2006). A range of initiatives and targets, backed up by funding, have been introduced to ensure that education is afforded a higher profile in care planning processes, and care and education staff are to work more closely together to ensure appropriate opportunities for children in care. Thus, children's homes have been provided with computers and fitted out to provide homework space.

Attempts to bring children in care up to speed educationally through improving examination results are all good and well. However, the means chosen to do so often fail to set low educational achievement in a social context. Clough et al (2006) note how the best efforts of staff in residential care can be compromised by the social circumstances of children's families or indeed by lack of support from local education authorities (LEAs). Staffing considerations in residential homes can further impede aspirations towards an educationally rich environment. Having parents who are themselves well educated is known to enhance educational achievement (Jackson, S., 2006). Yet the corporate parent, the residential care workforce, remains poorly educated compared with other professional groups, a trend reinforced by low-level qualifications frameworks. This has implications in terms of the capacity of many staff to help children with homework, for instance. It also limits their ability to advocate on equal terms with other professionals such as teachers to ensure that children are properly supported in schools. Disempowered staff groups are unlikely to empower the children in their care.

A feature of current approaches to educating children is that they are set within the context of the social investment state identified in Chapter One and betray a dominant view of education as a commodity with extrinsic worth, which can be expressed and measured according to examination results. Such a utilitarian view of education fits with wider policy agendas of children as becoming citizens (and responsible and reliable ones at that), who will work to boost the economy. There is no emancipatory or transformational view of education here. Improvements within what have until recently been tightly prescribed curricula are lauded as the key to educational improvement. Yet in the scheme of things achieving one or two basic level qualifications is unlikely to substantially improve a child's life chances. It might just build in a level of discontent among those who remain consigned to menial work or who cannot get a job even with their qualifications. Moreover, despite the various initiatives and the scale of investment in the education of children in care the reality is that there has been only a marginal improvement in their exam results and in fact the gap between children in care and the wider population is actually increasing (DfES, 2006).

On the other hand children may derive lifelong benefit from the influence of particular teachers who might instill a passion for reading, music or sport. Jackson et al's (2005) research into those who went to university from care settings highlights the importance of an adult who took an interest in their education. A fixation with curricular attempts to raise standards may in fact have the opposite effect from that intended as children and teachers are restricted in the degree of creativity and personal commitment they can bring to the experience of learning.

Health

Research (Grant et al, 2002; McCluskey et al, 2004) highlights the poor health outcomes for children in care. Many children suffer from neglected health needs while living at home and this does not necessarily improve in care settings, often due to frequency of placement moves and lack of continuity of carers. This can result in failure to attend routine health checks and missed immunisations due to irregular school attendance. Lifestyle factors such as smoking, poor diet and sleep patterns, misuse of alcohol and drugs, and problems with sexual health compound health problems. Addressing these health needs has not always been well done in residential child care due at times to a lack of priority being accorded to them or access to appropriate services being unavailable. Problems with physical health inevitably impact on emotional well-being. Seemingly small problems such as failure to ensure adequate dental treatment can result in rotten teeth by teenage years with a knock-on effect on self-esteem; problems such as bed-wetting can be similarly devastating. Failure to treat routine medical problems at the proper time can also have long-term medical and social consequences.

The culture of a home is vital in ensuring positive approaches to health. Staff have a role in encouraging and modelling appropriate behaviours around issues of smoking and drinking, for instance. One of the difficulties in the present climate is that they are not allowed to model any behaviours in relation to drink; to be seen drinking near a child is likely to result in disciplinary action being taken against them. Yet in the past it was common for staff to engage in controlled drinking in front of children and in some cases, perhaps on holidays abroad or meals out, to allow them to have a glass of wine or a bottle of beer. This is surely a healthier way to approach and to model appropriate attitudes towards drink than to issue denial ordinances, which are to do with organisational protection more than concern for children's health.

Mental health

Mental health problems affecting children in residential care are generally manifest in 'emotional and behavioural problems'. Studies suggest that between 15% and 20% of children and young people in the UK have mental health problems and that about 9% of all children and young people have a diagnosable mental health disorder (Meltzer, 2000). Figures for looked-after children suggest that 45% suffer from a mental health disorder.

Among the emotional and psychological problems reported in recent years are increasing rates of eating disorders, an increase in suicide rates among young men and considerable increases in hyperactivity among younger children. There has also been a big rise in the diagnosis of specific difficulties such as autism and Attention Deficit Hyperactivity Disorder (ADHD). Many, although not all, mental health problems can be linked to social circumstances. The diagnosis and medicalisation of ADHD in particular is subject to considerable debate.

Picking up on the prevalence of mental health problems, Anglin (2002) identifies the primary task of residential child care as responding to pain-based behaviours. Children's pain can be internalised or projected in ways from self-harming to violent acting out. Thinking about residential child care in this way places particular demands on carers. They need to demonstrate that they can contain or 'hold on to' the emotions which children themselves find unbearable or uncontainable. This sense of emotional containment becomes a fundamental element in the residential task.

Misuse of drugs and alcohol

Children's wider social and emotional difficulties can be projected through recourse to drink and drugs. Despite the profile that illicit drug use has at the moment, the effects of alcohol are equally damaging for children and their families. Drug and alcohol misuse is a way of life for many children in residential care, either through their own direct use or that of their families. It can be implicated in many of the difficulties such as offending or family difficulties that bring children into residential child care in the first place. It may also contribute to problematic behaviours such as absconding and bullying while children are in residential care.

Questioning the focus on outcomes

While the aspiration to improve the life chances of children in care is laudable it can proceed from the simplistic premise that outcomes are poor because staff are not doing their jobs properly. This strips the reality of children's situations from their wider context. As Clough et al (2006) note: 'Too often staff in residential establishments have been castigated for failing to remedy long-standing problems' (2006, p 2). They go on to say: 'The children who move into residential homes and schools as a consequence of social services intervention are likely to face pervasive problems that have not been easy to manage in other settings' (2006, p 2). To base policy conclusions on outcome studies of a sector that, by its nature, caters for the casualties of other parts of the child care system is at best disingenuous and may act to reinforce the failure of the sector by demotivating and demoralising staff. Garrett (2008) goes further, arguing that the condemnation levelled at a failing state system is calculated to justify the increasing recourse to private care providers.

Any consideration of the outcomes of residential child care needs to be understood in the context of the backgrounds of children admitted (Berridge, 2007). The odds are stacked against children long before they reach residential care. This is the reality that is not adequately addressed in New Labour's discourse on children, based as it is on a wider ideological shift that seeks to downplay the structural dimensions of poverty.

Managing an underclass of disadvantage: poverty and its effects

Cameron (2003), quoted in Chapter One, speaks of residential child care as managing an underclass of disadvantage. Goldson (2005), in respect of youth justice services, identifies the task as being one of processing the children of the poor. Poverty and inequality are perhaps the defining features of children in care and their families. The current government has set targets to eradicate child poverty, and while it is beginning to make inroads in this respect, it continues to fall short of its own targets (Joseph Rowntree Foundation, 2006). Sharp local concentrations exist in the spread of poverty. Dorling and Thomas (2004), for instance, found that 41% of Glasgow households were living in poverty.

At a simple level poverty is conceptualised as being absolute or relative. Absolute poverty is where individuals, families or communities lack the basic resources required for subsistence. Relative poverty exists when individuals, families or communities lack the resources to obtain the living conditions and amenities or to engage in the activities that are customary in the societies to which they belong, the effect of which is to exclude them from what might be considered everyday living (Joseph Rowntree Foundation, 2008). They may not be starving, but cannot enjoy what most people can take for granted – things like being able to organise a birthday party for their children or going out to the cinema or for an occasional meal. Increasingly, the lifestyles of many children involve parents driving them to and from different activities. The kind of social contacts available through involvement in a football club or a dance class, for instance, are not available to many poor families. Not being able to do things like this can lead to a grinding existence and often recourse to drink or drugs to alleviate this. It also affects children's current and future life chances.

Children in care are particularly affected by poverty. Bebbington and Miles (1989) compared the backgrounds of children admitted to care in the 1980s with a previous study from the 1960s. They found that levels of deprivation in this population had increased over this period. Only one quarter of the Bebbington and Miles cohort lived with both parents, almost three quarters received Income Support, only one in five lived in owner-occupied accommodation and over half lived in poor neighbourhoods. Berridge and Brodie (1998) considered children in residential child care to be among the most disadvantaged in society.

The effects of inequality

The effects of poverty are not only apparent in an inability to access the good things in life. Structural inequalities impact significantly on a range of social problems, for example, health and poor educational attainment, relationship difficulties, drug or alcohol misuse, mental health problems and offending. They are also apparent in softer indicators of social cohesion such as the levels of trust that exist in a society. It is not just poverty but the degree of inequality within a population that has the major impact on levels of health (Jack, 2001; Wilkinson and Pickett, 2007). Thus, reducing poverty while presiding over widening gaps between the rich and the poor is likely to compound the impact of structural disadvantage. Widening inequality has been apparent across OECD (Organisation for Economic Co-operation and Development) countries in the past decade with the highest levels to be found in the US, Ireland and the UK (Moss and Petrie, 2002). UNICEF (2007) notes a stark divide between North European countries, where child well-being is at its highest, and the UK and the US, those countries that have embraced neoliberalism most enthusiastically, and that find themselves in the bottom ranking on measures of child well-being. This is manifest in more fractious inter-generational relationships and in children's subjective accounts of their sense of well-being.

Poverty and the unequal distribution of wealth in society contribute to social exclusion. People who cannot access some of the finer things in life are unlikely to buy into the values of that society. Bringing up children in such circumstances can become a drudge for parents. Children brought up in such environments are likely to lack the kind of stimuli they need to consider alternative lifestyles. They are unlikely to buy into mainstream societal values, a point recognised by the *21st century social work review* which notes that 'Society is facing the consequences of rearing a group of disaffected, alienated young people with little stake in our society' (Scottish Executive, 2006, p 23). Workers in residential child care will recognise the existence of such groups, whereby children adopt particular countercultural identities – chavs, neds or whatever the current trend may be all of which generally involve demands for particular designer clothing. This might be thought of as an aggressive and showy assertion of some status, in a society obsessed with status.

From poverty to social inclusion

While the role of state care as a preserve of the poor is all too apparent, politicians increasingly seek to obscure this reality. While poverty is the foremost cause of state intervention in the lives of children in families, the 1989 Children Act fails conspicuously to identify this in its definition of children in need (Jackson, S., 2006). Poverty has been repackaged as social exclusion, requiring policies, not to tackle poverty, but to bring about social inclusion. Levitas (1998) identifies social inclusion as being politically constructed, enforcing social cohesion around market forces while regarding deprivation and inequality as consequences of individual deficit. Thus the focus of social policy has shifted from poverty and structural inequality towards raising individual opportunities and emphasising individual responsibilities. Policies such as those to improve the education of children in care need to be understood in this context.

Social workers can collude with this airbrushing of poverty from the centre stage of social welfare by failing to name it as central to family problems. Despite the structural origins of these problems the response of care systems is to individualise and address them as though they were a product of personal or family pathology. Children in care are subject to a range of technologies of intervention, such as counselling, anger management, cognitive skills or family therapy programmes, in order to smooth cognitive distortions so that they might return to a normative fold. Another conceptual problem with a focus on outcomes of care is that in many cases these only become apparent over the long term, often 10 or 20 years after a child might have left care. So while the language of outcomes might imply a cause and effect dynamic, the actual processes through which children negotiate the care system are convoluted and decidedly non-linear.

The wider problem

The problem with the raft of policy initiatives directed at children in care is that they treat every problem as one to be managed through technical/rational injunction and increasing micromanagement of homes. Failure to remedy problems through regulation seems only to result in renewed regulatory effort. This has been responsible for administrative burdens that have become impossible for practitioners to keep up with. And the effort expended in keeping up with regulatory requirements focuses practitioners' attention on the technical to the exclusion of identifying the wider moral and political aspects of caring for children.

Conclusion

What is immediately apparent in any cursory examination of residential child care is the multifaceted and interlinked nature of the difficulties faced by children placed there. Irrespective of their manifestation, these generally have their roots in social disadvantage and adversity. Assertions as to the poor outcomes of residential care need to take into account the nature of the inputs to the system, in terms of the complexity of the problems facing children admitted. In that context policies that profess to bring about improvement through individual opportunity alone are misguided and unlikely to be successful. The social context of children's situations presents staff in residential child care with a challenge: is their task merely to stick plasters on social problems or do they also need to name the structural and political origins of these? Rethinking residential child care demands a more explicit social justice orientation to be brought to bear on caring.

FIVE

Theorising residential child care

Introduction

This chapter attempts an overview of some of the theories and approaches that have been applied to residential child care over the years and in different practice settings. Theory is defined as a body of ideas that help explain or illuminate our observations and experiences of the world around us (and which hopefully is useful in informing practice). Although I use the words 'theory' and 'approaches' fairly interchangeably I think about an approach as being a more specific application of a particular theoretical orientation.

There can be a tendency for practitioners to claim that they are eclectic in their use of theory. It may be right that they are; there is no theory that holds all the answers of what goes on in residential child care and it is wise to draw on a range of insights. However, claims of eclecticism can mask distinctly hazy understandings of any theoretical body of knowledge. In order to pick and mix approaches appropriately practitioners need a basic knowledge of their theoretical underpinnings so as to be able to evaluate their relative merits. A lack of appropriate theoretical knowledge among those operating and managing homes was implicated in the maintenance of the Pindown regime in Staffordshire and in the failure of colleagues and managers to see the dangers in Frank Beck's claim to be using regression therapy in Leicestershire. At a more prosaic level over-reliance on a particular theoretical orientation can detract from the provision of good everyday care.

Particular approaches are introduced rather than gone into in any depth. For this, readers will need to follow up with more specific reading. (Whitaker, 1981, provides a particularly comprehensive account of the major approaches to residential care work, although inevitably, given its date of publication, it does not cover some more recent ideas.) While not professing to pedal any particular theoretical orientation I believe that the concept of lifespace, which I will go on to discuss in more length later in this chapter, must underpin any other theoretical application; practitioners might claim to be guided by insights from attachment theory, for example, while applying these in a lifespace context. Having offered a background to and brief outlines of a number of theoretical approaches that might cast some light on practice in residential child care I then go on to discuss some questions that practitioners might want to bear in mind when considering the role of theory. I conclude the chapter by suggesting that residential child care needs to cast its net more widely in seeking out an appropriate theory base.

Theory and residential child care

It would be fair to say that theory does not get a particularly good press among workers in residential child care. This reflects two things: firstly the structural position whereby the focus in many qualifications frameworks is on carrying out instrumental tasks and when theory is introduced it is at a fairly rudimentary level. The second reason is that many of the theories that have been and still are applied to residential child care, generally drawn from other fields of practice, often do not speak to the experiences of practitioners. Phelan states that:

> Treatment language reflects frameworks that do not have a 'fit' for the kind of work which child and youth care practitioners do. The language of psychology, social work and mental health does not resonate with the day to day experiences of doing effective child and youth care work. (2001a, p 1)

While many theories may not prove useful to workers, residential child care needs, nevertheless, to be able to draw on theoretical understandings. These, however, should be grounded in and developed from the experiences of those who have worked in the field. That way they may be of some practical use. The absence of an appropriate theory base does not mean that theory does not impact on residential practice. As Moss and Petrie note: 'Theories – whether in the form of academic, political or professional ideas, or offered in the guise of "common sense" – shape our understandings and govern our actions, whether we recognize this or not' (2002, p 17). In failing to recognise the presence of theory in their everyday practice residential workers are prey to theoretical assumptions from other disciplines, or else they fall back on a default position of crude behaviourism, whereby they believe that through imposing consequences to actions they will somehow change children's behaviours. If residential care is to achieve professional credibility and capability then practitioners need to be able to engage with theories, to challenge those that do not fit with what they do and to claim those that do.

History of theory in residential child care

Because of its association with parenting and more specifically mothering, care was not, historically, felt to require theory; it was just something that those in caring roles did. Carers learned how to care through caring; it was an oral tradition 'within which practice information was transmitted by word of mouth and apprenticeship ... from one generation of workers to the next' (Garfat, 1998, p 11). When it was considered that children needed more than basic care, specialist intervention was sought from outside 'experts': psychiatrists, psychologists or social workers. Treatment was conceived as being offered separately from care.

Maxwell Jones' experiments with therapeutic communities for those with mental ill health in the 1930s provided a challenge to this view. The therapeutic community was established as a living situation, which emphasised the principle that learning and growth occurred in the context of daily living. In the US, Bettelheim's *Love is not enough* (1950) and Redl and Wineman's *Children who hate* (1951) reflect a similar direction in respect of residential child care. This was echoed in England with the opening of the Mulberry Bush School in 1948 under the direction of Barbara Dockar-Drysdale. Pioneers such as Bettelheim and Dockar-Drysdale drew on a strong psychodynamic orientation.

Psychodynamic theory

Psychodynamic thinking has its origins in the work of Sigmund Freud in the 1920s. It has since been developed by, among others, Anna Freud, Sigmund's daughter, Melanie Klein and W.R.D. Fairbairn. Psychodynamic perspectives are concerned with the 'inner world' of the developing person. Early articulations proposed that personality was governed by powerful internal 'drives' or 'instincts' or libido (a term which now has particular sexual connotations but which originally referred to all psychic energy). As psychodynamic theory developed greater emphasis was attached to relationships with others and the ways in which a sense of self evolves through these. This process is not merely a product of conscious and rational decisions but is also influenced by the 'unconscious' feelings and desires in a person's inner world.

The inner world is shaped by early experience, providing a template for how subsequent experiences and relationships are played out in the here and now. A central concept in psychodynamic thinking is concerned with how individuals defend their 'selves' from anxiety or emotional pain. To do so they employ a range of psychological defence mechanisms such as projection or denial. Psychodynamic theory has been particularly influential in professional social work where models of psycho-social casework have their roots in such an orientation. It can undoubtedly provide some valuable insights into why an individual might behave in a particular way as a result of past experiences and, through highlighting the complexity of the origins of behaviours, it takes us beyond unhelpful attempts to understand children within rational and normative frameworks.

Psychodynamic approaches have been criticised on the grounds that while they might give a framework for understanding, they are less effective in providing practical ways through which to intervene to effect change. Those from a more radical social work tradition (Bailey and Brake, 1975) also claim that they lend themselves to psychological reductionism whereby problems are identified as having an internal focus, thus failing to give sufficient weight to structural determinants of individual functioning such as poverty and disadvantage. In the context of residential child care, the specialist nature of regimes run on strictly psychotherapeutic lines can be criticised on account of their inaccessibility to most child care workers and their incongruence with more mainstream thinking about child care and education.

Behaviourist approaches

The 1950s and 1960s witnessed a reaction to psychodynamic approaches, with their focus on an individual's past. Psychologists drawing on the work of Skinner (1938) developed theories of behaviour and personality that were determined by current circumstances. Behaviour was learned as a result of environmental stimuli and could, similarly, be unlearned. A central idea in this respect is that of operant conditioning, which is based around a belief that behaviour can be controlled through its consequences. Undesirable behaviours can be eliminated through the imposition of punishment or negative consequences; positive behaviours on the other hand can be reinforced by reward.

Behaviourism was influential in residential child care over the 1960s and 1970s, most notably in youth justice settings such as Glenthorne in Birmingham and Aycliffe in County Durham. Massud Hoghugi, the principal at Aycliffe, was an influential advocate of behaviourist approaches. Behaviourist regimes were often based on token economies, whereby acceptable behaviours were reinforced through the award of a token, which could be exchanged for privileges, such as access to particular activities or even home leave. Conversely, failure to behave in ways deemed to be desirable did not bring the reward of a token and thereby children were denied access to areas of a home's programme. Points systems whereby children have points amassed or deducted on account of good or bad behaviours also derive from behaviourism.

Behaviourist approaches can be seductive in that they resonate with a common-sense idea that many staff hold about the impact of punishment on behaviours. As I noted earlier in this chapter, they can be the default position in many residential units. The term punishment tends to be replaced by consequences, but the underlying assumption is the same. Such approaches can be criticised for failing to acknowledge the complexity of human behaviour. Those who work with children should realise that changing behaviour is not as simple as the award of sanctions or rewards. In fact sanctions, punishments, consequences or whatever one chooses to call them are at best ineffective and may well be counterproductive in work with troubled children (Taylor, 2005).

Additionally, despite their surface simplicity, behaviourally based systems can actually be complicated to operate. They are open to staff confusion and indeed collusion, which may result in the 'wrong' behaviours being reinforced. Moreover, the degree to which particular behaviours modified inside an establishment may be generalised to the world outside is questionable. At another level, ethical objections can be raised on account of the tendency of behaviourally based systems to treat children as objects rather than agents of self-control. As a result of such critiques 'classical' behaviourist approaches are now far less apparent in residential child care, although some of their assumptions persist in everyday practice.

Developmental models

While over the course of the 1960s and 1970s England sought to apply ostensibly 'scientific' approaches, drawn from either psychodynamic or behaviourist traditions, to working with children, Scotland, under the influence of a group of psychologists attached to the List D schools, adopted a model of human growth and development (Forrest, 1976). A simple developmental model proposes that, from birth, children have a range of physiological, social and emotional needs. If these needs are adequately met a child will experience trust and hope and will grow into a healthy, autonomous adult. Conversely, failure to meet these needs will result in an inability to manage anxiety and this will be projected outwards through delinquent or otherwise troubled behaviours. The focus on inner feelings and anxiety within such a model draws on psychodynamic thinking but there is also a social dimension. Growth and development takes place in what Rayner (1978) calls conducive contexts. The social circumstances of many families, evident in their experiences of poverty, disadvantage and family disharmony, are not conducive to children's healthy growth and development.

Mia Kellmer-Pringle's book, *The needs of children* (1983), provides a model of how children grow and develop that is readily accessible to staff in residential child care. She identifies children as having four basic needs: love and security, new experiences, praise and recognition and responsibility. White (2008) introduces a spiritual dimension to a consideration of children's needs by including needs for significance and community, thus appropriately identifying children as existing in relationship with others.

An interesting and inspiring take on a developmental model is developed from a native American tradition by Brendtro et al (1990) in their book *Reclaiming youth at risk*. Drawing on the tribal medicine wheel of the Lakota Indians they identify domains of belonging, mastery, independence and generosity to highlight the needs and characteristics of children. This book has led to the development of a Reclaiming Youth Network (www.reclaiming.com) to provide a strengths-based forum for professionals to approach work with troubled youth.

A useful aspect of developmental models such as those above is that they provide a readily accessible framework within which residential care workers might conceive of their task. At one level it is a fairly simple one: to offer children compensatory developmental experiences within conducive contexts so that they might grow and develop. While on the one hand this assertion may seem straightforward, it actually has some fairly profound implications. It identifies the task of residential child care to be an essentially educational one, where education is understood in its widest sense of social development, as opposed to a treatment one, where the task is conceived as addressing psychological disturbance (this point is developed in Chapter Ten).

Stage models

Residential child care works predominantly with adolescents. In that sense it is useful for workers to have some understanding of what might be considered normal or appropriate adolescent behaviour. Stage theorists posit particular levels of functioning and developmental tasks that might be expected at different ages and stages. An understanding of these and of preceding and subsequent developmental stages can allow us to assess an individual against what might be expected for a child of a particular age. Without going into this literature in any detail it is worth signposting some of the main theorists associated with particular types of development.

Cognitive development

Adolescence is a time of significant development across a range of domains. This begins at a biological level and its attendant push towards physiological and sexual maturity. This in turn kicks in cognitive changes. According to Piaget (1971), a Swiss psychologist who is associated with identifying the stages of children's cognitive development, adolescents shift from a stage of 'concrete operations' to 'formal operations'. This transition enables them to conceive of the world in less black and white terms and to deal with increasingly abstract ideas. Workers may be able to identify this in their experiences of working with younger children and adolescents. The latter are generally more amenable to reasoned discussion, assuming workers have the basic relational skills to be able to engage with them.

Moral development

Kohlberg (1984) applies a similar stage model to children's moral development. Adolescence should see a shift towards what Kohlberg terms 'post-conventional morality', which is associated with conscience development and perhaps a tendency towards taking ideological stances.

Psycho-social development

The main writer associated with human psycho-social development is Erik Erikson. He identifies the primary task of adolescence to be that of identity formation, within which answering the 'Who am I?' question is central. Adolescents have to negotiate the tension between what Erikson (1995) terms 'identity' and 'identity diffusion', where they are unsure who they are or want to be. Adolescence involves a process of individuation as the developing child starts to consider themself as an entity separate from their parents. In this quest for their own identity adolescents may turn away from and appear to reject their family of origin and shift towards peer groups. Their desire to assert their independence may lead them to acting out behaviour as an expression of their own uniqueness.

While stage models of development may be of some use in understanding how children grow and develop they should not become too deterministic. As Magnuson (2003, p xxii) tells us, 'Development and growth is a mysterious, asynchronous, nonlinear process and dynamic'. Again, workers might be able to think of children with whom something just seems to click and their whole outlook and response can change. We have to take care not to try and fit this into some psychological straightjacket or other; sometimes change and growth just happen.

Derivatives of psychodynamic approaches

Attachment

Attachment theory is associated with the work of John Bowlby, which came to prominence in the years following the Second World War. Until this time the emotional dimension of care were undoubtedly present but largely unacknowledged; care was conceived primarily as a functional task. Bowlby (1951) conceptualised attachment as a fundamental human need. Attachment is defined as the affectional bond which develops between an infant and their caregiver and which endures over time. For Bowlby, this initial bond was conceived to be with an infant's mother as the primary caregiver, although later articulations of attachment theory broaden this to include other potential attachment figures such as fathers, siblings or other carers.

A central tenet of attachment theory is the arousal–relaxation cycle whereby a baby communicates their distress or need by crying. In adaptive relationships this will elicit a comforting response from the caregiver, thus establishing feelings of trust and security within the relationship. Taylor (2005) outlines the next stage in attachment theory, the positive interaction cycle, where the caregiver initiates interaction with the child, which elicits a positive response. From this interaction the child's self-esteem and self-worth are established. These early and repeated experiences with caregivers set a foundation for our internal working models of self, others and relationships between self and others. They provide us with a belief about whether we possess qualities that attract caregiving and whether we believe in the capacity of attachment figures to provide us with nurture and protection. Thus the nature and quality of early relationships provides a template for subsequent ones.

Ainsworth et al (1978) identified ideas of attachment that appear to result from early patterns of response from caregivers. Essentially these are secure attachment whereby a child can use the secure base established by trusting early relationships to explore their world with some confidence and surety. Insecure attachments, conceptualised by Ainsworth et al as either avoidant or ambivalent, result when the initial bond is less available or consistent. Such attachment patterns are manifest in difficulties in interpreting and responding to situations. More recent research (Gerhardt, 2004) identifies neurological consequences of poor early attachment experiences to the extent of identifying what is termed as a virtual black hole in the area of the brain responsible for managing emotions.

Children will seek to engage in relationships in ways that are consistent with their past experiences of being cared for. Children in residential child care, whose past experiences may have been inconsistent or involved neglect or abuse, may have learned that aggression, violence and emotional pain are integral to close relationships. Therefore, they may develop aggressive approaches in their attempts to force a response from their caregiver. Attachment theory offers workers some analytical purchase through which they might make better sense of the behaviours they encounter from children. It also offers some pointers for intervention, some of which may appear counter-intuitive. We all perhaps have a tendency to respond to the behaviour we see in front of us. Yet if, for instance, a child's aggressive behaviours provoke a negative response from their caregivers this is likely, on the basis of past experience, to replicate past responses confirming in the child a belief that they are bad and unlovable and that caregivers are rejecting. This is likely to inhibit the development of healthier relationships, which might in time provide the basis for learning more adaptive and trusting ways of relating and behaving. Working from an attachment perspective, therefore, requires workers to be concerned with the causes and meanings of behaviours rather than just their manifestations. They need to be mindful of the need to separate out these meanings from the behaviours themselves in their interventions with children. Of course, this is an inexact science and locating the roots for behaviours in past experience should not be used as a reason not to address unacceptable behaviours in the present. In fact the need, within attachment theory, to present as strong adults who are able to soak up and deal with children's anger demands that staff do confront and address behaviours.

Developments in attachment theory have led to a resurgent interest in psychodynamic and relationally based approaches to practice, in some cases as an antidote to the more technical/rational approaches that have come to dominate social work practice in recent decades (Ruch, 2005). They are gaining adherents in residential child care and in the right conditions might provide helpful theoretical insights for practice. There can be difficulties, however, in professing to operate from attachment perspectives in wider social policy contexts which can act to disrupt emerging attachments through multiple placement moves and ideological assumptions that seek to minimise time spent in residential care.

Resilience

Although it does not have roots in psychodynamic thinking the concept of resilience is often linked with attachment ideas in considerations of child development (see Daniel et al, 1999). Not all children deal with the effects of poor early experiences in the same way. The ability of some children to cope and come through adversity is called resilience. A number of factors are identified with resilience, some to do with individual temperament and others linked to environmental features. Internationally, the concept of resilience and its process and outcomes is being studied cross-culturally through the work of the Resilience Research Centre led by Michael Ungar in Canada (www. resilienceproject.org). This is beginning to uncover some of the processes and indeed the stories and journeys that lie beneath individual experiences of resilience. The work of the Search Institute in the US (www.search-institute.org/assets) provides good evidence of the effects of particular developmental assets in enhancing a child's life chances.

The concept of resilience is one that is easily grasped by workers and residential homes ought to be in a position to implement resilience-based programmes. According to Gilligan, it is not so much a theory in its own right but a:

> ... valuable organising frame for thinking about the role of the carer in residential care.... It is enhanced ... by some of the fundamentals of good care – close relationships, purposeful engagement in valued tasks, opportunities for enriching social and educational experiences. (2005, p 105)

Derivatives of behavioural approaches

Social learning theory

Criticisms of classic behaviourism led to a rise in the popularity of social learning theory (Bandura, 1977). Rather than using environmental stimuli to punish or reward behaviours, social learning theory utilises role models to teach a person how to behave in a pro-social way by means primarily of example and reward. The emphasis is on rewarding pro-social behaviours rather than punishing anti-social ones. Pro-social approaches need to be applied consistently by all the staff in an establishment who become trainers, modelling and reinforcing particular standards of behaviour on a day-to-day basis. Personal attributes of honesty, concern and commitment on the part of the worker and a clear definition of roles are central to the efficacy of this model (Trotter, 1999). Obviously working in a lifespace context and the opportunities available, for instance, through the use of activities (Steckley, 2005a, 2005b) provides fertile ground for the utilisation of social learning approaches.

Cognitive behaviourism

Cognitive behavioural approaches are a development from classic behavioural theory and have been prominent in psychological interventions in recent years. In social work they are central to the 'what works' agenda (McGuire, 1995) in the field of criminal justice and provide the theoretical basis to many of the programmed interventions utilised in residential child care, especially perhaps in secure accommodation or residential school settings, where they might focus on aspects of cognitive skills, anger management or offence-focused work. Cognitive behaviourism is based on a premise that it is not events or situations themselves that trouble people but the view they take of these events. The way they think about things will affect their emotions and behaviours. Negative thinking can lead to emotional difficulties that can in turn result in self-defeating behaviours. Many of the precipitating thoughts within a cognitive behavioural perspective are identified as irrational and distorted, leading to 'all or nothing' thinking, overgeneralisation or magnification or minimisation of the perceived problem (Gabor and Ing, 1991).

Irrational or distorted thoughts are the focus of intervention in cognitive behavioural approaches, on the grounds that tackling these will lead to a reduction in stress and in disabling emotions and ultimately a reduction in problematic behaviours. Unlike other therapeutic approaches the role of the worker in cognitive behavioural approaches is de-emphasised (Gabor and Ing, 1991) and is focused on a more didactic teaching role in which they directly challenge cognitive distortions and offer particular techniques to help alter these.

There are some problems in using cognitive behavioural approaches with children. At one level these relate to children's capacity to process their own thoughts at a level required to then act to change these. At another level behaviours and their causes can be decontextualised and presented as value-free, especially in a climate where children's behaviour is subject to heightened political scrutiny. What might once have been considered normal adolescent behaviour can now be pathologised and brought into the sphere of an increasing array of psychologically based interventions. The dominant professionals in this situation are vested with the power to decide what is or is not a cognitive distortion. Yet, in many cases, the behaviour of children in residential child care may reflect perfectly understandable and adaptable responses to past life circumstances or events. Cognitive behaviourism in this sense needs to be considered within wider social and political trends to individualise behaviours and to separate them out from their sources or context (Ferguson, 2008).

While ideas from cognitive behaviourism may have some applicability to working with children in residential child care, they certainly do not provide the silver bullet that some proponents thought they might when they first entered into the lexicon of professional interventions. If used, they should only be considered as one component of a centre's overall programme (Stevens, 2004).

Solution-focused approaches

Solution-focused brief therapy is associated with the work of de Shazer (1985) and his colleagues in Milwaukee. No single framework is drawn on to understand a person's problems. Indeed, a focus on problems and their origins is eschewed in favour of one that emphasises current resources and future hopes. These are brought to the surface in a limited number of sessions in which the therapist encourages a client to think about a future when the problems that brought them to therapy are gone. The approach makes use of what is called the miracle question to explore what would need to change to bring this about. An assumption is that there have been times when problems have been less oppressive and that people, with appropriate prompting, can identify some of these more positive moments and what contributed to them.

Ideas deriving from solution-focused ways of thinking can be employed in residential work (Murphy, 2001).These involve reframing the ways that staff approach and address children's everyday behaviours. A solution-focused approach is predicated on a belief that children respond better to raised expectations rather than to warnings and sanctions. Staff then need to learn ways of identifying ways forward for children when they get caught up in negative behaviours rather than getting hung up on the behaviour itself and the consequences that might result from it. Employing such ways of working requires a 'whole team' approach that should percolate and inform the overall ethos of a centre.

Vygotsky

The brief overview of psychological theory provided in this chapter needs to at least mention Lev Vygotsky. While most western psychological theory focuses on individual developmental processes, Vygotsky, a Russian whose work was undertaken in the 1920s but only 'discovered' in the West and resurrected towards the end of the 20th century, suggests that learning and development are not solely or even primarily to do with individual cognition but are inherently social. Development takes place firstly through social interaction that is then incorporated into an individual's cognitive schema.

Vygotsky's (1962) work is increasingly utilised in approaches to learning. A central theme relates to what he calls the zone of proximal development (ZPD). Essentially, children grow and can be supported in that growth towards the level of their potential development through appropriate adult or peer guidance. The ZPD is socially mediated, formed through relationship. There are obvious points of contact between Vygotsky's work and Bandura's ideas on social learning. The identification of learning as a social process supported by more expert adults or peers adumbrates interesting prospects for applying Vygotsky's thinking to residential child care. Adults are accorded a role in working with children to help them identify and develop their skills in particular areas. Peers likewise can play a role in mediating this development (Emond, 2000).

While little work has been done to explicitly apply Vygotskian perspectives to residential child care (in an anglophone context at least), the setting would seem to provide fertile ground from which to do so. Such perspectives lend themselves to work with groups; they are fundamentally social and broadly educational rather than individual and problem-focused.They also foreground the relationship established between children and the adults who work with them. Vygotsky provides a robust psychological underpinning to models of social education or social pedagogy (as discussed in Chapter Ten).

Lifespace

Chapter Two identifies how residential child care began to look to itself rather than to outside professionals to provide therapeutic care for children, culminating in the publication of *The other 23 hours* (Trieschman et al, 1969), which embedded the idea of lifespace in the child care literature. Lifespace might not be a theory at all in the same sense as some of the other theories discussed here. It is more a way of thinking about how workers and children coexist in sharing everyday living and working space. Lifespace can be described as:

> ... the use of daily life events as they occur to promote children's growth, development and learning. Working in the 'lifespace' is what workers in residential child care do, on a day by day, shift by shift, minute by minute basis. It recognises the potential for communication with troubled young people that is provided by shared life experiences. Daily life events, as shared by care staff and residents are used to help children make connections between and make sense of the various areas of their lives. (Smith, 2005a, p 1)

A lifespace approach can be difficult for some, schooled in a social work mode of thinking, to get their heads around. Social work students are often eager to do 'real' social work which they think involves interventions around anger management or planned groupwork programmes. Lifespace work is about being with children where they live their lives, engaging in seemingly mundane everyday activities. It 'is neither individual casework nor groupwork, nor even individual casework conducted in a group context, but a therapeutic discipline of its own' (Keenan, 2002, p 221). Lifespace approaches are at the heart of North American child and youth care approaches.

Developmental care

A defining contribution to the literature on child and youth care is Henry Maier's paper *The core of care* (1979). Maier links child care and child development – basing how we care for children on knowledge of how children grow and learn. Residential child care offers powerful opportunities to understand how children grow in relation to those they live alongside. *The core of care* introduces seven components essential to the provision of developmental care. In many respects it resonates with ideas on attachment. Maier says that we need to start by ensuring the provision of good basic care or *bodily comfort*. This needs to take into account the differences or *differentiations* that exist between children. Maier describes some children as 'human radars', others as 'go-go kids'. The first are the active scanners, the second those children whose only way to find out about the world is to bump into it. How we respond to a child demonstrating one character trait is unlikely to suit the other. Consistency, says Maier, is neither possible nor desirable, thus laying down a challenge to those who would propose this to be a central tenet of residential child care.

In building relationships with children, workers need to take into account their individual differences and to enter into a *rhythmic interaction* with them. This is essentially about getting onto a similar wavelength. It might be easiest to think about ideas of rhythmic interaction in terms of a table tennis ball bobbing on either side of a table. There is a certain comfort to be had from the pattern of such movements. Out of the experience of rhythm comes a level of *predictability*, where children are able to anticipate the responses of a worker in a situation. Once they have reached this stage they can begin to experience *dependency*. Dependency can be frowned on in a social work discourse, where the aim seems to be to promote independence. It is only through the experience of a healthy dependency, however, that children can move on to achieve meaningful independence, or interdependence. The development of dependent and reciprocal relationships makes *personalised behaviour training* possible. Many residential facilities attempt to impose appropriate behaviours through sets of house rules. In Maier's model this is starting at the wrong place; good behaviour results from good personal relationships.

The final element in *The core of care* is *care for the caregiver*. Bringing children up, whether as a parent or carer, is incredibly difficult and needs support. Carers can only care for children if they too feel cared for and valued, something that many do not in current organisational cultures.

Over the years writers have developed thinking based around lifespace-based approaches (Krueger, 1991; Garfat, 1998). Garfat and McElwee (2004) identify core elements of a child and youth care approach as centring round the use of daily life events as a focus of intervention and being with people as they live their lives. They go on to list other characteristics of such an approach, all of which stem from this central premise of practitioners sharing the lifespace with those they work with. The central tenets of lifespace approaches seem to resonate with what practitioners in residential child care do. Potentially it gives them a language through which to articulate the everydayness of their job and to locate this within a suitably robust theoretical framework.

Conclusion

There is no one theory that provides any sort of silver bullet in residential child care, no one theory directly associated with better outcomes for children. The connection between theory and effectiveness is a more indirect one. Visser (2002) and Clough et al (2006) highlight how staff groups that work to a particular theoretical model are likely to be more focused and effective in their work. Berridge and Brodie (1998) suggest a strong association between the quality of care and the ability of managers to articulate and stick to a clear theoretical orientation. The nature of the theoretical orientation seems to be of less importance than the fact that they have one. Ideally, a range of understandings and possible ways of intervening will be brought to bear according to the unique circumstances of individual children and staff groups. Any particular theoretical model should be embedded within an understanding of ideas around lifespace. In considering the role of theory in residential child care or in settling on a theoretical rationale for the work they do, practitioners might want to consider some of the following points:

- Is the theoretical model deficit- or strengths-based? Many psychologically based theories can lead workers to try to identify and solve problems. This in turn has implications for the sources of power within professional relationships, the individual (usually the worker) who identifies the problem, and by implication a solution, holds the upper hand. Strengths-based perspectives (Saleebey, 1997) call for a paradigm shift in the way we approach our work, requiring a mindset that looks for strengths and competencies and considers how these personal resources can be applied to help children grow up. It demands that children become equal partners in the helping process.
- Is a model useful in providing insights into the individual or the group? Again, most psychological theory that has been applied to residential work tends to focus on the individual. Social learning theory and, increasingly, Vygotskian ideas make more explicit use of the group in promoting learning and development.

- Are chosen theories most useful in explaining or intervening? Many psychologically based theories provide considerable insight into the origins of current difficulties although they do not always help in pointing a way forward in terms of how we might intervene. Solution-focused approaches on the other hand place little emphasis on understanding what has gone on in the past and concentrate on helping children deal with the present and the future. Theories around attachment might be used to help us both understand and respond. It can be useful to make this simple distinction between understanding and intervening (Collingwood, 2005), if only in our heads, as it helps us to a clearer picture of the role of theory in what we do. Residential workers need to both understand and intervene. Phelan notes that 'child and youth care work is simple and complex in the same moment. The ability to create simple responses based on complex understanding is the heart of effective practice' (2006, p 27).

Over the years residential care workers have sought to gain professional legitimacy through borrowing from the discourses of other professional orientations and groups. All of the theoretical perspectives identified in this chapter betray origins in psychology. While valuable, these are insufficient to capture the essence of caring for children. This is far broader than being merely or even primarily a scientific task but incorporates powerful moral dimensions around the nature of care itself. Theorising residential child care through such a lens takes us into the realms of other professional and intellectual activity such as education and philosophy. In the final chapter I begin to think about care through a broader theoretical lens.

SIX

The residential environment

Psychodynamic perspectives always recognised the inherent complexity of residential child care, a complexity that needed to be understood and appropriately negotiated. Managerial regimes have sought to reduce complex relational and psychodynamic processes to a series of procedures. This is fundamentally misconceived; attempts to manage relationships through regulation detract from the essence of care, a point I develop in the final chapter. They also assume that residential child care can be managed structurally and functionally, whereas it really requires to be understood organically. White (2008) offers a useful metaphor when he likens residential care to a compost heap. A compost heap is a particularly complex organic structure where constituent parts interact with one another to produce compost. When this interaction goes well the result is a medium for growth; when something within the biochemical process goes wrong it can let off a stench. It does not take too much imagination to extend this metaphor to residential child care; as a form of intervention with children it can be a powerful medium for growth or at worst it can become decidedly rotten. Within an ecological model interventions in one area may well produce unintended consequences elsewhere in the system.

This chapter considers the care environment. Discussion is located within Fulcher and Ainsworth's definition of group care as involving a 'group focus, using the physical and social characteristics of a service centre to produce a shared lifespace between those in receipt of care and those who give it' (1985, p 4). The interaction of the human and environmental dimensions in a lifespace context produces unique cultures of care.

The milieu

This overall medium created when staff and resident groups come together in a particular physical environment is referred to as the milieu. The concept is not particularly tangible; it can be thought of as 'particles in the air'. It is the 'feel' of a place. As you enter a residential care home you pick up very quickly what it feels like, whether there is a tension or a 'buzz' or a sense of calm. What a place feels like, while it might be hard to measure, is likely to have a profound effect on those who live and work there. A positive milieu is likely to give children the message that they are cared for and valued by the staff who look after them.

I now move on to consider in a bit more detail the variables in Fulcher and Ainsworth's above definition: the resident group, the staff team and the physical environment. The same authors go on to say that interventions should be arranged, 'which exploit the total environment of a programme ... involving the disciplined use of time, space, objects, events, activities and exchanges between children and significant others, be they staff or children' (1985, p 9). These factors act to enhance or inhibit the experiences available to children. Practitioners therefore need to be aware of and to shape those elements that together constitute the milieu in order to enhance the opportunities a group care centre provides for children's learning and growth.

The resident group

In earlier incarnations of residential care, especially in therapeutic communities, the group was seen as integral to the overall residential experience as a conduit of growth and healing. In residential schools, the house or cottage meeting provided a regular forum through which issues of daily living could be addressed. In that sense it was a vehicle for maintaining community cohesion and equilibrium. It is symptomatic of increasing individualism that the group is rarely mentioned in mainstream residential care nowadays other than as a negative force, being implicated in peer bullying and abuse (Kahan, 1994). In the past, experienced staff picked up how to work with groups through an apprenticeship model where they learned the tricks of the trade from older hands. Nowadays staff have become more fearful and less confident in working with groups of children, often considering them as a threat to order or possibly to their own safety.

Fear of the group has led to some odd developments in the name of residential child care, where particularly difficult-to-place children have been accommodated in so-called special arrangements where, in some cases, a staff team is brought together for a single child. Aside from the prohibitive expense of such arrangements, they are oppressive to any child subject to the gaze of changing shifts of adults, denied the spontaneous company of other children. Other less extreme examples can involve homes making individual holiday arrangements for children rather than organising group outings. Valorising the autonomous individual is of course reflected in policy where care planning processes impose an individual focus to work, rarely taking into account the opportunities provided by group living (Emond, 2000).

The difficulty staff can have in working with groups is hardly surprising. Social work education fails almost entirely to provide students with practical ways of working with groups, focusing, as it largely does, on casework and care planning. Some courses may include a groupwork element but this is rarely undertaken from a lifespace perspective. Practical advice on aspects of everyday practice such as being adequately prepared to start a shift, on techniques to maintain order, and on positioning oneself to ensure appropriate supervision, are conspicuously lacking in most social work training.

The second point that makes working with groups more difficult is that groups have themselves become more difficult. When residential child care is a residual service catering primarily for children who are hard to place and poorly integrated, many will struggle to function in groups; the misbehaviour of one may spark a response from another and the business of trying to manage the resultant dynamics can be beyond the ability of even the best workers. Within better-balanced groups the more socialised children can act as culture carriers and can help create and sustain group norms that allow the living experience to be a positive one.

A classic study in group functioning in residential child care is Howard Polsky's *Cottage six* (1962), which examined the social organisation of boys in a treatment facility in the US. From a sociological perspective Polsky describes a peer group system constructed hierarchically by means of violence and intimidation. The group is conceptualised within a diamond structure. At the top of the diamond are a few of the most powerful characters and at the bottom end the scapegoats. In the middle is a range of individuals who owe their status to attributes such as humour or affiliation to more powerful characters. There is little movement between levels. For Polsky the peer group was more influential than formal systems in regulating group norms and behaviours and delinquent subcultures were passed on from resident to resident.

More recently, Emond (2000) has reappraised Polsky's analysis of the resident group through an ethnographic study that involved her living as a resident in two different children's homes in the North of Scotland. From this experience Emond suggests that group roles and relationships in residential care are far less fixed that in Polsky's model and are subject to subtle and ongoing negotiation and realignment. To capture some of this subtlety, she draws on the work of the French social scientist, Pierre Bourdieu, to provide an analytic framework through which to understand the group. The ways in which residents operate are considered within Bourdieu's idea of 'habitus', which is described as a 'feel for the game' (Emond, 2004, p 199), the sort of unconscious understandings we develop of our world and our place within it. Another way of thinking of this might be in terms of a sense of timing. Residential workers will be able to think of children whose interactions with others and with their immediate environment are just not quite right in terms of timing or pacing and who consequently struggle to fit in.

Emond (2000) identified particular social competencies or currencies around areas of knowledge (of systems and of cultures of care), and environment (such as humour and practices around, for instance, touch and physical space), which, when appropriately employed, confer on individuals status within the group. Verbal and physical violence did not confer status; indeed bullies had little status. A striking feature of this study is the extent to which resident groups valued positive behaviours and provided support for one another. Practice experience brings to mind children who have positions within a peer group without being heavy-handed or intimidatory but also those who try and throw their weight around but are still not accepted. It also identifies the acts of care from young people to one another.

In both of the children's homes studied children demonstrated more positive and caring behaviours than they did negative or aggressive ones. This holds out the possibility of the group as a positive force, capable of channelling its members away from dangerous or socially unacceptable behaviour. The realisation of this potential, however, requires a shift in the mindsets of workers and managers away from the current focus on the individual to an appreciation of the possibilities that working with groups might present. The idea of positive peer culture (Vorrath and Brendtro, 2000) provides an example of a practice model that consciously utilises children's capacity to provide support to one another. A positive peer culture approach is based around encouraging children to demonstrate positive, caring values and concern for others and to reject behaviours that hurt themselves or others. The emphasis in such a model is on adults guiding rather than attempting to directly control children's behaviours and doing so from an appreciation of children's capacity to care for one another.

Gender and care

The overall functioning of any resident group will also be affected by factors of gender and 'race'. A cursory glance at the residential child care sector reveals it as a gendered site of practice, although this fact and its implications are only beginning to be recognised. Around 70% of the population of residential child care is boys, yet the gender split within the workforce is in inverse proportion to this, with around two female carers for each male (Smith, 2003b).

An awareness of the gendered nature of care is increasingly recognised in ensuring appropriate experiences for children, who demonstrate gendered patterns of behaviour. Offending, for instance, is still largely a boy problem, a way perhaps of 'doing masculinity'. Boys and girls also appear to process experiences of abuse differently and exhibit different patterns in seeking help (Daniel et al, 2005). They also seem to respond better to different staff characteristics and approaches (Nicholson and Artz, 2003). Despite evidence of the differential needs of boys and girls most policy and practice in residential child care has persisted, largely, in a gender-blind approach. Since the decline in residential schooling it has conspicuously failed to address 'the boy problem'. Adolescent boys are the majority population in residential care and they throw up significant challenges in respect of their care and control. Responding to these issues needs to take gender into account. Yet as Biddulph argues, in a position that might be applied to residential child care, 'For 30 years it has been trendy to deny masculinity and say that boys and girls are really just the same. But as parents and teachers know, this approach isn't working' (1998, p 3). The Gender Equality Duty (GED), which came into force in 2007, acknowledges the gendered aspects of bringing up children, requiring public bodies to take gender into account in their education and socialisation.

Minority ethnic children

Children from black and minority ethnic backgrounds and those of mixed parentage are disproportionately represented in the care system in England (Singh, 2005) and further so in secure accommodation (Pitts, 2005). Minority ethnic children from other backgrounds such as Eastern Europe and those seeking asylum from various parts of the globe are likely to figure more prominently in future years. Jones and Waul (2005) point to the experience of racism in residential care as elsewhere in society. Children from different ethnic backgrounds are also faced with assumptions and practices that derive from specifically western bio-psycho-social perspectives (Fulcher, 1998; Singh, 2005). These impose a particular image of family, for instance, locating it at a nuclear rather than an inter-generational level.

Whatever the backgrounds of children, they will be best cared for when they feel that staff seek to acknowledge their cultural experience. An awareness of issues of 'cultural safety' is increasingly identified as important for child and youth care workers (Fulcher, 1998). Cultural safety is defined as:

> ... that state of being in which the child knows emotionally that her/his personal well-being, as well as social and cultural frames of reference, are acknowledged – even if not fully understood. Furthermore, she/he is given active reason to feel hopeful that her/his needs and those of her/his family members and kin will be accorded dignity and respect. (Ramsden, 1997, cited in Fulcher, 1998, p 333)

The staff team

The second element in the overall group care environment is the staff team. This invariably introduces its own complex dynamics to the care task. It is not just children who demonstrate a sense of 'habitus'. Workers also need to develop their own feel for the game and for what is going on around them. This is rarely a rational or conscious process; it is something that is learned experientially rather than taught directly. And just as there are children whose sense of timing is that bit off, so too are there staff who do not get their interactions quite right and who grate with their environment and with those around them. The nature and functioning of staff teams is an area that requires further research (Fulcher and Ainsworth, 1985) and what is offered here barely skims the surface of an incredibly complicated aspect of group care. Any staff group is likely to consist of individuals from disparate backgrounds holding a range of views and value positions on how best to care for children, especially so in residential child care where there is still no pre-entry professionalisation or socialisation process.

The reality too is that there is not just one staff team but a number of different teams in most care homes (Ward, 1993); there might be a separate night staff team, a domestic team, a senior team; in larger establishments there will be separate unit or house teams. There are also the informal groupings that form around common interests or backgrounds. Such informal teams can have a positive or negative effect on the overall functioning of a home; they can be a force for creativity or disaffection depending on the personalities involved.

Influences on staff team functioning

The way a staff team operates is influenced by a number of factors. Three of these, stages of worker development, gender and the composition of staff groups, are discussed below.

Stages of worker development

Phelan (1990) identified three stages that a child care worker goes through in their first three years. Phelan's model is summarised by Garfat:

> ... early in the first phase the worker is overwhelmed, seeking pragmatic control techniques, and lacking in confidence. With progress the worker shows increased confidence, is more able to exert influence and is ready to begin the application of therapeutic techniques. During the second phase the worker is able to practice what has been learned in both school and experience, demonstrates greater competence, feels more confident and appears to see self as a competent technician. It is at this stage, he argues, that the worker can become 'stuck' in professional development and runs the risk of engaging in constant repetitive interventions. Without further growth, the worker either stays at this level of development (paraprofessional) or begins to search for other work. In phase three, the worker becomes energized by the nuances of the messages from the youth, shows an appreciation of the need for skill, knowledge and self to be integrated in practice and respects the clinical expertise necessary to work effectively. (2001)

Any properly functioning staff team will include a mix of workers at different stages of development. These different stages need to be understood otherwise new workers can become anxious and frustrated by their difficulties in exercising control and might resent or become suspicious of those more experienced workers to whom this comes more naturally. The process of becoming more relaxed and competent in post probably cannot be cut short; it just happens for most workers over time.

Gender

The nature of children's care experience will differ significantly depending on the gender mix in staff teams. As is the case when seeking to understand the resident group, gender-blind approaches are not sustainable. Men and women care in different ways and children should experience both sexes in caring roles. The residential workforce is predominantly female, however, and recruitment practices appear to reinforce this dominance. McPheat (2007) notes a marked difference in the success rates for male and female applicants for posts in residential child care, suggesting perhaps that assumptions made in the recruitment process privilege the appointment of women. Coming to any meaningful understanding of the role played by gender in residential care needs to move beyond the rhetoric of patriarchy, within which debates are often cast.

Group composition

The qualifications profile of residential child care is touched on in Chapter Three. It is not just the level but also the nature of qualifications that is important. Many training programmes appear to overemphasise a counselling-type orientation. While this has a place, it may steer a centre towards individualistic and problem-based ways of working. The overall profile of staff teams benefits from a variety of life experience and theoretical orientations, perhaps around activity or other youth work-type approaches. Competency-based approaches to recruitment risk the emergence of a breed of 'Stepford' care workers, with the result that staff teams lack the requisite balance of background, qualifications and indeed personality type to contribute to the team-oriented nature of residential child care. Greater attention needs to be paid to the combination of personalities, skills and life experiences engaged in any care team. It is:

> ... far more important to assess what skills, interests, and attributes are missing in a team at the time of a vacancy. In so doing, the principle of 'interchangeable parts' instead of 'replaceable parts' is built into team recruitment, where the contributions of each worker provide something that others in the team cannot provide. Teamwork is thus more likely to produce a service that is greater that the sum of the individual parts. (Fulcher, 2007, p 34)

This can be difficult to achieve within the rather unimaginative equal opportunities policies of most bureaucracies.

Managing anxiety

The intensity of residential child care can bring tensions and differences within a staff group into sharp relief. Even in the best functioning teams the nature of the task is a stressful one, likely to provoke anxiety. A psychodynamic understanding of anxiety is helpful in trying to understand what can happen in staff teams. Menzies Lyth (1970), in her studies of nursing systems in hospitals, provides a classic conceptualisation of how organisations generate and respond to anxiety. She argues that proximity to children's pain arouses a primitive, in the sense of being childlike, and not necessarily rational, anxiety. Brearley (1985) describes anxiety as a fear of what might happen in the future. This is particularly apt in the case of residential child care, where staff often find themselves dealing with group or individual dynamics that appear to be simmering, or teetering, on the brink of a loss of control. There may be a fear of emotional intimacy, physical violence or of the consequences of a failure to deal with a situation satisfactorily.

To protect themselves from the pain and anxiety generated by the job, staff employ a range of psychological defence mechanisms, such as splitting off the relational aspects of caring from the instrumental tasks, leading to detachment and a denial of feelings. (Such defences against anxiety can actually be valorised as being appropriately professional in current conceptualisations of care.) Another strategy is to delegate responsibility to superiors; residential child care workers seem to be particularly prone, and perhaps not without reason, to laying the blame for inadequacies elsewhere.

While the strategies utilised in responding to anxiety may be understandable, they are not adaptive and can themselves lead to levels of secondary stress. In extreme cases this can lead to the concept of burnout (Mattingly, 2006), where workers essentially move beyond being able to offer care meaningfully. In other cases, the job still gets done but more energy can be spent in maintaining psychological defences against anxiety than is committed to the primary task; task can readily slip into anti-task (Menzies Lyth, 1979).

The compost heap metaphor

A useful feature of White's (2008) compost heap analogy is that it identifies residential care as an organic rather than a technical endeavour. If we consider a small residential home of, say, six children and 12 staff, then the possible interactions between the various players runs to hundreds of thousands, with the likelihood in many of these relationships of personal animosity, sexual attraction and all sorts of complex psychodynamic processes of transference and counter-transference.

Within the compost heap particular individuals can exert particular influences. Some children, through their extreme pain and behaviours, can single-handedly bring a staff team to its knees. Individual staff members can also create havoc within a team, often through what Webster (2005) describes as a psychology of righteousness, a belief that everyone is out of step but themselves. The aftermath of the various abuse scandals has allowed such individuals, who, in some cases, may have struggled with the demands of residential care, to cast themselves as 'whistleblowers' and in so doing to fundamentally disrupt and often fatally undermine the functioning of a home. A tendency to perceive of such situations rationally and linearly, shorn of any of the complex psychodynamic processes that are an inevitable feature of residential homes, is invariably unable to respond to such complex dynamics.

Power

Power differentials exist in any care or indeed work setting. They exist among and between adults and children in residential care. Their operation is generally not as simple as can be portrayed. On the surface staff are vested with power over the children they work with. They are able to leave the home at the end of a shift; they are not dependent on children for every aspect of their functioning in the way that children in care might be on them. Carers of course need to take questions of vulnerability and dependence into account in their interactions with children and to act ethically in these. However, power rarely operates in only one direction. While residential workers may hold positions of power, they rarely feel this to be the case. When abuses of power occur this can owe as much to feelings of powerlessness as to the overt expression of power.

It is generally unhelpful to seek to understand or address complex relational difficulties around bullying, for instance, through recourse to policy. This is invariably a blunt instrument with which to manage the unique dynamics that are present in most instances of bullying and responses based on policy alone may only serve to aggravate a situation. Relationships between staff and residents are equally complex. Again their messiness and ambiguity can rarely be satisfactorily resolved through recourse to complaints procedures. Power is relational and ideally power imbalances and infractions need to be addressed relationally, through adults and children speaking to one another. In most cases an adult acknowledging their faults is far more empowering to a young person than recourse to procedural routes to problem resolution.

Leadership

The intensity of the dynamics in residential care settings requires strong management. Unfortunately, ideas of strong management within a managerial climate can be manifest in procedural attempts to control and discipline the workforce. In many respects this is the antithesis of what is required as it actually provokes anxiety, through creating climates of fear and blame, reinforcing the maladaptive spiral of inadequate performance it professes to address. The proper job of a manager is to contain the anxiety that is an inevitable feature of such settings (Bion, 1961). Some of this containment can be provided through the personal characteristics of the manager; there is a symbolic dimension to the role, which again caters for a primitive need staff have for a parental figure. Formal and informal systems of supervision and support are also crucial. Just as providing parents with support is crucial in ensuring appropriate care for children in families, care for the caregiver is a prerequisite for effective group care (Maier, 1979). This demands that those in positions of leadership understand, negotiate and nurture staff groups. Without an interpretive understanding of the complexity of the residential milieu 'the systems, guidance, procedures and targets which are brought to bear on residential child care are unlikely to be sufficient' (Hicks et al, 2008, p 16). Crucially, managers also have to manage the boundary between the home and the outside world. This is not always easy when there can be a lack of congruence between the internal philosophy of a home and that of the imperatives of the wider organisation (Anglin, 2002).

The physical environment

The final component of the overall milieu is the physical environment. Patterns in the use of space, time and activity are now considered, as are concepts of rhythm, ritual and developmental intervention.

Use of space

According to Maier (1982, p 153), 'The space we create controls us'. The physical environment impacts fundamentally on the personal interactions and processes of a centre, determining those activities that are possible and those that are not. Maier suggests that attention needs to be given to what constitutes public and private space. Public space, according to Redl and Wineman, should be 'an area which smiles, with props that invite, and space which allows' (1957, p 6). Staff need to mediate the public and private spaces. There is a need to strike a balance between ensuring continuous proximity while simultaneously assuring residents a sense of intimacy and private experimentation (Maier, 1981).

To achieve this all who live and work in a home need to feel an investment in its layout and appearance. They should share in everyday chores and consider ways they might contribute to the 'feel' of a centre. Small and simple gestures such as placing a vase of flowers on a dining table can convey a powerful message of care to children and to staff and visitors alike.

Use of time

The use of time in a home is largely determined by the staff rota. Since the demise of live-in staff in the 1970s and 1980s residential care has operated to what Douglas and Payne (1981) call an 'industrial model': it is essentially a time and motion exercise. The way the rota is structured is a bone of contention in all residential units. The kind of discussions that occur in staff meetings across the land generally proceed from a basis of staff preferences and taken-for-granted assumptions of what is a good rota. They rarely include any consideration of how the rota might actually support the developmental goals of a home.

Some of the assumptions that serve to maintain the standard late-onto-early shift pattern do not hold much water. The defence offered for such systems is that they ensure that the staff who put children to bed at nights will also get them up in the mornings. But of course, taking that line of argument forward, those who get children up in the morning will not be the ones putting them to bed that night. Besides, the early–late shift pattern requires staff changeovers in the middle of the day, just the time to get in the way of day trips or other out-of-home activities.

There is no such thing as the perfect rota. The priorities of young, single staff will differ from those of staff with young children. Those charged with constructing rotas might do well to bear in mind some basic principles: essentially, the rota should be based around a unit's programme. It ought to support and reinforce the development of teamwork practices and consistency of relationships. Good quality care demands predictability and the rota should as far as possible model this. Anyone who has worked in residential care will be familiar with the refrain, 'Who's on the back-shift?'. And the follow up, 'Aw naw' or 'Sound'. 'Who's on' allows young people to know what to expect. Staff also need to experience some predictability in the rota. They should know when they are on and off duty to allow them to plan their lives outside of work. Rotas that chop and change all the time do not allow normalising opportunities away from work.

Activity

The way in which activities in a centre are organised again influences the milieu. These should be structured to ensure changes of pace through the course of the day. Opportunities should be built in for physical activity, for social interaction and for moments of quiet reflection. Consideration should be given to the kind of rhythms of the day, to ensure, for instance, a sense of purpose in the mornings when children are getting ready to go to school and a sense of winding down as it gets nearer to bedtime. The evening programme might involve offering an activity or a choice of activities after tea, then an opportunity for children to get bathed or showered or otherwise ready for bed, followed by supper and some time with staff watching the television or playing quiet games or just chatting, before it is time to go to bed. Like the rest of us, children benefit from slowing down before going to sleep, yet sometimes in residential child care they are expected to go from a period of heightened activity, directly to bed. Staff can vary the tempo of a shift and the atmosphere of a unit through simple interventions in the rhythms of daily living. Actions such as drawing curtains or dimming lights or playing relaxing music can give the message, 'It's time to slow down now'. Likewise they can encourage children's involvement in activities by actively engaging in these themselves.

Rhythm

The concepts of rhythm and ritual have become central to child and youth care practice (Maier, 1979). Rhythm is important in bringing a measure of stability, security and predictability to children whose lives have often been out of control. It is the process through which workers and children find a common and comfortable way of being together. We all find a sense of comfort from being 'in tune' with the environment around us, but even more so in experiencing the sense of safety and intimacy that comes with being on the same wavelength as someone else and being comfortable in their presence. When that happens, it says something about the 'fit' between an individual and their environment. Jackson explains:

> ... rhythmicity is an essential ingredient in human communication and development. In attempting to communicate effectively with a child the carer has to fall into step with the child so that they dance to the same tune. The child and the caregiver then search for ways to establish and maintain that joint rhythm in a mutually inclusive way.... It is important for us to learn to listen, to look and explore in a new way the pulse of groups with which we are working. It is argued that only by living one's work can one become sensitized and respond appropriately to these rhythms. (Jackson, R., 2006, p 70)

The idea of rhythm might also be applied at an organisational level, to convey the sense of order and predictability in the patterns of daily living in a home. Rhythm is less rigid or prescribed than the kind of routine that might (or might not) emerge from procedural attempts to impose order. When appropriate rhythms are established in a centre, things can seem to run like clockwork. Rules and expectations become implicit rather than needing to be continually re-inforced. New residents pick up on the rhythms of a home and readily fit into them. However, it is worth maintaining an awareness of the rhythms of a centre lest they become too embedded and routinised. Staff may consider introducing a bit of variety to established rhythms to ensure that they do not become stale. They might decide, for instance, to dispense with cooking on a particular night and get everyone a takeaway meal. Or they might allow children to stay up past their bedtimes to watch a particular programme on the television, making popcorn and hot chocolate long after the normal suppertime. Such deviations from established routine can threaten the need some staff have for order. However, rather than compromising a sense of order, these deviations from the norm, so long as they are properly thought through, actually contribute to it. They also avoid children becoming overly institutionalised, by introducing an element of flexibility into their lives in safe and managed ways. Having a 'feel' for appropriate rhythms can ensure the smooth operation of critical everyday events in the life of the centre, such as the transitions between unit and school, mealtimes and bedtimes.

Rituals

Rituals are practices that become embedded in the fabric of a place and which have meaning and significance for the workers and children who engage in them. The kind of rituals that can develop might be things like 'high fives' or nudges. Such simple and seemingly mundane rituals can become a powerful means through which adults and children can convey a sense of affection for and connection with one another. Children may need to follow their own unique rituals at bedtime for instance, involving particular patterns or sequences of doing things. Unless such rituals are understood and accommodated they might have difficulty settling for the night. Appreciation of the seemingly simple rituals in the everyday lives of those we work with speak of a connection and a sense of care.

Rituals also operate at an organisational level. The importance of mealtimes as a focus of community life is fundamental. In every culture, the taking and sharing of food has a particular significance, one that is often ignored in residential child care settings where the priority at times can be to feed and water children with the minimum of disruption and to minimise any community dimension for fear of the group getting out of control. Events in the social calendar such as Christmas or Halloween are also important and should not be allowed to pass without celebration. Just as in families, there should be a sense of 'This is how we do Christmas here' (or whatever festival is being marked). In larger establishments, rituals can build up around particular areas of a centre's programme, such as membership of the football team, with all that might entail in terms of cleaning boots and lining pitches. These rituals are more important than any formal set of house rules in setting the tone and culture of a place.

Developmental interaction

Ainsworth suggests that a defining feature of group care is the fact that 'practitioners take as the theatre for their work the actual living situations as shared with and experienced by the child' (1981, p 234). This sharing of the lifespace introduces opportunities for relationships to develop between adults and children that can enhance opportunities for learning and growth. Bronfenbrenner (1979) offers a three-stage model through which this might happen. The first stage involves observation of one another's activity. A skilled worker may initiate the opportunity for such observation through, for instance, shuffling a deck of cards and thus inviting a child to move closer and become involved with them. Conversely, an adult might consciously choose to become involved in a child's actions, perhaps involving throwing a ball. One way or another, the observation leads to shared participation in which adult and child become involved in each other's activity. There is a reciprocal, rhythmic aspect to this interaction and a relational dimension begins to emerge, whereby enduring feelings between the parties can develop. It is this relationship that can become the conduit for learning. While many of these interactions happen naturalistically their impact can be optimised if workers have a conscious understanding of the processes involved. Failing to understand these might result in interactions being built around the wrong stimulus, such as staff continually intervening to tell a child off. In these cases the relationship that develops is likely to be negative, rather than one which holds out opportunities for positive learning.

Conclusion

Residential child care is, by its nature, an organic domain of practice, which is rarely amenable to linear and prescriptive ways of thinking or acting on it. Creating healthy cultures of care involves an appreciation of staff and resident group influences and of the staples of group care practice; the rhythms, rituals and routines of the centre, which are fundamental to facilitating the sense of security and purpose required by children and indeed staff. An understanding of the complexity of the residential environment is crucial. Without this 'feel for the game' the target setting and audit initiatives of the past couple of decades will be to little avail.

SEVEN

Assessment, care planning and programming

This chapter considers the key stages in a child's stay in residential care: assessment, care planning and programming. The *Children who wait* report (Rowe and Lambert, 1973) identified a situation where children stayed in residential child care settings with little sense of purpose to the placement, other than that of providing everyday care. This report posed fundamental questions as to the suitability of residential child care to provide long-term care for children; this, axiomatically, being assumed to be located in natural or increasingly in substitute family settings. The publication of *Children who wait* coincided with the professionalisation of social work in the early 1970s. Within a casework model, the basic social work process was considered to comprise stages of: referral, assessment, planning, intervention and evaluation. Assimilation into professional social work in the 1970s placed an onus on residential child care to fit in with such a model, to articulate a sense of purpose and progress through the system, rather than merely to provide everyday care.

Reports throughout the 1980s highlighted specific flaws in the care system. Parton (1991) identified the absence of a logical link between what was happening in care settings and hoped-for outcomes for children. And within increasingly managerial cultures questions of cost became uppermost; was the government getting value for money in respect of resources directed towards care provision and children's welfare more generally? At another level the introduction of the category 'children in need' in the 1989 Children Act demanded some mechanism through which these children might be identified. In residential child care reports such as those by Utting (1991) and Skinner (1992), asserting that residential child care should be a positive choice for some children similarly required some means of assessing those for whom it might be so.

Assessment

Coulshed and Orme identify assessment as being core to social work practice. They define it as:

> ... an on-going process, in which the client or service user
> participates, the purpose of which is to understand people
> in relation to their environment; assessment is also a basis
> for planning what needs to be done to maintain, improve
> or bring about change in the person, the environment or
> both. (2006, p 24)

Assessment in this sense provides a platform for decision making and for
intervention. This is true in respect of reports prepared for outside bodies
such as courts or children's hearings. In residential child care it is equally
true in a lifespace context where staff continuously observe and reflect
upon what might be going on with a particular child in a particular
situation and perhaps are called to act on the conclusions they draw
from such observation and reflection. If assessments are based on wrong
information or an inability to interpret that information appropriately
then it is likely that subsequent decision making will be flawed.

An ecological approach

The Coulshed and Orme quote above notes the purpose of assessment
as being to understand people in relation to their environment. This
demands that the focus extends beyond the individual to also take
account of their wider social circumstances. This focus on the individual
in the context of the wider social systems within which they operate
is called an ecological approach and is based on the work of Uri
Bronfenbrenner (1977), who sought to apply ideas from biological
sciences to human development. Bronfenbrenner was also, during
his life, a child and youth care worker, so his insights are grounded in
personal experience of working with children. He describes the ecology
of human development as involving:

> ... the scientific study of the progressive, mutual
> accommodation between the active, growing human being
> and the changing properties of the immediate setting in
> which the developing person lives, as this process is affected
> by relations between these settings and by the larger contexts
> in which these settings are embedded. (1979, p 21)

He conceptualises this model as either a set of concentric circles or as
Russian dolls, one embedded within the other. The inner circle or doll
is described as the micro-system, the pattern of actions and relations
between the developing person and their immediate environment.

In most cases this will be a child's immediate family. The next layer out is the meso-system, which is concerned with interrelations among different settings in which a developing person participates; this may involve relations between home, school and peer group. If such relations are harmonious, this is likely to encourage healthy development. Conversely if they are fractious, developmental conditions become less conducive. The third layer in Bronfenbrenner's model is termed the exo-system. This acknowledges that events or decisions occurring outside of a child's immediate setting can impact on their developmental opportunities. A parent losing their job, for instance, may have implications for a child in respect of changing material circumstances or status within the community. Similarly, local authority policies around the placement of under-12-year-olds in residential child care, for instance, or decisions about educational mainstreaming, neither of which involve individual children directly, nevertheless have a significant impact on the kind of services they can expect and hence on their developmental experience. The final layer in the ecology of human development is the macro-system. This consists of cultural and subcultural norms around parenting styles, for instance. Cultural mores around authoritarian or laissez-faire parenting and perhaps increasingly around the kind of uneasy relationships which exist between adults and children (UNICEF, 2007) all impact on the kind of upbringing a child will encounter. Issues of poverty or the distribution of wealth in particular societies will also impact fundamentally on children's experiences.

A welcome feature of Bronfenbrenner's system is that it is dynamic or, in his own terms, bidirectional. Children (and indeed parents) can be seen as agents within their own ecological systems. At a simple micro-systemic level, for example, an infant who is sickly and whiney is likely to elicit a differential response from their caregiver than one who is smiley and engaging. Similarly, in residential care children who are engaging and likeable will elicit a different response to those who may be surly or vexatious. The reality is, however, that the further removed people are from social and political systems the less likely they are to be able to affect them. They will, however, be affected by them.

Assessment frameworks

The growing concern in the 1980s to ensure value for money and the linking of what happened in care to the outcomes for children led to the establishment of a working party under Professor Roy Parker to create a system of assessing outcomes for children in substitute care. The resultant looked-after children system was launched in England and Wales in 1995 and subsequently introduced in Scotland and Northern Ireland. The idea behind the system was to collate all the information available on a child within a common framework. It included assessment and action records that were intended to guide staff to identify gaps in particular domains of a child's development and to formulate plans as to how these might be addressed.

The looked-after children material in some respects fell prey to the very problem it sought to remedy. For it to work required that every part of the system fitted together. However, staff in residential child care found the system to be cumbersome and time consuming; many forms were not forwarded from referring agencies, with the result that gaps in knowledge of particular children persisted. One of the criticisms of the system was that it overly focused on the needs of individual children and specifically, as the title indicates, on looked-after children. The New Labour government sought to extend the role of assessment. The *Framework for the assessment of children in need and their families* (DH et al, 2000) introduced an ostensibly ecological approach based on three broad dimensions represented by the sides of a triangle: a child's own developmental needs, parenting capacity and environmental factors. Although the assessment triangle requires social workers to address environmental issues, the shift away from structural concerns towards a greater focus on individual deficits in recent decades, and presumably a belief that they can do little to address structural issues, means that issues of poverty are rarely named in any meaningful way in social workers' assessments. The framework also extends the scope of assessment away from only looked-after children to include any child who may be in need.

The assessment framework in some part paved the way for the government's integrated services agenda. This was taken forward by the 2003 Green Paper *Every Child Matters* (ECM) (DfES, 2003) and its Scottish counterpart *Getting it Right for Every Child* (GIRFEC) (Scottish Executive, 2005b). Both of these identify the multifaceted nature of children's needs, which require multi-systemic approaches to addressing them. ECM identifies five outcomes for children: that they are healthy, stay safe, enjoy and achieve, make a positive contribution and that they experience economic well-being. GIRFEC identifies seven outcomes, namely that children are: safe, healthy, achieving, nurtured, active, respected and responsible, and included. ECM has led to the development of the common assessment framework (CAF), a standardised approach to conducting an assessment for use by practitioners across children's services in England. CAF is thus a tool through which to take forward integrated services. In Scotland GIRFEC calls for a single assessment, record and plan overseen by a key children's services worker.

Problems with assessment frameworks

Milner and O'Byrne caution that there are 'too many linear, prescriptive and stylised assessment formats that come nowhere near meeting the complexities, uncertainties and ambiguities of current social work practice' (2002, p 3). Practitioners need to bear in mind that any assessment framework should be considered as being primarily for guidance. They do not provide any objective account of an individual in context merely through the ticking of particular boxes. And they are likely to throw up a number of false positives or negatives. Workers need to exercise considerable professional skills and judgement in making sense of the data that assessment frameworks might provide them with. In the wrong hands assessment has the potential to harm as well as to help, and requires an intelligent understanding of its purpose and an ability to engage and to interpret information appropriately. A criticism that can be made of models such as those identified above is that in breaking down assessment into a series of discrete areas, it risks losing the dynamic and holistic nature of a properly ecological assessment and becomes an exercise in information gathering.

There is also a political dimension to assessment frameworks. Harvey (2005) identifies the contradictions in neoliberalism: on the one hand professing greater freedom while on the other demanding more and more information on individuals and groups. Parton (2006) identifies assessment frameworks as being fundamentally implicated in wider moves towards greater social surveillance. Frameworks also speak of a particular view of children. While few might argue with the principles of initiatives such as ECM and GIRFEC, they reflect what Moss and Petrie describe as 'technologies for acting upon children ... to produce specific, predetermined and adult-defined outcomes' (2002, p 9).

Assessment in the lifespace

As mentioned earlier, assessment is not just something that is done in a casework context; it is something that residential workers are doing all the time. They observe situations, try and work out what is going on, whether or not they need to intervene and if so how best to. In this sense the kind of casework processes identified at the beginning of the chapter become truncated and condensed to the moment. Adrian Ward's framework of 'opportunity led work' (2000) provides a useful model of how a residential worker might process lifespace events. Ward breaks down what goes on into stages of assessment, decision making, actions and closure. In some respects the various elements of thought and action involved can seem to come together in an indeterminate muddle, often requiring split-second processing, which can inevitably involve a worker getting things wrong. Garfat (2003a) identifies a process that involves workers giving meaning to what they see, attempting to work out the meaning the same event might have for the children involved and, crucially, what he calls 'checking in with self'. This entails reflecting on what a particular situation might trigger in a worker and how best to bring the 'self' into the chosen response.

Some approaches, in the name of objectivity, seek to take the 'self' out of assessment. This is not possible; the self of any practitioner inevitably influences what people think and how they act in particular situations. Personal values and whether or not we like those we are working with will inevitably flavour the conclusions drawn. While we might like to claim some level of professional detachment, if a member of staff likes the subject of their assessment, the result is more likely to read positively; conversely a fractious relationship is likely to manifest in a more negative assessment. To deny the inevitable subjectivity of assessment is not helpful. What is more helpful is that practitioners adopt a reflexive turn in their thinking about children and families, acknowledging what they might bring to the whole process of sense making but also being aware of the wider systemic and discursive influences that will inevitably influence how they view and report situations.

Assessment in the lifespace might best be thought of in terms of a 'getting to know you' process at a relational rather than just an instrumental and information-gathering level. It is about getting into a common rhythm, finding out what makes children (and ourselves) 'tick' and how best to use any emerging 'fit' to build and sustain a relationship. It is part and parcel of caring for a child:

> The child care worker is a player immersed in the game of caring for the child. In the process of the game, the child care worker seeks to understand the child, not explain him or predict him. In the process of the game the child care worker is able to do this, to some extent, because he and the child are partners in the game, they share the game, the game does not exist without them. (Austin and Halpin, 1988)

Summary

While accepting that assessment is a core process in social work and a continuous task for workers in residential child care, some caveats should be attached to the increasing demands placed on practitioners to undertake assessments and the expectations policy makers might have as to the results of these. Some of these are of a practical nature; others are more philosophical.

Assessment is postulated to be benign; who could take issue with the collection of information in order to provide an individual with the best possible service? However, in many cases assessment does not lead to the provision of services; it begins and ends with the collection of information. Indeed assessments are increasingly used to ration or deny services. In residential child care they can be used to make a case for bringing a service to an end, to limit liability to care. If an assessment is not used as a platform to provide services, it becomes little more than a data-gathering exercise and becomes almost voyeuristic.

Assessment frameworks incorporate a normative aspect. In coming to judgements about particular behaviours or situations we inevitably do so through an evaluation of what we see or are told against what we consider to be normal and acceptable. Yet what is normal and acceptable is of course historically, culturally and personally contingent. It may also betray particular social class and cultural biases.

Assessment can also be deterministic and risk labelling children. In the present climate we have become increasingly prone to categorising behaviours. The trend towards specific units for so-called sexually aggressive adolescents, for instance, might do little more than reflect heightened societal anxiety about all things sexual and risks pathologising normal adolescent sexual behaviour. Rather than helping young people move on, such an approach risks confirming them in an identity as a sex offender, which does them and society no good.

The final point is perhaps more ethereal but may be worth introducing nevertheless. It concerns the extent to which we can or should know 'the other'. Levinas, a French philosopher of the 20th century, whose work I return to in the final chapter, alleges that 'the other' is unique and ultimately unknowable and that the only way we can attempt to know them is to impose our own beliefs and assumptions on them and through so doing 'murdering' the self of the other. This argument has ethical implications for the power dynamics within any assessment relationship but it also has a practical resonance. Practitioners are often confronted with situations where they think they know what is going on for a child or their family, only to be surprised by some new, unexpected information. There are serious practical and ethical limitations to the quest to know 'the other', which need to be borne in mind in the assessment process. However much or little we know about the children we work with, this does not detract from an ultimate responsibility to care for them.

Risk assessment

Perhaps the most prominent construct to have entered social work discourse in recent years is that of risk assessment. Staff in residential child care cannot, it seems, do anything from running a bath to boiling an egg without having to conduct a risk assessment. They are not allowed to make a sandwich without having undertaken food hygiene training and they certainly cannot decide to take off for the day to the hills or the beach. I have called risk assessment a construct for that is what it is; despite claims or perhaps hopes that it is vested with some scientific validity or that it has any meaningful predictive qualities, the very concept of risk assessment may ultimately be little more than 'a smoke screen to convince ourselves and others that we are doing something positive in a situation over which we have little control' (Cree and Wallace, 2005, p 126). Risk assessment tools may in the right hands help support professional assessment and judgement. However, they are never likely to move beyond this to provide any scientific means on which to base complex decisions.

The concept of risk assessment can only be understood within the wider context of the risk society (Beck, 1992), as outlined in Chapter One. As previously noted, political discourse shifted in the 1980s from a predominant concern for social welfare and family support to one which sought to identify and target social work intervention at 'dangerous' families through more clinical application of risk assessment tools. This was an ideological decision reflecting a concern to limit the role of the state with families and a parallel concern to cut costs. Criminal and youth justice social work has witnessed a similar shift in focus from one that sought to minimise the risk of recidivism to the individual offender to concerns to reduce reoffending and enhance community safety. This led to the development of risk assessment tools, which it was thought might better identify the potential for reoffending or serious harm, thus enabling resources to be targeted more proactively at these cases. Kemshall (2002) argues that social work is now primarily involved in assessing and managing risk, to the detriment of concerns around social need and justice. As Barry argues:

Culpability is focused on the family (rather than external factors such as poverty in terms of child neglect, for example) and/or on the practitioner, and there is little evidence of corporate responsibility for child protection issues. This often results in practitioners working defensively and applying objective and often compulsory measures to families rather than building trusting relationships with families. (Barry, 2007)

In residential child care the risk assessment agenda is manifest in the development of safe caring perspectives that have assumed a taken-for-granted status over recent years. Some unhealthy practices have emerged from discourses of safe caring. These include injunctions or, perhaps worse still, inchoate practice cultures that have evolved, for instance, around staff not offering children physical comfort or touch, not being on their own with children and not engaging with them in particular activities or during out-of-work hours. Considerations of healthy developmental experiences are subsumed beneath those of risk. Safe caring perspectives of this sort are more often about protecting individual staff members from allegations (Horwath, 2000) or about protecting organisations from litigation than they are about protecting children from harm. As Barry puts it, 'the relationship between worker and client is paramount to effective working and yet is being eroded by the language and politics of risk' (2007).

Those who advocate the idea of risk assessment often do so on the grounds that an appropriate risk assessment need not inhibit practice but can provide workers with arguments through which they might justify taking particular risks. Notions of defensibility, of having thought through and articulated possible risks in a situation, may allow a worker to defend his or her decision making rather than offering any predictive certainty. This is as much as might realistically be hoped for from risk assessment. However, such arguments assume a rational worldview. Yet Munro (1999) highlights intrinsic irrationality in decision making in risky situations and shows that social workers' decisions are informed by their beliefs and values rather than available evidence. Moreover, in the current political climate social work, and in particular any aspect of practice that might have a child protection dimension, operates from a more primitive basis, one often rooted in fear and uncertainty. This gets in the way of more rational consideration of the role and limitations of risk assessment.

When it comes down to it, risk assessment is actually something that any responsible parent or carer does on an ongoing basis. They make decisions as to whether children can go into the sea to swim or how deep they can go in, possibly having checked the depth and current themselves. They make sure that children are suitably clothed and equipped for any activity and, most of all, they ensure that they supervise them. This does not require forms or score sheets; it is part and parcel of what it is to care and is rooted in cultural norms and understandings rather than abstract formulas requiring workers to identify and quantify particular dangers and hazards.

In the current climate, however, anyone seeking to challenge practices promoted in the name of child safety risks accusations of being naive, cavalier or worse. However, some sense of perspective needs to be brought to bear on how we interact with children. Safe caring as it has emerged creates and reinforces a dissonance and a mutual suspicion between adults and children. Moss and Petrie (2002) claim that the best safeguard against abuse is a culture of listening to and respecting children. Children so treated will be assertive in their dealings with adults who they will trust to take their concerns seriously. This situation will come about through getting relationships rather than procedures right.

Care planning

As already mentioned, assessment ought to provide a platform for the formulation of a care plan setting out how best to intervene with children and their families, identifying who will be responsible for carrying out particular tasks and setting out some idea of timescales. Local authorities are now expected to complete overarching care plans identifying their strategic direction in a case, such as long-term foster care or rehabilitation. Sometimes care plans in the context of residential child care are called placement plans. These should relate to the specific goals of a placement. In some cases there needs to be a sequencing of particular care or placement plan objectives; for instance, children generally need to feel safe and settled and to establish trusting relationships with those working with them before they can move on to address some of the more difficult areas in their lives. It is increasingly an expectation and almost goes without saying that care plan objectives are more likely to be successfully met if children can contribute to them.

Care plans cannot be written in tablets of stone and should not become linear or over-prescriptive. While we all like a bit of predictability in our lives and some sense of knowing where we are going, we would not want our every movement circumscribed and scrutinised. There needs to be some flexibility within overall goals, which themselves need to be reappraised from time to time. There is little point continuing down a particular path with a child just because it says so in a care plan when whatever is being done is obviously not working. There need to be mechanisms through which care plans can be discussed and reviewed on an ongoing basis. Linked to the above point, care plans also need to be manageable. There is no point, for example, taking a decision to confine a child to the home if the staff group cannot practically or physically carry through that plan. The credibility of the whole care planning process is compromised in such circumstances.

The idea of programme

Fulcher (2004) notes that the term 'programme' has been used extensively in North American child and youth care since the end of the Second World War. When the term was first introduced in the UK in a primarily developmental context (Fulcher and Ainsworth, 1981) it was met with suspicion on account of connotations of social control (Fulcher, 2004). Ironically the notion of programme has become resurgent in recent years, having entered the social work lexicon through criminal justice services. As such it is now very often associated with social control. In a residential child care context programmes have become associated with particular treatment packages aimed at reducing or extinguishing specific problematic behaviours (for example, anger management programmes, programmes for sexually aggressive young people or cognitive behavioural therapy programmes). The official imprimatur is accorded to the idea of programmes in reports on residential schools by Audit Scotland (2002), which recommends the development and accreditation of a range of programmes based around 'what works' principles to address issues of youth offending.

Policy injunctions such as those proposed by audit bodies have led in some residential homes to the appointment of separate teams or workers charged with implementing particular programmed interventions with children. There are practical and ethical questions that can be asked of such one-dimensional conceptions of the idea of programme. At a practical level such an approach separates out the tackling of particular targeted behaviours from children's everyday experiences and thereby cuts across the potential of the lifespace as the preferred medium for addressing behaviours. Ethically the application of proprietary interventions to address problematic behaviours as though these were somehow generic in origin and manifestation is antithetical to the principles of a differential assessment of children and their needs

(Fulcher, 2004). Perhaps the most telling critique of an over-reliance on programmed interventions, however, is that there is scant evidence of their effectiveness (Pitts, 2001; Audit Scotland, 2002). Indeed, recent research into secure accommodation (Walker et al, 2006) suggests that the most effective units were those relying on relational skills.

The foregoing critique of programmes as they have been developed in recent years should not be taken to discount the idea of programme per se. One of the legitimate criticisms that can be levelled at residential child care is that it has lacked an appropriate sense of purpose. A programme which sets out what a centre purports to offer and how it intends to go about this provides an invaluable focus for a staff group. As I have argued elsewhere, 'a well articulated programme provides a unifying framework within which staff can make sense of and against which they can be required to justify their interventions with youth' (Smith, 2005a, p 121). I conclude this point by stating that 'the focus needs to remain on the whole child and the opportunities to effect change that are offered in the course of daily living' (2005a, p 121).

Activities

A central consideration in the programme of any residential unit ought to include the role played in it by activities. Despite the fact that staff are likely to spend more time engaging in activities of one sort or another than in any formal interventions with children, activities are rarely given the attention they deserve. Yet they are probably the most important tool in the armoury of those who work with children.

There are perhaps two reasons why we fail to capitalise sufficiently on what activities might offer. The first of these is a throwback to a less eligibility mentality; activities are fun and we do not want to be seen to be offering children in care too much fun – far better to be seen to be targeting them with interventions aimed at ironing out some behavioural difficulty or other. A second reason staff do not make the most of activities is that they have failed to develop appropriate activity-based skills. In line with normalising philosophies, children were often encouraged to spend recreational time in the community rather than in organised activities alongside staff. And of course practical training around activities does not feature on social work training programmes where the focus is on social science-based perspectives. In this wider context, activities in residential child care have in many cases become expensive ways of filling time rather than a vehicle for well thought-through developmental opportunities. Scott (1999) sums up a central tension between these two perspectives when he asks:

Is it possibly a sign of our own tendency to expect the worst that we offer all these cliché skills to troubled children – conflict resolution, problem solving, anger management, self-defense...? I wonder how necessary these things would be if we offered them experience in sailing, vegetable growing, soccer, playing bongo drums or fixing bikes. (Scott, 1999, p 3, quoted in Phelan, 2001a, p 1)

A result of this is an impoverished childhood experience for many children denied access to the cultural capital that involvement in communal games or physical activity can bring and in the development and therapeutic benefits that can accrue from such involvement (VanderVen, 1985). I now consider what some of these might be.

Growing through play

We are well aware of the importance of play in helping young children grow and develop. Play allows them to tap into their creative side and helps them to negotiate and learn the importance of rules and conventions. Properly planned activities can fulfil the same purpose for children of all ages, sometimes presenting those in care settings with these opportunities for the first time. Albert Camus, the French/ Algerian philosopher and one-time goalkeeper, stated: 'All I know most surely about morality and obligations, I owe to football' (*Guardian*, 2008). Team games confront children with the need for collaboration in an immediate and, if well managed, non-threatening way.

Experiencing competence

Phelan (2001b) identifies the potential of activities to provide a free space for children where they can put aside the constraints of past adversity and the uncertainty around future prospects for the duration of the activity. However, activities in Phelan's model are not merely a form of escapism. He reconceptualises the task of residential child care workers quite radically, identifying a central role for them as experienced arrangers charged to put in place opportunities that allow children to experience a state of cognitive dissonance, to feel competent and to re-script self-defeating narratives into ones that include hope for the future. Thus the central therapeutic tool of residential child care workers becomes the conscious and purposeful use of activities as opposed to traditional controlling- or counselling-type relationships which Phelan argues stick children in self-defeating narratives.

Building relationships

A recurring theme in this book is around the centrality of adult–child relationships in effecting change. Shared involvement in activities provides a powerful conduit through which children and adults might experience one another in different ways and is implicated in developing resilience (Gilligan, 2005). Activities can provide what Phelan (2001b) describes as a place in the present where the usual roles do not apply. Relationships in this place are less hierarchical and more authentic. The nature of the relationship is one of 'doing with' rather than 'doing to or for', of being alongside one another. Too often residential work is concerned with 'doing to' children, about doing 'the work' whatever 'the work' might be (it is usually about chastising children for misbehaving or seeking to address emotional distress through counselling-type interventions). 'Doing with' them is somehow insufficiently 'professional'.

Often the most powerful activities are those that assume a personal dimension, when staff can share their own passions with the children they work with and, similarly, can enter into the particular interests of children. This personal involvement adds another dimension to their joint involvement. The type of relationship that is facilitated by involvement in activities is what Phelan describes as analogue communication; it is sensuous and non-verbal rather than counselling or didactic, forged through shared activity. This contributes to the strength of the resultant bond and to the nature of any power dynamics, which become far less pronounced.

Activities in the lifespace

The shared lifespace, which is a unique feature of residential child care, is replete with opportunities to engage in activity-based work. Some of these activities are seemingly naturally occurring. A pack of cards and a few well-rehearsed tricks can have a Pied Piper effect in drawing children towards the dealer, presenting opportunities for shared interaction. Board games such as Monopoly or Risk can span days or weeks and can become a central focus in the life of a centre. Arts and crafts constitute another important aspect of activity programming and in the hands of skilled and enthusiastic members of staff can contribute, if displayed, to the overall fabric and feel of a place.

The very term 'activities' might suggest those of a physical or sporting nature and these should be integral to the life of any group care centre. The promotion of physical activity is an important strand in current initiatives to tackle children's health and fitness needs. And while there is little hard evidence to support wider social benefits of children's involvement in sport, there are strong theoretical and experiential arguments that point to a range of these such as enhanced self confidence and esteem for those who take part. Steckley (2005a), for instance, identifies the benefits that accrue through boys' involvement in organised football in a residential school setting.

In many cases the benefits of involvement in activities can be incidental. Because staff often fail to conceptualise activities as bona fide interventions with children in care they can remain consigned in official discourse to a cameo role, one that supports the real work of counselling children. Activities in many respects *are* the real work of residential child care; they provide the platform to support the development of competence and strength. As Phelan argues, 'work with youth and families is best done in an activity, not in a conversation' (2001b, p 1).

The ordinary and the everyday in residential child care

If the notion of programme is considered to include the overall purpose and ethos of a residential home, the question arises as to what extent any programme should emphasise the ordinary or everyday and to what extent it should provide special or therapeutic experiences for children (Ward, 2006). Ward argues that current ideological discourses favouring normalisation and policy preferences based around inclusion valorise the ordinary and in so doing downplay the extent of the social and mental health problems that children have encountered prior to admission to residential child care. Offering only everyday experiences to children who are often extremely damaged fails to address their specific needs. Increasingly, bodies representing children's rights or claiming to represent the voice of the child are the most vocal advocates of a 'normalised' approach to children's care. Adopting such a stance can present an unrealistic picture of the real needs of children and underplay the realities of their difficulties.

On the other hand, too great a focus on the therapeutic is equally unhelpful. Overemphasising children's emotional problems can inhibit staff from providing them with the basic care they need. Yet children who are emotionally disturbed, perhaps more than most, need the safety and security that comes from well-structured daily routines and rhythms of care. Good daily care is a prerequisite for any treatment approach. Anglin (2002) identifies the central tension of children's behaviours being rooted in painful past experience, yet within this they struggle for normality. Ward (2006) advocates that residential child care should provide special everyday living experiences that include a compensatory or reparatory dimension.

Conclusion

As residential child care has become ostensibly more 'professional', the tendency has been to impose ever more systemic demands on it. There is, of course, obvious merit in residential homes and workers having a sense of purpose, in understanding the needs of particular children and intervening accordingly to meet these. In that sense workers having some understanding of ideas around assessment, care planning and programming is important. There are risks, however (and increasingly these risks seem to have become realities), that attempts to 'professionalise' the processes of residential care can lead to overly procedural approaches to everyday practice. This redefines the job away from direct caring and leads to practitioners spending more time writing about children than being with them. Ideas of care planning and programming also tend to be problem-focused and as such fail to acknowledge the potential benefits of the staples of residential child care, such as activities, in promoting placement goals.

Increasingly, policy documents such as *Care Matters* (DfES, 2006) liken the task of caring to parenting. While most parents have a sense of what makes their children tick, and have particular hopes and aspirations for them, they do not write these down at regular intervals. And while there may be some inevitable distinction to be made in respect of the private and public dimensions of caring, demands for technicism and accountability in public care have gone far too far and now detract from the act and the art of caring.

EIGHT

Working at the boundaries: the personal–professional relationship

Previous chapters have looked at the residential environment. For anything worthwhile to happen there needs to be a catalyst. In this respect the relationship established between carers and cared for is fundamental; any programme is only as good as those who carry it through. To put it another way, there is a need to reframe the managerial zeitgeist of 'what works' to one of 'who works' (McNeill et al, 2005). Putting the personal at the heart of work with children introduces a range of boundary issues. This chapter addresses some of these, asking, essentially, how we can place the relationship at the centre of what we do while recognising and addressing the challenges this presents. I address some of the more sensitive issues that confront practitioners on an everyday basis – issues such as love, touch, sexuality and physical restraint. Ultimately, it is argued that ensuring healthy and productive relationships comes down to workers operating from an appropriate ethical base rather than merely adhering to sets of codes and procedures.

The personal–professional relationship

Perhaps the best-known line in the North American child and youth care literature is Uri Bronfenbrenner's assertion that 'every child needs at least one adult who's crazy about them' (1977, p 5). Research into what has helped young people who have made successful transitions from residential child care backs this up, indicating the importance of at least one adult who formed a special relationship with them (Jackson et al, 2005). Theories of resilience similarly foreground the importance of appropriate adult–child connections and inter-generational role-modelling (Gilligan, 2005). The importance of relationships and the possibilities opened up by relational approaches to practice are particularly pronounced in residential child care, which is perhaps unique among professions in placing the personal qualities of adults at the forefront of the task. While it might be desirable for other professionals, teachers and doctors, for instance, to build relationships with those they teach or treat, ultimately teaching and treating are the primary tasks. In care settings, building appropriate relationships and using these to help children as they grow up is the primary endeavour. Care is what Phelan (2001b) calls a 'self in action' task. We need to consider how that 'self' can become a positive force in connection with other 'selves'.

The worker–client relationship was central within traditional psychosocial approaches to social work, although there was a persistent concern among social work managers that such relationships should not become so close that workers might 'go native' and identify with the structural oppressions in clients' lives (Jones, 1983). The relationship was therefore contained within an 'expert'–client model. Even such limited relational approaches have become marginalised in recent years, deemed within managerial discourse to be too 'woolly' and unable to demonstrate sufficient evidence of the outcomes of intervention. As a result case management approaches have become dominant. In residential child care the personal relationship took a particular 'hit' following the various abuse scandals and organisational responses to these. Stuck within managerial and procedural paradigms, policy makers and managers might publicly agree that relationships are a good thing while becoming very jumpy when actually confronted with a close adult–child connection. In many organisational cultures it can be deemed 'unprofessional' for a worker to admit to any personal feelings for a child. This is unhelpful in respect of the task and can be seen as a case of collective denial; essentially pretending that adults can come into the intimate contact that residential care involves without developing powerful feelings of all sorts for the children they work with. The issue facing residential care is not to deny the strength of these relationships and emotions but to validate them and to ensure that they remain healthy and centred on the needs of the child.

There is now a resurgent interest in relationally based practice, both in terms of its greater congruence with social work values but also in light of emerging evidence that it is effective. Nicolson and Artz cite research by Clark (2001), which looked into 40 years of psychotherapy outcomes for youth. It concludes:

> ... relationship factors (the strength of the alliance that develops between the youth and the worker, built upon perceived empathy, acceptance, warmth, trust and self-expression and defined by the youth as a helpful connection) and the ability of workers to work positively with the clients' ways of understanding themselves and others, account for

70% of behaviour change. Two other factors, hope and expectancy that change will occur, account for 15% of behaviour change (and also depend on a positive relationship between worker and youth); while intervention model and technique account for only 15%. Fundamental to any prevention or intervention that has a chance of success, is a strong positive relationship. (2003, pp 41-2)

Relationships in the context of care

Discussion of relationships in care settings requires some understanding of the nature of care. Is it an instrumental task, driven by contracts, targets and outcomes, or is it an affective endeavour, a disposition, 'a general habit of mind', as Tronto (1994) puts it? We have seen that the dominant professional discourse can veer towards the former view. Care can be conceived of as a commodity that can be measured in the dimensions of a bedroom or the thickness of a home's procedures manual. Of course care cannot and must not be reduced in such ways.

Maier (1979) has considered this distinction between the hotelling function of residential care and a more rounded conception of caring. He differentiates between physical care and 'caring care'. What transforms the former to the latter is the personal connection, that sense of a carer being truly present in the moment, attentive and responsive to a child's needs. This caring presence can be manifest in small ways such as the ruffling of hair on getting a child up in the morning or remembering what they take in their tea. Such experiences of caring care are, according to Maier (1987, p 110), 'our whispered moments of glory, our Camelots'. In a similar vein, Noddings notes that 'the cared-for "grows and glows" under the perceived attitude of the one-caring' (1996a, p 29). Care only becomes meaningful when it is personal. Ricks (1992) claims that an ethic of care takes:

> ... professional caring into the personal realm and require(s) that both parties show up, be present, be engaged at a feeling level for each other. The presence of feeling(s) provides the link which connects the worker and client. Very simply put, without this connection, without the feeling(s) in the relationship, the people do not matter to each other.

While relationships are argued to be fundamental to effective practice it is not enough merely to assert this without any wider consideration of the nature and purpose of relationships; they cannot afford to be indiscriminate. Fewster has suggested that 'the personalized relationship continues to be the greatest challenge in professional child and youth care' (1990, p 26). He discusses the difficulty workers can have in developing a relationship with a child in which the experience of intimacy and connectedness can be present, while appropriate boundaries are maintained. However, he goes on to say that in the absence of relationship, the care worker's ability to affect a youth's values, beliefs, attitudes or behaviours is extremely limited. Elsewhere, Fewster (2004) talks of working at the 'contact boundary', the place where the self of the worker and the self of the client make authentic connection. He considers this to be the nexus of the personal relationship, the crucible in which the most profound and transformational learning takes place. Accordingly residential care workers must seek out opportunities to work at this contact boundary if their involvement is to effect change in the lives of children.

Who are you? Characteristics of the effective child and youth care intervention

Having asserted the importance of effective personal and professional relationships, what is involved in these? Tronto's (1994) conception of care suggests that to be well intentioned is not in itself enough. Care also needs to include elements of purpose and competence. The caring relationship is responsive to the needs of the other, so carers need to know these needs and respond to them with appropriate professional rigour. One dimension of this requires an appreciation of the limits of the caring role depending on circumstances. For instance, workers need to negotiate the complexity of having sufficiently close and caring relationships that do not inappropriately eclipse the potential for a child to rebuild and/or maintain loving attachments with parents. To do this workers need to know themselves. It is perhaps the central question asked of residential staff, to know who they are if they are to work effectively with children. Effective work with difficult young people demands certain personal qualities of staff.

So how do the qualities of effective residential care workers manifest? Garfat (1998) explored workers' and children's views of what was meaningful in their experience of particular interventions, and identified several themes. These included adults having a high degree of care for and commitment to those they work with, high levels of self-confidence and responsibility, and a general and immediate sense of themselves. Good workers also possessed an awareness of the wider context, understanding the individual child within the context of the issues or situations facing them. The latter in particular seems to be promoted by the ongoing process of sharing and working together in the lifespace. Finally, a young person's experience of continuity in the relationship with the worker emerged as a theme in the study.

Working at the contact boundary with children, sharing their lifespace, is an intimate experience and one that throws up all sorts of questions about where that contact boundary might be located and how personal the personal relationship should become. One thing that is certain is that the contact boundary is in a different place for those who share the lifespace with children than it might be for social workers and other professionals whose relationship is less intimate. This is often not recognised by those whose view of professionalism and professional boundaries derives from a casework orientation. Despite the best efforts of employing agencies to lay down lines of where boundaries should lie through procedural edict, there are no simple answers; the questions are irredeemably nuanced and will shift inevitably from one set of relationships to another. The best workers can do is to grapple with this complexity and attempt to act ethically within it. I now turn to addressing some of the complex boundary issues that practitioners must grapple with day to day.

Love

A question that persistently surfaces in residential child care is whether workers can or should love those they work with. In many respects that question should be turned on its head and reframed as, can they not love them? We have seen in Chapter Five that love is identified by Kellmer-Pringle (1975) as one of the needs of children essential to their healthy development. The famous educator Pestalozzi claimed that 'Love of those we educate is "the sole and everlasting foundation" in which to work. Without love, neither physical nor intellectual powers would develop naturally' (quoted in Infed, 2007). Yet in the current climate love is a word that can ring alarm bells when applied to the care of other people's children. Part of the problem may be that the term 'love' in the English language encompass a whole range of emotions, some of which are essential to bringing up children and some, those with more romantic or sexual connotations, that would be inappropriate. As a consequence of our unease about the term, or our difficulty in defining it, we tend to throw the baby out with the bathwater; love is deemed 'unprofessional'. Yet we should be able to justify the concept of love professionally. The intensity of the feelings developed for others should be able to be understood through reference to attachment theory, which tells us that there are innate drives that draw human beings together in affectional bonds that endure over time. When we share the lifespace with children, we are inevitably prone to such attachments. Residential care involves what Lynch (2007) calls 'love labour', which is not reducible to considerations of pay and conditions.

The call to reach out to the other in love is embedded in religious and philosophical traditions. An exposition of the place of love in the human condition is provided by the Scottish philosopher John Macmurray. His biographer, Costelloe, argues that:

> We come to be who we are as personal individuals only in personal relationship. The positive form of that relationship which goes by many names: love, friendship, fellowship, communion and community.... Because the meaning of the word 'love' had become so distorted in western societies, Macmurray frequently chose to speak of 'positive' personal relations in contrast to negative ones, that is, those based on fear and/or hatred. (2002, pp 326-7)

Macmurray goes on to claim that 'the fulfilment of all meaningful action is in friendship, that is, in our capacity to love others for their own sake' (Costelloe, 2002, pp 326-7).

There is perhaps yet another level of love that should be taken into account in work with children – its political dimension. Workers in residential child care should express a preferential option for those they work with, generally those on the bottom of society's ladder, and do this with what Freire (1995) calls an 'armed love' – the love required to name and denounce oppression. Love therefore assumes some of our deeper hopes for humanity, a quest for social justice, a philosophical concern for 'the good life' and a desire that those children we work with get a share in it. For this to happen requires that we side with them in challenging the oppressions and injustices of the systems that hold them back; love can be the fire in our belly for change. In that sense it poses a significant challenge to dominant instrumental views of care.

Of course, there are boundary issues that will be expanded on later in this chapter in any expression of love in a professional context. Adults should not enter into loving relationships with those they care for in the expectation that they will be reciprocated. Levinas argues that our call to care is one-way and infinite. However, although adults should not enter relationships with any expectation of a return, one of the joys of working with children is that they regularly do get something back. The warmth with which we are generally greeted when we meet those we once worked with, and their memories of seemingly mundane ways in which we made an impression, speak of affectional bonds that endure over time.

Sexuality

Sexuality is the elephant in the room in work with children. The subject is often shrouded in collective unease or hidden behind instrumental sex education programmes and a tendency to farm this out to 'experts' such as health professionals or specialist agencies.

The concept of sexuality reflects a person's sexual and romantic attractions. How they define their sexuality is largely socially constructed, influenced by social norms and assumptions and defined differently in different cultures and periods in history. Notions of sexuality are changing rapidly. Traditional assumptions of heterosexuality as the norm are becoming increasingly difficult to sustain in light of a greater awareness and acceptance of same-sex partnerships and a realisation that sexual identity is not fixed but may find different expression at different points in an individual's life cycle. More recent perspectives on sexuality consider the term 'sexualities' to be more appropriate in reflecting this complexity. Children we work with are likely to experience and may express a variety of sexual feelings. Nonetheless, despite the complex and dynamic nature of sexuality, there are powerful and sincerely held social forces which promote what might be considered to be 'normative' views, which assume a moral position on issues such as same-sex partnerships. The moral and political dimensions to debates around sexuality make it an area where practitioners need to tread carefully.

The fundamental developmental task of adolescence is to deal with the 'Who am I?' question. Addressing issues of sexual identity is integral to this. Adolescence is also a time of heightened sexual interest and activity as a result of the hormonal impact of puberty. In the confines of a residential home this means that some powerful sexual energies will be around. Children in residential care can confuse sexual drive with wider aspects of sexuality such as the desire for intimacy and validation and this can be manifest in their involvement in a range of inappropriate relationships. More than any of this, however, sexuality is integral to 'self'. It is part of who each of us, staff or child, is. It encompasses gender identity, sexual orientation and much social behaviour. When we connect with others in our everyday encounters, our sexualities inevitably enter into that engagement (Fewster, 2000). We need to become aware of this to ensure that our sexual selves become a healthy rather than a damaging force in work with children.

We are not generally good at this. Many workers lack confidence or feel uncomfortable addressing issues of sexuality. A recent UNICEF report (2007) suggests that attitudes towards sexuality in the UK and the US, in particular, are unhealthy and actually contribute to the very concerns around child safety they purport to avert. Northern European countries have more liberal and relaxed views on sexual matters, and they also have lower levels of sexual activity among children, significantly lower rates of teenage pregnancy and abortion and lower rates of divorce.

Engaging with children about matters of sexuality is rarely neutral. Because we are all sexual beings, when we talk to them it inevitably touches on aspects of our own sexual selves and can trigger a range of emotions. To deal with these safely and comfortably, workers need to reflect on their own sexuality and reflect on why particular situations may throw up the feelings they do. This can be a tricky area to get into, especially in foreclosing organisational cultures. As a result, many workers find it easier either to deny these feelings or else not to get involved in such areas of engagement. Yet because sexuality is such a fundamental part of our developing selves, it might be argued that we fail properly to promote the holistic development of young people if we do not acknowledge and engage with them as sexual beings.

With practice and support, workers can engage in positive ways around issues of sexuality. Trying to be as open and matter of fact as possible is likely to be the best way to proceed. Using appropriate humour may make it easier for staff and young people to deal with the issue without becoming too embarrassed. However, jokes should not trivialise the subject or be used to hide discomfort altogether. Some reflection is also required as to what assumptions lie behind any humour or behind our use of language more generally and how young people might interpret this. The most powerful way to encourage healthy attitudes towards sexuality is to ensure that staff model appropriate attitudes and behaviours in the lifespace, ideally providing different images of both femininity and masculinity and of sexual identity that young people might draw on.

Touch

One of the most disturbing features of residential practice over the past decade or so has been the development, in the name of safety, of 'no touch' policies (in many cases these are less policies and more inchoate practice cultures that take on the strength of policy). Such policies or assumptions are ridiculous because, as anyone who has worked with children will know, they are impossible to implement – children operate in perpetual motion; they bump into adults, hit against them, hang on them, become involved in scraps that require adult intervention and sometimes even demonstrate affection. It is disturbing when adults are fearful to respond when children initiate physical contact. It is equally disturbing that adults feel that they cannot initiate such contact. This is noted by Kent (1997), who expresses his horror that there are homes where adults feel afraid to comfort a child by putting their arm around them.

One of the reasons why no touch injunctions are so disturbing is that, by avoiding abuse, they are themselves abusive. Children need touch to grow physically and emotionally. To deny them appropriate human contact expressed through touch will stunt their overall development in one way or another. Kent notes that 'it is essential that we provide the necessary warmth, affection and comfort for children's healthy development if we are not further to damage emotionally children and young people who have usually had a raw deal from life' (1997, p 18).

Residential homes and schools may attempt to address the fears that exist around touch through guidance, demanding that adults seek permission to touch. Henry Maier (2002) is dismissive of such developments. '"May I touch you?" Nonsense! Asking that question implies that the worker is apt to be dangerous, possibly lecherous.' Maier is right. Asking for permission to touch misunderstands the whole nature of touch, which is spontaneous, often unconscious and reciprocal; it is an expression of normal personal interaction. What is comfortable and appropriate within that is something that is subtly negotiated in social context. And what is appropriate for one child or adult may not be for another; not everyone is touchy-feely in personal relationships, nor should they strive to be if it does not come naturally. Where our own boundaries lie is something we can only learn through interacting with others. Locating practice around touch within formulaic guidelines denies children the opportunity to learn appropriate social conventions and boundaries.

Maier's point about workers being considered dangerous is an insightful one. Piper et al (2006) identify how the paranoia that surrounds touch can bring to adult consciousness feelings they might otherwise not have had. One teacher in their research notes 'a definite hesitation and suspicion of myself', and, more worryingly, 'a feeling that this implanted awareness alerts any proclivity I have towards "the taboo"; that it might awaken otherwise non-existent desires' (Piper et al, 2006, p 152). This comment reflects more than healthy self-awareness and raises questions about whether no touch policies may actually generate the kind of problems they seek to avert. Piper observes: 'It's those who police themselves who end up feeling like perverts, rather than those who engage in unthinking and innocent touching' (cited in Appleton, 2006).

One area of practice that inevitably involves touch is toy fighting or horseplay. This can elicit all sorts of hand-wringing in residential child care; it is deemed to be implicated in inappropriate shows of strength and power or as a potential source of sexual arousal and exploitation, and no doubt in a small minority of cases it could be. As a result, many agencies have moved to ban such practices. Yet from a developmental perspective, Whyte suggests that 'if you want to get along with boys, learn to wrestle' (cited in Biddulph, 2003, p 74). Rough and tumble, like other play, is a vehicle through which children (perhaps especially boys) can let off steam, have fun and, importantly, learn to play by the rules and know when to stop. When allowed in a controlled fashion it can be entirely appropriate and healthy.

Piper and Smith (2003) claim that fear of touching is turning classrooms and nurseries into minefields. How much more is this the case in residential care settings? The consequence of the current paranoia is that carers fail to engage with children in care in the same way that they might respond to their own children – to the detriment of the children's development.

Restraint

Questions of how to ensure appropriate authority and control in a home are possibly the foremost consideration of staff in residential child care. Any aspirations they might have of creative or innovative ways of working, any attempt to address emotional or educational needs, are going to flounder in the absence of a suitably controlled environment.

The extreme end of the spectrum of ensuring control is the use of physical restraint. Restraint introduces powerful feelings of anger and fear into working with children and for many staff is the most disturbing aspect of working in residential child care. Perhaps only those who have been involved in restraint understand how emotionally draining the experience can be. Steckley and Kendrick (forthcoming) capture this in an interview with a member of staff: 'I can normally deal with the situation itself but immediately afterwards, immediately as it's safe to do, um, my stomach's churning, my hands are sweating, um, I can shake, I can cry' (staff member, quoted in Steckley and Kendrick, forthcoming). The intensity of this experience can be compounded when staff have to then countenance defensive organisational responses to restraints gone wrong. The emotion that restraint generates can get in the way of more measured consideration of the complexity of the issue. As in other areas of practice, organisations have sought to frame restraint within technical and legal discourse to try and remove it rather than facing up to its inherent messiness.

One of the least helpful discourses framing restraint is that of rights, which states that children should have the same rights to freedom from physical interference as adults. Such a perspective decontextualises restraint, separating it out from the care task; within a caring relationship adults are called to do many things for and with children that they would not do within a different context, from becoming involved in their intimate care to putting them to bed at 10 o'clock. From a care perspective, the question ought to be not one of whether a child's legal rights have been breached but whether a particular action was morally and ethically justifiable in the context of a mandate to care. The ability and preparedness to confront the out-of-control bits of a child is central to an adult's capacity to care for them and ultimately to attach with them. We would all like to think that we could exert that control through the strength of our relationships with children or through reasoned discussion. Some staff can indeed get to that stage in most of their encounters with children but it is an unhelpful conceit to think that we can get by without restraint on the strength of personality alone.

Encroaching legalism, often based around rights discourses alongside the scandals that came to the surface over the course of the last couple of decades, have led to a changing climate governing the use of restraint. The 1990s witnessed a proliferation of proprietary methods of care and control. What used to be done, for better or worse, trusting to staff's common sense has now become an industry, complete with turf wars fought out between the proponents of various systems. Such systems can create an unhelpful impression that there is a nice, clean, technical way to conduct restraints if only we could find the right one! Making restraint a technical endeavour also risks routinising and sanitising it, stripping it of its complex interrelational dynamics. And of course when restraints do not go according to the textbook then individual staff members involved can be held to account for not following the manual.

While there has been an expansion of proprietary systems of control, wider governmental guidance on the subject has been conspicuously lacking, perhaps reflecting the fact that the area is a legal minefield. Guidance was only eventually published in Scotland in 2005. The political interpretation of this guidance reflects a worrying, although in the current political climate typical, faith in technical and procedural solutions. The ministerial foreword proclaims, rather grandly:

> This guidance offers what might for some seem a radical approach to the care of children, based on a partnership between staff and children and young people, to ensure that those children and young people are safe and able to develop constructive ways of living. And this guidance will help people in residential child care across Scotland, with the appropriate training, to review if, and when, why and how they restrain children and to arrange matters so that the welfare of those children and young people is always given paramount importance, even and especially where they are likely to harm themselves or others. (Robson, quoted in Davidson et al, 2005, p 3)

By this account, ideas of partnerships between adults and children are radical and care and control is all a matter of guidance and appropriate training, with appropriate review mechanisms built in, of course. This political perception fails to acknowledge that the practice of restraint is not readily reducible to a set of principles. It is visceral; based around a primitive fear staff have of losing control. Indeed this fear of losing control can become more pronounced in a climate where the control of youth has become a political fixation.

A procedural approach to matters of restraint looks for universalisable principles: physical restraint should only be used as a 'last resort', with minimum force and for the shortest possible duration. None of these principles are unproblematic, however. As Burton notes, 'It is all very well using minimum force with someone who is considerably weaker than you but it soon becomes maximum force when they are big and strong' (1998, p 65).

Another problem is the notion of last resort. It is easy, from a distance, to use terminology of de-escalation, but in some situations, what might be claimed to be de-escalation can equate with a failure to take appropriate action to bring a situation under control. The dilemma this can cause is reflected in this quote from a member of care staff:

> And the window smashed, and then the window smashed again and by this time I had entered the room and I took hold of him. Now maybe if I'd done that in the first place he wouldn't, you know, and that's the bit where your professional judgement, I guess, comes in and maybe I was wrong in that case. Maybe I wasn't, it's hard to say. (quoted in Steckley and Kendrick, forthcoming)

There is no easy answer as to whether an intervention might be either precipitous or indeed too late. Steckley's research begins to uncover some of the complexity of restraint in residential child care. It is not merely the technical application of a well-honed procedure which if misapplied can be cast in terms of an abuse of power. It is significantly more nuanced than this.

The strength of relationships between the young person and staff involved is central to the meaning a child makes of their experience of restraint and of the reasons for and the way it is carried out. Properly carried-out restraint can also be formative in establishing these relationships, a point linked to the idea of restraint constituting one aspect of the overall experience of containment children need in relationships. Again one of Steckley and Kendrick's respondents makes this point: 'you could think a member of staff is a weak one and then when you get restrained you might like them because you know they are not going to take any of your crap' (quoted in Steckley and Kendrick, forthcoming). This could be interpreted as this young person being able to trust that a member of staff is capable of dealing with and responding to some of their behaviours that they might find frightening.

There are also maladaptive reasons why some children might initiate restraints. One young woman in Steckley's research spoke about the cathartic experience of being physically restrained. One girl interviewed said 'I think I just needed a cuddle … that's my way of dealing with anger', thus raising 'the concern that young people may become entrenched in a destructive dependency on physical restraint as a coping mechanism for their emotions' (quoted in Steckley and Kendrick, 2007). Questions of whether restraint might be the only way to attract physical contact from staff in the current climate where more natural expressions of touch are frowned on need to be considered.

Concluding comments on restraint: some personal reflections

When I began in residential work in the early 1980s, and despite a tendency to portray residential schools as being characterised by violence and conflict, restraint was rare. When I left it almost 20 years later it could be an almost daily occurrence. In some respects the increase in the use of restraint is a consequence of the residualisation of residential care; when only the most difficult children are placed there then restraint is more likely. Related dynamics also come into play. When a greater mix of children were placed in residential care, staff could depend on a number of reasonably well-socialised 'culture carriers' to convey the message 'this is how things are done around here'. This can no longer be relied on. A very unhelpful dynamic can emerge, whereby disturbed children begin to act out their pain and disturbance externally. A disproportionate amount of time is spent dealing with them, often involving physical restraint. Other children can then pick up the message 'this is how you get attention around here'. Cultures emerge where a sense of 'firefighting' and regular restraints become the norm, not because staff are mishandling situations or because they are heavy-handed but because they are confronted with impossibly difficult situations and often do not have the time to step back and reflect on what might be going on. Such an opportunity is essential in such circumstances. But of course it is only possible if staffing and other considerations allow.

When staff feel confident in what they are doing and in the support they receive there are likely to be fewer restraints. A culture where staff are fearful of the ramifications of becoming involved in restraint and of the constant scrutiny involved saps this confidence. When staff are fearful, paradoxically, this may make them more likely to resort to restraint. And when children pick up a sense that staff are unsure they are less likely to feel safe and more likely to engage in behaviours likely to result in restraint. The complexity of such experiential dynamics of restraint are again captured by Steckley and Kendrick (forthcoming):

> Staff not only appear to feel the weight of making a truly child-centred decision under extremely difficult circumstances, but also to be seen by other young people, colleagues and managers as competent. For some, this competency applies beyond the confines of restoring

safety in the immediate situation to maintaining the overall structure (ie rules, expectations, routines) and even the physical environment of the unit. A general lack of ability, either by individuals or staff teams, to effectively maintain fair and predictable boundaries can in itself contribute to a diminished sense of safety amongst staff and young people, potentially leading to higher incidents of physical restraint. By the same token, an inability to respond to young people in a manner that helps them to de-escalate their behaviour and diffuses the situation will also increase incidents of physical restraint.

Managing the relationship boundaries

The subjects discussed in this chapter highlight complexity, ambiguity and at times paradox, all of which are integral to working with children in residential child care. It is also indisputable that there are sensual and emotional dimensions to this work. A central paradox is captured by McWilliam who asserts that *eros* is part and parcel of the caring relationship. It is what drives us to care in the first place. She argues that:

> The caring relationship, like the pedagogical relationship, is ambiguous and duplicitous, because it is produced out of desire. Moves to separate the 'good/ethical/unsex' bits of desire from the 'bad/unethical/sex' bits of desire cannot help but misrecognize the nature of eros in the care giving relationship…. In the rush to end abuse, we have waged war on eros, with the result that one set of tyrannies has given way to another. The new order is characterised by the safety of blandness. (McWilliam, 1999, cited in Piper and Smith, 2003, p 879)

A safety of blandness is induced by managerial and bureaucratic paradigms. These attempt to eradicate ambivalence from relationships through increasing recourse to regulation, but such approaches are fundamentally misconceived. They are akin to attempts to grab porridge – it oozes and slips through your fingers. Bureaucratic and managerial approaches are further flawed in that they detract from the very essence of care by miscasting an essentially relational and emotional endeavour as a technical/rational one. Fewster makes the point that 'The more a relationship is defined in terms of roles and rules, the more the subjective experience of both parties will be excluded and the more rigid and impersonal the relationship will become' (2004, p 9).

The fact that there are sensual and emotional dimensions to providing care introduces boundary issues that need to be addressed if residential child care is to be a positive and ethical experience for children placed there. Practitioners need a reflexive relationship with their 'selves'. Ricks (2001) claims that without knowing yourself you can never know the other. Without this knowing, there can be, perhaps, engagement, but there will never be connection.

Until now organisations have sought to impose these boundaries through regulation and behavioural codes. However, prescriptive approaches are, according to Piper et al, 'negative rather than positive, products of fear rather than a characteristic of a confident profession or workforce'. Codes give no space for context or good professional sense, and so were generally 'ignored or became unworkable', creating 'guilt at their non-compliance'. The more specific codes become, the more ridiculous they are, and the more they cast teachers under the veil of suspicion (cited in Appleton, 2006).

In place of ever more prescription Piper et al propose 'a return to notions of professional trust and agency' (cited in Appleton, 2006) – a trust in teachers to do the right thing and decide on the appropriate way to behave. This locates ethical practice not within codes of conduct or procedures manuals, but in the actions of those who work directly with children. It requires that ethics are re-personalised (Bauman, 1993). McBeath and Webb (2002) argue for ethical approaches that emphasise the personal qualities or virtues of individual carers' 'judgement, experience, understanding, reflection and disposition', rather than on adherence to externally imposed rules of behaviour. Ricks and Bellefeuille, citing Blum (1994), make a similar point, arguing that ethics have to be constructed in relation to 'self'. Ethical and moral connection with another involves:

> ... getting oneself to attend to the reality of individual other persons ... while not allowing one's own needs, biases, fantasies (conscious or unconscious) and desires regarding the other persons to get in the way of appreciating his or her own particular needs and situation. (2003, p 120)

Ethics, according to such a formulation, does not deny the complex range of human emotions that can be present in caring relationships but requires that workers are aware of these and can make informed moral decisions to foreground the needs of the person being cared for. The upshot of denial of emotional content in care relationships is not safe or ethical adult–child relationships. Indeed such approaches might even make unethical behaviour more likely. Webster draws on Martin Luther's paradox of purity, observing that:

> … 'the more you cleanse yourself, the dirtier you get'. What he [Luther] was implicitly recognising was the fascination of sin – that the more any appetite or impulse is cast into the realm of the unclean by those who pursue purity, the more psychologically compelling it becomes. The pursuit of purity thus actually serves to promote an imaginative obsession with anything that has been explicitly or implicitly defined as obscene. (cited in Webster, 1994, online)

A conclusion of this way of thinking is that the more we obsess about purity, or in this case safety, the more we create conditions where the impure (or unsafe) parts of ourselves are likely to come to the surface.

Re-personalising ethics

For workers to take responsibility for acting properly in relationships requires that they know themselves and their own boundaries. Boundaries are essential to self and to interpersonal work. They are expressed and felt cognitively and emotionally (Fewster, 2004); we know both intellectually and at a feeling level when children (and indeed we as individuals) are uncomfortable with particular aspects of our relationship. Fewster makes the point, 'no boundaries, no self – no self, no relationships' (2005, p 13). Fewster also claims, however, that we confuse boundaries with barriers in the current climate – boundaries are individual and personal, barriers reactive. The better a worker knows her or himself the closer they can become to the children they work with, and the closer they can become the more productive any relationship will be. The contact boundary, as noted earlier, is not fixed in one place – what is appropriate and comfortable for one person in a particular situation might not be for another. This highlights the need for staff to become reflexive, to continually reflect on what is going on in a situation and how their presence is impacting on it. It also requires an organisational culture where staff can be supported in this reflection, through appropriate supervisory structures but perhaps more so through open and discursive cultures where they feel they can take risks and be supported in these. This demands greater recognition of the complex and demanding nature of the job.

Embracing complexity

The personal–professional relationship is fundamental to work with children; it is also nuanced and, as McWilliam (1999) asserts, duplicitous and ambiguous. There is a need to embrace this complexity. Hiding behind procedures or injunctions towards some mythical best practice has sapped the essence of residential child care. Decisions on everyday practice issues need to be considered on a case-by-case basis rather than subsumed beneath blanket injunctions. Examples of this might be around areas such as staff taking children to their own homes, a practice that used to be common but is now frowned on to the point of being considered as tantamount to an intent to abuse. Of course there are questions to be asked, considerations to be taken into account around motivation, around the possibility of raising expectations, about perceptions of possible favouritism. But properly managed, such practices can provide children with a powerful message of their acceptance and worth; they can become their moments of glory, their Camelots (Maier, 1979). In other situations injunctions in respect of privacy may be unnecessary and possibly harmful for particular children and may prevent staff from engaging in perfectly healthy activities with them. There is no one size fits all, no universalisable best practice. What is required is for individually negotiated relationships and practices which reflect the comfort levels and the needs of particular children and of the adults who work with them.

Conclusion: supporting proper professionalism

Caring requires a rethink of what it means to be professional in the human services. In current discourse, to be professional is to be objective, rational and unengaged at any emotional level (Meagher and Parton, 2004). This version of professional confuses professional with professionalisation (Noddings, 1996b). The quest for professionalisation is about the status that goes with the title 'professional'. Actually being professional is about getting the job done, competently and ethically. So any proper consideration of what is professional needs to start with what the job is. If the job is to make intimate human connections with those we work with to help them grow and develop then conceptions of the professional ought to support this. Assumptions that inhibit such relationships can be argued to be unprofessional; they get in the way of what we should be doing when we care for children.

NINE

Residential child care in a continuum of care

One of the legitimate criticisms levelled at residential child care historically is that it cut children off from the outside world. In many respects this merely reflected prevailing ideologies, particularly those deriving from a rescue philosophy, which decreed that children were best removed from their families and communities. Thus, homes were situated apart from centres of population and family contact was actively discouraged or restricted. Awareness of theories of attachment and of the central importance of families in children's lives has brought about a reappraisal of the role of the family in work with children in care. Similarly, ideas of community ascribe an importance to 'place', even if for many children communities of origin might not always be safe or happy places.

Like any child, children in care should be able to access a range of services according to need. Chapter Four has outlined some of the particular needs that children in care experience. These can rarely be addressed by one individual or agency alone but require that links be established with other professionals to ensure an effective whole child response. This chapter is concerned with how residential child care facilities need to take account of, and work effectively with, a range of family, social and other professional networks.

What is family?

The concept of family can take on very different complexions beyond that of the nuclear model that we might be drawn to think about when we hear the term. The reality is that despite increasing levels of single parenting and rising divorce rates, the majority of children growing up live with both biological parents. This figure reaches 90% in countries such as Greece and is around 70% in the UK and 60% in North America (UNICEF, 2007). However, once children become involved in child protection proceedings these figures drop dramatically, a trend that continues as child protection proceedings continue (Daniel and Taylor, 2001).

Trends in recent years suggesting increased levels of family breakdown, and the fact that residential child care is likely to work with children who are well down the road of child protection or other social work proceedings, might infer that few children in residential child care can expect to live with both biological parents. Many parents will not themselves have experienced nurturing and effective parenting and are hence unable to provide their own children with these qualities. Many children will experience various configurations of reconstituted family relationships. Some of those who enter into children's lives through reconstituted parental relationships may prove to be significant to the children and become part of what they might consider to be family. Others will be figures of disdain or indifference, never likely to be accepted as such. Ideas of family are therefore subjective and incorporate whoever children consider to be family. This may or may not involve biological relatedness. In many cases the families of children in care will experience inter-generational patterns of dysfunction.

Wade (2008) indicates a range of what he calls 'key kin' family members with whom children leaving care have a close relationship. These include siblings, grandparents and aunts and uncles as well as parents. One of the tasks that workers might want to undertake with children is some kind of life story work to ascertain who children consider their family to be and who is important within their family networks. How they make meaning of family histories, biographies and relationships is integral to their own identity formation.

The importance of family

The most important relationships for most children in care are likely to remain with their families of origin. The fact that the care some families have offered may not be considered to have been good enough and may even have been positively abusive does not necessarily diminish a child's relationship with their parents or other family members. Indeed, ideas of insecure attachment (Ainsworth et al, 1978) might make a child crave the approval and affection of family members all the more. And there are, in fact, very few families where parents do not actually love and want the best for their children, however inadequate or distorted their efforts may be in this regard. Taylor advises that 'it is very important for young people in care to know that they are cared about even if they can't be cared for' (2005, p 16).

There are also strong practical reasons why residential workers should seek to engage with families throughout the course of a child's placement. Despite care plans that may have written them off as having little to offer and identifying objectives of independent living, the reality is that most children who leave care gravitate back to their families of origin at some point. Bullock et al (1995) put this figure as high as 87%. Wade's (2008) study puts the figure for those who return home far lower, at 13%, but nevertheless notes that around 80% maintain some sort of contact with family members. Ongoing family contact also improves a child's chances of returning home. A good residential placement may in fact help family relationships. Often at the point of admission to care nerves are frayed on both sides and need some time to settle down before appropriate contact can be re-established. For this to happen effectively seems to depend on children experiencing some structure and routine, allowing their behaviour to settle sufficiently to take the heat out of family tensions (Smith et al, 2004).

Involving fathers

While mothers remain the primary and often the sole carers for most children in care, there has been a growing awareness in recent years of the importance of fathers in children's lives (Lamb, 2004). Positive involvement of a father is implicated in a range of enhanced outcomes for children including educational attainment and socially acceptable behaviour. Children and particularly adolescents have an emotional need to know who their father is in order to come to terms with their own identity formation (Daniel and Taylor, 2001). The figures above show most children in care will not live with fathers, many will have little or no contact and some may not know who their father is. It is too easy to put this down to fecklessness on the part of fathers themselves or a belief that they do not care. The reality is generally more complicated than this (Mandell, 2003).

Fathers' involvement in families and in communities is also entering into political discourse where there is a move to identify them as resources rather than merely as problems (Featherstone, 2003). While fathers are increasingly identified as important in their children's lives they are still too readily identified and treated as though they were problems in social work and especially in child protection discourses (Daniel and Taylor, 2001). As a result they can be marginalised in professional discourse. If residential workers are to begin to see themselves as working with families, they need to include fathers within this thinking.

Increasingly grandparents are also becoming important in children's direct care, often in kinship care arrangements where parents have drug problems. Accepting children's needs for roots and some sort of family identity, grandparents fulfil this role in a way that other carers might not (Gilligan, 2005). For other children relationships with grandparents can be a significant protective factor against poor outcomes (Gilligan, 2001).

Becoming parents

Many of those who leave care will themselves go on to early parenthood (Wade, 2008). Inevitably there are pressures in this that again do not lend themselves to stereotyped understandings. This is reflected in this interview excerpt with a 19-year-old young father talking about his former partner (Smith and Cavanagh, 2002, p 13). This young man:

> ... wanted to be there for her – 'don't know if I love her – don't think so, but just feel responsible'. He goes on to say, 'They [the mother's parents] want her to stick in at college – get a decent job – they see me as a waster – not good enough for her. I'm starting to feel they are right and maybe I should just drift off the scene'.

This was a father who felt a responsibility to his child, and indeed to his former partner, but was unable to negotiate a role for himself. His sense of just drifting away was a symptom of despair rather than evidence of irresponsibility. It is not difficult to imagine that many of the fathers of children in residential care may 'just have "drifted off the scene"' not knowing how to assert and maintain a place in their children's lives. Similarly many young people, both boys and girls, leaving care are statistically more likely than others of their age to become young parents with all this entails.

Working with families

The idea of family work can assume an esoteric ring for many residential workers. It can be confused with family therapy and thought to require a range of specialist skills and understandings. One of the reasons for this way of thinking is structural. Family work is something that can be thought of as, and can often be claimed to be, the responsibility of social workers in community settings and by implication requiring the skills of a qualified social worker. Yet residential workers are often in a better position than social workers to engage effectively with families. They are not the ones who are seen to have removed a child from their family and are less likely to bear the brunt of any resultant animosity.

They are also charged with the everyday care of children and can be aware of the difficulties and frustrations inherent in this, which may encourage a common bond with parents.

Garfat (2003b) extends ideas of lifespace which are characteristic of direct work with children to incorporate how residential workers might approach work with families. In his model, child and youth care workers become involved not in a formal authority or counselling role, but alongside families as they live their lives. They become attuned to the patterns of interaction that operate in any family situation and are able to respond to these using daily life events as they occur to promote change. In many respects workers within such an approach encourage good parenting through modelling qualities of nurturing, accepting, limit setting, appropriate expressions of emotion and practical help. As in any lifespace-based approach workers need to operate from an appropriate awareness of self and of their role and boundaries in any situation.

Family group conferences

Family group conferences provide a useful model through which family and wider networks might be harnessed to support children in care. The model originates in Maori and Inuit communities where concerns about the over-representation of indigenous populations in welfare services led to exploration of more traditional community-based means of problem solving. Family group conferences bring together members of a child's extended family along with friends, neighbours and other parties with an interest in a child's welfare. In the UK such conferences are facilitated by an independent coordinator, often employed by a children's charity rather than directly by a local authority. The child is encouraged to be an active participant in the process, the intention of which is to develop a care plan that maximises the kind of supports that might be put in place for her or him, often drawing on the informal supports of participants in the conference. Although family group conferences are primarily used to make decisions about a child's care arrangements before they might be admitted to residential care, the principle is one that perhaps should be considered for every child admitted to a residential facility. A family group type forum arranged in the early stages of a placement would provide an opportunity to build in family involvement in the care of children from the outset, placing the residential unit at the heart of that work. Family group conferences might uncover resources previously not thought about to support a child. They also give staff a feel for the interactions and rhythms within any family situation.

Undertaken according to the principles on which the model is based, family group conferences require a fundamental shift in power relations between professionals and families, where families are vested with the responsibility for children's care, perhaps sharing this with the residential home or a selection of other members of a child's network. However, these principles are very often mediated to fit in with the bureaucratic and risk-averse cultures of child protection agencies. In such circumstances they risk becoming merely another social work intervention rather than a mindset that informs how we might best work with families as partners in their children's care.

Social networks

While children's primary attachments, generally to immediate family members, are important, Gilligan (2001) suggests that an overemphasis on these can obscure the significance of other relationships in children's lives, especially perhaps as they enter adolescence and widen their spheres of social influence. Informal social networks and relationships such as those that emerge through involvement in various sports or recreational activities can be instrumental in determining which path a child may take through adolescence and into adult life. Involvement with a caring, non-parental adult is identified as a component of resilience. This involvement is enhanced if based around a particular skill or activity (Gilligan, 2001, 2005). The developmental assets framework, developed by the Search Institute (1997, 2007), similarly identifies non-parental adult relationships and the constructive use of time around sports and other youth activities as essential elements in children's upbringing. High achievers who had grown up in care identify a special relationship with at least one adult who spent time with them and encouraged them (Jackson and Martin, 1998; see also Gilligan, 2005).While some schemes seek to formalise such mentoring arrangements, those that emerge through everyday social contacts seem to be the most fruitful (Gilligan, 2001). It is concerning in light of this kind of evidence that many agencies seem to actively discourage the establishment of such relationships, a situation that is compounded by legislation extending the requirements for vetting adults who come into contact with children.

Integrated services

The 1989 Children Act and the 1995 Children (Scotland) Act broadened responsibility for looked-after children beyond social work departments, locating it with local authorities as corporate parents. In this the legislation sought to highlight the fact that children's care required a range of services to be brought to bear, including education, recreation and health. These services were vested with a corporate responsibility to ensure that the needs of children in care were adequately met.

As discussed in Chapter One, the election of a New Labour government in 1997 introduced a 'modernising' agenda to social work services. Central to this was a drive towards partnership working so that users or 'consumers' of services might experience seamless service delivery across the range of their needs. A focus on collaborative and joined-up inter-agency, partnership or integrated working has been a feature of social work discourse since then and one that has gathered pace in policy initiatives such as ECM (2003) and GIRFEC (2005).

While it is difficult to argue with the general principle that different services should come together to respond to the wide range of children's needs there is a distinct lack of clarity about the current political agenda. Part of this comes down to questions of terminology. Easen et al point to the 'conceptual elusiveness of terms such as co-ordination and collaboration' (2000, p 56, cited in Milligan and Stevens, 2006, p 28). Some activities apply to individual professionals within distinct disciplines working more effectively together; others apply to entire disciplines establishing protocols for working together. In other cases professional boundaries appear to be blurred as erstwhile separate professional groupings are brought together within new organisational structures such as those apparent in the merging by many local authorities of social work and education departments into combined children's services departments. Yet despite such significant differences in what is or can be meant by these various initiatives, terminology is often used interchangeably.

Aside from the conceptual elusiveness of this agenda there are also contradictions within it. Orme (2001) identifies a tendency for social work services under New Labour to be fragmented rather than integrated. This is apparent for instance in youth justice services which have been hived off from mainstream social work. A similar point can be made in respect of aftercare services, mental health services and specialist counselling resources, each of which have proliferated in the form of discrete, often short-term funded projects. Children in residential care can be faced with a range of different workers each charged to focus on a particular area of their functioning. So at one and the same time we witness the fragmentation of services alongside political injunctions that these services work more effectively together. This in itself fails to understand a primary tendency of any bureaucracy to define and defend its own territory.

One of the difficulties of the joined-up working agenda is that it proceeds from an assumption that organisational changes alone will bring about shifts in practice. In respect of the trend to integrate children's services, a colleague and myself have argued elsewhere that:

> ... given the historical bifurcation of education and care, so long as these changes take place only at policy and organisational levels, without any underpinning or commonly understood conceptual base, bringing social work and education together will fail to bring about the kind of integrated service to children and families that is intended. Teachers will continue to process children through crowded academic curricula and examinations and pass on the casualties of that system to social workers who, if they respond at all, will do so within the child protection meta-narrative which has come to dominate practice over the past decade or so. The complex needs of the whole child will be lost in the professionalisation of two distinct disciplines – and the political zeitgeist exhorting them to work together will come to nothing. (Smith and Whyte, 2008, p 13)

The evidence for integrated services

The move towards more effective integrated working is driven by a desire to improve outcomes for children and families. The weight of political injunction behind the policy is such that the linkage between integrated working and better outcomes can be represented as axiomatic. It is not. In fact the evidence in this regard is equivocal (Brown and White, 2006). Much of it is based on the negative evidence gleaned from child protection reports that highlight instances where a failure of professionals to work together has resulted in tragedy. There is little solid evidence to suggest that working together necessarily leads to better outcomes. Indeed in some cases increased collaboration can be seen to have a negative effect on practice outcomes. In their review of the evidence for and against collaborative practice, Brown and White (2006) identify studies that suggest that agency culture is of greater import than staff working together with other professionals. Outcomes for children and families are better in agencies where staff report greater job satisfaction, role clarity and fair organisational practices.

The importance of cultural determinants in any discussion of outcomes is significant in respect of residential child care, where Berridge and Brodie (1998) note that residential workers do not have a positive view of themselves in relation to other professionals and where Heron and Chakrabarti (2002) describe workers as experiencing considerable ambiguity in terms of what is expected of them. This is compounded by the setting of qualifications requirements at a vocational level that is not conducive to authentic or equal interdisciplinary dialogue between residential workers and other professionals such as teachers, doctors or nurses. In this context injunctions calling on workers in different disciplines to collaborate more effectively are unlikely to move beyond the level of political and professional rhetoric to result in better outcomes for children in care.

Having identified flaws in joint working discourses is not to argue against it. There are, of course, examples of it being effective, particularly perhaps in relation to health. Health inequalities experienced by children in care are well documented and include a range of long-term illness, mental ill health and sexual health issues (Grant et al, 2002). These are compounded by the chaotic lifestyles many children have experienced. For children in residential child care placement moves lead to discontinuity in medical records and medical care. This in turn can result in health problems not being identified or addressed in any sustained way, manifest in, for instance, missed inoculations.

Practice traditionally was for children admitted to residential child care to be registered with local GPs, allowing them routine consultations as required. However, there was rarely any coordinated or comprehensive attempt to assess or address their health needs. In the wake of the kind of thinking that emerged from the Quality Protects agenda and a more general political concern with social inclusion, a number of initiatives sprung up to address this situation. A healthcare project in residential care for instance, located in Edinburgh and surrounding authorities, was established to address these issues. This involved nurses working alongside residential staff in each children's unit, supported by a community paediatrician, a mental health worker and a GP researcher. The results of this project have been twofold: firstly it allowed for a concerted and holistic attempt to address the health needs of children in the care system for the duration of the project's existence. It also shifted the culture within residential units in a way that allowed workers to become more aware of and more confident in following through children's health needs. The cultural shift such initiatives can bring about can also lead to a greater emphasis on health promotion in units rather than on mere treatment (Grant et al, 2002).

Similar trends in multi-agency responses are apparent in relation to children's mental health needs through the establishment of child and adolescent mental health services (CAMHS) teams, including psychiatrists, psychologists and mental health nurses. Some of these teams attempt to cater specifically for the needs of children in care (Van Beinum et al, 2002), although access to these teams by children in care can be patchy.

There are also examples from education of professionals working together to support children in care, although progress in this respect is again variable (Brodie, 2005). Additionally, schools face competing pressures to improve qualification levels and can regard the efforts required to maintain children in care who may require considerable educational and behavioural support as impeding this objective. Bringing together education and social work into integrated children's services departments should theoretically help this, although, as previously noted, this is less likely unless there is a conceptual shift which broadens current conceptions of education beyond mere classroom learning.

Caring for the whole child in residential care

While current discourses invoke different professionals to work together to address a range of children's needs Fulcher and Ainsworth highlight the need for a holistic approach to children's needs in residential settings. They identify four societal resource systems within which group care facilities are located: healthcare, education, social welfare and criminal justice. The purpose of each of these systems is respectively to treat, teach, nurture and control. 'All of these systems', they argue, 'embody value preferences, organisational features and occupational characteristics that reflect these purposes' (1985, p 6). They observe that:

> ... any group care centre has in various way to incorporate aspects of treatment, teaching, nurturing and control according to the specific needs of children referred there. Yet experience has shown that the ethos of most group care centres is heavily dominated by the single yet simplistic

purpose that underpins the resource system sponsoring a centre. This often results in the overall developmental needs of children being overwhelmed by a single purpose which although important, is an incomplete response at best.... It is worth noting however that facilities which seek to transcend or overlap boundaries, and in that respect respond to a broader conception of children's development needs are invariably the most controversial programmes. Public debate frequently surrounds the operation of these programmes, with strong pressure being exerted from many sources for these group care services to concentrate on a single purpose rather than operating from a multi purpose orientation. (Fulcher and Ainsworth, 1985, p 6)

These observations highlight a point often overlooked in the integrated services discourse, suggesting that conceptions of need in respect of children are not neutral but are likely to be subject to political, professional and ideological preferences. In the current climate services often reflect dominant child protection, rights and youth justice meta-narratives and thus skew services in these directions. Locating residential care services around the broad range of children's needs and mandating and empowering staff to take these forward in a quasi–parental role may be of more benefit than presiding over a proliferation of workers each dealing with only part of a child. Residential workers are well placed to assume this essentially parental role in respect of children in their care. It should involve them having knowledge of local services and personal qualities of commitment and tenacity in advocating for and accessing and negotiating these.

Residential workers as transition workers

Given the transient nature of the residential experience for most children and in particular the experience many of them have of multiple previous placements, Maier (1979) highlights the need for child care workers to be 'transition workers', facilitating children's transitions from one life situation to another. Smart (2006) highlights the importance of workers understanding themes of transition in the context of residential child care. Facilitating transition is not the same as undertaking the practical tasks needed when children move from one care setting to another. Change is the alteration of physical state. Transition relates more to how a person deals with such changes and as such is a psychological process. It requires more than life skills training in how to boil an egg or wire a plug to prepare a child to move on healthily and effectively.

Many transitions in our lives are predictable, such as moving from primary to secondary school, from home to university or getting married. As such we generally adapt to these without too much difficulty. However, for children in care transitional experiences are often accelerated and compressed in comparison to those of peers who are not in care (Caulfield-Dow, 2005). They may, for instance, experience multiple changes of placement, school and community and have to deal with the emotional effects of this. Understandably many will appear numbed by and inured to the whole experience of transition. Bad experiences of transition are likely to provide a template of what children expect in future transition. The effects of transition can be likened to those experienced in situations of grief and loss and may include emotions such as denial, anger, bargaining, anxiety and sadness before any new state of being can be accepted (Kubler-Ross, 1973; Marris, 1974).

It falls to residential workers both to minimise the number of transitions children experience and also to help them make some meaning of these. Amidst the emotional turmoil of transition, children need to feel safe. This can be provided through the appropriate rhythms and routines of residential child care. Again, the idea of rhythm explored in Chapter Six is important in providing a framework that enables often disoriented residents to experience a measure of stability, security and predictability in their lives.

Any successful transition needs to celebrate or at least acknowledge the past (Bridges, 1991). In that respect workers should make efforts to ask about where children came from, who they know, what football team they support. This need to make connections with the past resonates with Fulcher's idea of cultural safety, outlined in Chapter Six, the sense children need social and cultural frames of reference to be acknowledged. Winnicott's (1971) concept of the transitional object whereby children take an object such as a teddy bear or a comfort blanket with them through various placement moves can help maintain the connection between their inner world and their changing outer world. Possibly of greater importance is the maintenance of particular relationships. Thus family members or previous foster carers should be encouraged to maintain contact when children are in residential care and members of staff who are significant to a child should maintain that relationship once the child has left care. Again, organisational paranoia over questions of child safety can result in policies that prohibit such ongoing contact. Again, such policies cut across an obvious developmental need and should be challenged.

Throughcare and aftercare

Picking up on concerns about the poor outcomes for children leaving care, manifest in high levels of homelessness, unemployment and health difficulties, the 1989 Children Act and the 1995 Children (Scotland) Act lay out the powers and duties of local authorities to provide throughcare and aftercare services. These obligations are taken forward in the English 2000 Children (Leaving Care) Act and similar legislation in the other countries of the UK. The actual provision of support for children leaving care remains patchy (Dixon and Stein, 2002b).

Within professional discourses which regard residential child care as providing only short-term provision, either preparing children for family placement or for more independent living, it has become an expectation that residential units begin at an early stage to plan for children moving on. Throughcare is the term given to the process whereby children are supported to develop a range of skills they are likely to need in moving on from care, such as life skills involving cooking, housekeeping and budgeting, information on resources, job opportunities and welfare benefits. Children should be involved with staff in this preparatory process.

Preparing children to move on from care is not merely a practical task. Children can only become properly independent if they have experienced appropriate dependency. As Maier (1979) says, dependency tastes good. Yet within a social work discourse we are often encouraged to minimise children's feelings of dependency and to prepare them for independence. The experience of children in residential care needs to emphasise their need for meaningful and appropriately dependent relationships as a platform from which they might gradually assume greater independence.

Workers in residential child care will be aware of situations where children have moved on from care back into situations from which they may have come, and any perceived benefits of residential care have quickly dissipated. In criminal justice/social work this is known as a washout effect. Aftercare policies are intended to support children in the period once they leave care. In most cases this involves residential units working with and passing on cases to local authorities or other agencies with a particular aftercare function. Some residential homes have developed their own aftercare services that make sense in light of the strong arguments that residential workers with established relationships should be central to the provision of aftercare. What such units are discovering is that aftercare is not a time-limited task. Many former residents avail themselves of support long into adulthood.

Conclusion

Residential child care needs to take into account and needs to instil in children a sense of both past and future, from whence they have come and to where they are going. Without this sense children can live only in the present with all that entails in terms of hope for the future. Family is generally significant in any consideration of past and future and residential workers need to become skilled in working with families. They also need to work with other services and agencies with whom children come into contact. In fact they need to be at the hub of inter-professional networks, arguing for and accessing services for children in the way that a concerned and articulate parent would.

TEN

Other traditions of practice

The UK is unusual in locating residential child care professionally within social work. In most European countries social pedagogy (the terminology and exact nature of the task changing according to national contexts but the overall principles being similar) is the discipline underpinning work with children and youth. This chapter considers what social pedagogy might offer to ways of thinking about residential child care in the UK. It also looks at other traditions of practice, particularly the North American model of child and youth care.

What is social pedagogy?

The word 'pedagogy' derives from the Greek *pais* meaning child and *agein* to lead or to bring up. A pedagogue therefore is someone who is involved in bringing up children. Social pedagogy is less a prescriptive practice method of how to do so than a way of thinking about children and childhood and how best to promote their upbringing. The use of the term 'social pedagogy' can be problematic in the anglophone world; when the word 'pedagogy' is used it tends to be limited to theories of learning and teaching. As a result the term 'social education' has been drawn on to capture the ideas contained within social pedagogy (Lane, 2001). However, this too can find its meaning limited by its appearance in school curricula, where it tends to be about social skills and health education. Increasingly, those interested in applying pedagogical ideas in the UK are becoming more assertive in their use of the term. In the context of improving outcomes for children in residential child care, the White Paper *Care Matters: Time for change* (DfES, 2007) proposed pilot projects to consider the applicability of social pedagogical approaches. Children in Scotland (2008), a major Scottish children's charity, is calling for the introduction of a 'Scottish pedagogue' to work across children's services.

History of social pedagogy

A progressive and romantic educational ideal can be traced back to Rousseau's novel *Emile*, which proposed that children should enjoy a naturalistic and experiential education and upbringing. Rousseau's ideas were developed by others such as the Swiss educator Pestalozzi in the early 19th century. Pestalozzi's aim was to educate the whole child, requiring the active involvement of the learner in the learning process and including three elements – hands, heart and head – principles that remain central to current notions of social pedagogy (Petrie, 2004). There was also a social dimension to the work of Pestalozzi and his followers. They saw themselves as 'educators of the poor', working in special schools but also in poor rural areas. Education in such a model became fundamentally linked with social development and the creation of community. It was a social as well as an individual endeavour, where social problems were seen as political and cultural rather than scientific or psychological.

The aim of social pedagogy is to promote social welfare through broadly socio-educational strategies. It developed as a profession following the Second World War and is now the model of practice applied to work with children and youth across most of Europe. In France the broad term is *educateur*, or *educateur specialisée*, the concept of *education* encompassing an idea of education that extends beyond the academic. In Germany the term for a pedagogue, *Erzieher*, translates as 'upbringer', capturing the holistic nature of the task as involving all aspects of a child's growth and development. Social pedagogy relates to the whole person: 'body, mind, feelings, spirit, creativity and, crucially, the relationship of the individual to others – their social connectedness' (Petrie, 2001, p 18). There is an obvious conceptual contrast between the focus on social connection central to social pedagogy and the individualistic and curricularly driven approaches to education favoured in an Anglo-American context.

Academics at the Thomas Coram Research Unit at the Institute of Education, University of London, have undertaken large-scale comparative studies of care work across Europe. This has opened up ideas around social pedagogy to an English-speaking audience and has been instructive in identifying points of comparison and departure between approaches across Europe and the UK. These studies and publications deriving from them provide much of the information on which subsequent discussion is based.

Principles of social pedagogic approaches

Petrie et al identify the following principles that define a pedagogic approach to practice:

- a focus on the child as a whole person, and support for the child's overall development;
- the practitioner seeing herself/himself as a person, in relationship with the child or young person;
- while they are together, children and staff are seen as inhabiting the same life space, not as existing in separate, hierarchical domains;
- as professionals, pedagogues are encouraged to constantly reflect on their practice and to apply both theoretical understandings and self-knowledge to their work and the sometimes challenging demands with which they are confronted;
- pedagogues should also be practical and creative; their training prepares them to share in many aspects of children's daily lives, such as preparing meals and snacks, or making music and building kites;
- when working in group settings, children's associative life is seen as an important resource; workers should foster and make use of the group;
- pedagogy builds on an understanding of children's rights that is not limited to procedural matters or legislated requirements;
- there is an emphasis on team work and valuing the contribution of others in the task of 'bringing up' children: family members, other professionals and members of the local community. (2008, p 4)

These principles speak of what residential workers perhaps used to do and might still do were they not so overburdened by bureaucracy and constrained by a protectionist discourse. Social pedagogy is essentially a practical task, not just describing and explaining social phenomena but acting on them to achieve change.

Social pedagogy and social work

The divergence between social work and social pedagogical approaches perhaps hinges around different understandings of the role of education in society. In the UK (Scotland, arguably, has traditions that align it more closely to European models; see Smith and Whyte, 2008), education focuses primarily on what happens in the classroom. It may be implicated in individual improvement, manifest in future economic productivity. Imagining a role for it in wider social change is a prospect viewed with some suspicion, however; education is about maintaining rather than challenging existing social relations. In Continental Europe education is conceptualised far more broadly and equates with holistic ideas of 'upbringing' or formation; 'education in its widest sense'. The more limited conception of education within the Anglo-Saxon tradition can lead to a bifurcation of education and care, with education taking place in schools and care in the home, whereas in most of Europe the boundaries between the two are more blurred. Care is a social and broadly educational as well as a familial task.

As discussed in Chapter Two, the development of social work in the UK has drawn heavily on Anglo-American rather than European models. The Poor Law roots of these embed models of practice based on individual deficit, detached from social and wider community context. The philosophical underpinnings of social pedagogy reflect a different history. Social pedagogy is rooted in a belief in social progress; it is essentially optimistic, being concerned with 'the good life' and with helping the poor in society to claim their share of this. Workers operate from an agenda for social change. This contrasts with a Poor Law hangover in the Anglo-American tradition that the poor should not be seen to be getting too much. This deeply embedded ideological constraint is manifest in a primary practice focus on behavioural control and on interventions calculated to address individual pathology rather than a more normative concern for a child's upbringing. The idea of 'upbringing' is the central one in social pedagogy; it provides the pedagogue with a sense of purpose and locates their task within a universal framework of child development.

Conceptually, social pedagogy seems to make sense if we really want to address the needs of the 'whole child'. It incorporates elements of teaching, treatment, nurturing and control within the one profession. It is a normative approach, which eschews the individualistic, stigmatising and pathologising effects of social work interventions drawn from increasingly correctional and blaming paradigms.

Differences in national context

The different histories and assumptions underlying social pedagogy and residential child care within a social work tradition are evident in the way services are thought about and structured. In the UK, despite the exhortations of various reports that residential child care should be regarded as a positive choice, it is invariably a last resort. Foster care is the intervention of choice for children unable to be cared for by their families. In England, only 13% of children looked after by local authorities are accommodated in residential care. In Germany, this percentage is 60% and rising. In Sweden, too, numbers in residential care are rising (Statham and Mooney, 2006).

The difference in proportions of children in different placements reflects different ideologies regarding the comparative value of these resources. In the UK there can be an uncritical acceptance of foster care as the option of choice when children have to be placed away from home. In other parts of Europe this perception is reversed. Professionally qualified staff groups in children's homes are considered to be better equipped to support children's upbringing than unqualified foster carers. The situation is a circular one: professionally qualified and socially valued staff groups will lead to a preference for the kind of service they can provide; poorly educated and ill-valued staff groups will lead professionals placing children to look towards foster care. So long as foster care remains the placement of choice there is likely to be a disincentive, conscious or otherwise, to boost the education and status of those working in residential child care, and a tendency to opt for the minimalist and reductionist approaches of vocational training.

The focus on an educational ideal, of education in its broadest sense, rather than on the individual psychopathology which social work struggles to break free from has a practical knock-on effect. An educational approach would tend towards larger homes, where the group experience and process is central to the overall experience of growth and learning. The small homes preferred in a social work model perhaps reinforce individualised and problem-based ways of working.

There are also implications for the type of alliances formed between workers and children. These become essentially educational rather than directly therapeutic. Social problems, considered from an educational perspective, stress human maturation and capacity for growth rather than individual pathology. Broadly educative rather than counselling methods are, therefore, used to assist individuals and where necessary equip them with the skills to overcome social problems. Social pedagogical models emphasise the importance of practical help and of 'being with' clients as they live their lives in the lifespace rather than through more 'expert' social casework models. They acknowledge the emotional aspects of the professional–personal relationship and are less concerned with the niceties of professional distance that social workers here increasingly fall back on to mediate their relationships with clients (see Chapter Eight).

The possibilities of a social pedagogical approach in a UK context

The emerging interest in ideas of social pedagogy stems in part from concern over the poor outcomes of residential child care placements. Policy trends are increasingly conducive to the adoption of social pedagogical approaches. ECM, the Green Paper on the future direction of children's services, and GIRFEC, its Scottish counterpart, begin to introduce pedagogical concepts to children's services in the UK. Ideas of 'the whole child' and of the need for multi-systemic and holistic approaches to meet these individual and social needs, which might be thought of as broadly educational and developmental, are evident in these documents. *Care Matters* (DfES, 2006) provides additional impetus in this direction, describing pedagogy as a theoretical and practical framework for understanding children's upbringing, focused on building relationships through practical engagement.

A concern, however, is that social pedagogy becomes seen as attractive to politicians as a framework to take forward other agendas such as those around inter-agency working rather than being grounded in any wider understanding of the concept. Many local authorities are already merging children's and families' social work and education services. To bring children together under the umbrella of a universal service such as education with additional support for those children who need it has obvious advantages. Yet given the historical bifurcation of education and social care in the UK, merely bringing together different local authority departments at policy and organisational levels without any underpinning conceptual base on which to ground this will fail to bring about the kind of integrated services intended; teachers will continue to cram students through the academic curriculum while social workers will remain stuck within the child protection meta-narrative which has come to dominate practice (Smith and Whyte, 2008).

Adopting a social pedagogic approach requires that children's services relinquish preoccupations with risk and protection to foreground ideas of growth through relationships. It also requires the return of professional trust and judgement, and the realisation that there are no 'one size fits all', 'best practice' interventions when it comes to working with children. According to the National Centre for Excellence in Residential Child Care (NCERCC):

> ... the pedagogical approach rests on an image of the child as a complex social being with rich and extraordinary potential, rather than as an adult-in-waiting who needs to be

given the right ingredients for optimal development ... for
the pedagogue, there is no universal solution, each situation
requires a response based on a combination of information,
emotions, self-knowledge and theory. (2007, p 5)

Thomas (2005) suggests that the social pedagogic model presents a
timely challenge to current care philosophy and practice. There are,
however, powerful interest groups and professional ideologies that
maintain an essentially protectionist stance in work with children.
Participants in NCERCC pilot projects, which followed from *Care
Matters*, identified practices around risk assessments, regulations in
relation to safeguarding procedures, and fear of false allegations as
impeding a more wholehearted adoption of social pedagogic ideas.
Nevertheless, they did see social pedagogy as a model through which
they might reclaim some of the essentially relational aspects of
residential child care. One respondent felt that:

... over the years, 'the head' for example, staff policies,
risk assessments, children coming in as a last resort, has
dominated how I perceive and work with the young people.
I have rediscovered 'the heart' and can see working with
these young people with a renewed perspective. (Bengtsson
et al, 2008, pp 3–4)

The workforce

Comparisons between European social pedagogues and residential
care staff in the UK are stark. Across Northern Europe pedagogues
undertake a professional diploma pitched at degree level; others go on
to complete Master's qualifications. In Denmark, 94% of pedagogues
are educated to degree level. In England only 57% of workers in
residential child care have qualifications at upper secondary school level
(including NVQ) or higher (Boddy et al, 2006). In Denmark social
pedagogy is the most popular professional training course, above even
medicine and teaching.

Like social work the professional training of pedagogues involves
practice placements. Once in practice staff retention is not a problem.
Pedagogues also have scope to move job within the overall field, perhaps
shifting from direct care to administration or training and development,
an occupational flexibility available to few residential workers in the
UK. In Denmark, pedagogues increasingly work in human services
across the lifecourse. The generally positive air around recruitment and

retention of staff carries through to reports of high morale in practice; pedagogues seem to feel that they are doing a worthwhile job.

It is not just the level of qualification that differentiates social pedagogy from current qualifications frameworks in the UK but also the nature of the educational experience. Locating training within a vocational framework in the UK means that it assumes an overriding instrumental and procedural focus. Social pedagogical training has three strands to it: a formal academic strand that centres around social science and education, a practice skills strand that covers areas such as teamwork and communication and a third strand focusing on sporting, aesthetic or cultural elements intended to equip students with the kind of practical and activity-based skills they might bring to their engagement with children. The concern throughout is to develop reflective practitioners able to work creatively and to use professional judgement rather than procedural guidance in reaching decisions about practice.

Advantages

The researchers responsible for the social pedagogy research studies at the Thomas Coram Research Unit are clear about the benefits of a social pedagogical approach. While recognising the challenges of introducing such a model in a different professional and cultural context they claim that residential child care would benefit from the professionalisation of the workforce through a social pedagogic education arguing that: 'The benefits indicated by our research lead us to conclude that the value of a professional educated workforce warrants the challenge of establishing a social pedagogic approach to care work for the future' (Boddy et al, 2006, p 109).

The benefits for staff in feeling part of a valued professional grouping have already been mentioned. There are also significant benefits in terms of outcomes for children. While direct comparisons are problematic in light of different traditions of welfare, children cared for under social pedagogic models enjoy significantly better outcomes across a range of measures, including educational attainment, employment, non-involvement in crime, health and related factors such as teenage pregnancy (Petrie et al, 2006).

Professionalisation need not cost more than current arrangements. Indeed there are financial benefits that might accrue from adopting social pedagogical models of practice. A German civil servant interviewed for the Thomas Coram Research Unit research commented that 'everyone should have it [the social pedagogy diploma] in order to have appropriate skills. This will save us money in the end because they will work well with the children and maybe they can return home earlier' (Boddy et al, 2006, p 96). This is an interesting point. The costs of residential child care in the UK are high – having a poorly qualified workforce caring for some of society's most difficult children takes its toll. Creating a residual service catering only for the most difficult children leads to continual demands for better staffing ratios and is reflected in high sickness and turnover rates, all of which add to the cost of the service.

Child and youth care

Child and youth care, with its roots in residential child care, is the discipline involved in direct care practice with children in North America and increasingly in developing countries such as South Africa. As identified in Chapter Two the care and treatment aspects of residential child care were conceived of, historically, as being independent of one another. Care was everyday, mundane and unskilled and those providing it were not considered to be doing a professional job. The 'professional' task was undertaken by social workers, psychologists or therapists who counselled children around particular difficulties. These external professionals also managed and shaped the discourse of residential child care, privileging medical models of care and treatment. This in many respects has continued to the present day, where in North America funding for residential placement often only follows from diagnosis of a particular medical or psychological condition. From the 1950s, however, a practice-based literature began to emerge which located the therapeutic task with those involved in caring for children. Residential settings, staffed by those with proper skills and knowledge of child development, began to be identified as possible sites to teach, treat and nurture children (Krueger, 1991). The idea of lifespace, the conscious utilisation of daily life events, as they occurred, for therapeutic purposes (see Chapter Five), became the foundational principle of child and youth care.

Ferguson and Anglin (1985) developed some defining features of a lifespace orientation to practice with children, involving four characteristics: a focus on the growth and development of children and youth; a concern for the totality of a child's functioning (a 'whole child' approach); a social competency (as opposed to an individual pathology) perspective; and the locus of such work being undertaken with children and youth within their environment (a lifespace approach). They later added a fifth characteristic: involving the development of therapeutic relationships. There are obvious similarities between these characteristics of a child and youth care approach and the principles of social pedagogy.

The professionalisation of child and youth care

Child and youth care has moved further along the road to professional status in Canada than it has in the US, where developments have been more patchy. In fact debate continues as to whether child and youth care is in fact a profession, whether it should even aspire to be and, if so, what kind of profession it might be. Profession, emergent profession, semi-profession, craft, whatever stage of development child and youth care might be at, its existence as a discipline has been largely practitioner-driven. In Canada the Council of Canadian Child and Youth Care Associations has been instrumental in defining a professional identity and an underpinning value base and in pushing for the certification and regulation of child and youth care workers and agencies. There is, however, no national accrediting body and each province has taken different routes towards professionalisation. Universities and colleges in each province provide either four-year honours or two- or three-year diploma programmes with a specific focus on child and youth care. The University of Victoria in British Columbia offers a thriving Master's programme and has instituted a PhD programme for child and youth care.

In the US the Association for Child and Youth Care Practice (ACYCP) and the International Leadership Coalition for Professional Child and Youth Care Work, working in partnership through the North American Certification Project (NACP), developed a Code of Ethics for child and youth care professionals in the mid-1990s (www.pitt.edu/~mattgly/CYCethics.html). This continues to serve as a practice benchmark. Through the NACP the ACYCP has detailed core competencies needed by individuals working in the direct care of children.

South Africa adopted an innovative approach to residential child care, setting qualification levels for work in the sector at a degree level, specifically in child and youth care (du Toit, 2000). However, as is the case in the UK and the US, social work has continued as the dominant profession in relation to children and in recent years child and youth care qualifications have struggled to attract the government funding needed to maintain a separate status.

While child and youth care has much to offer, the concept of 'lifespace' being one that practitioners in the UK can readily identify with as giving a name to the job they do, the approach, in a North

American context, might be thought to have some limitations in respect of its relative lack of a social dimension. Although there is an explicit thrust to de-medicalise children's difficulties, these continue to be seen primarily in the context of the individual child and family. South African approaches, reflecting the nature of social and political structures there, adopt a greater social justice orientation.

Social care

In the Republic of Ireland the term 'social care' is used to describe direct care workers across a range of client groups including residential child care. Social care is now a degree-level qualification undertaken in institutes of technology. The Irish Association of Social Care Educators draws explicit links between social care work there and social pedagogic and child and youth care traditions, noting: 'In the broader European context, social care work is usually referred to as social pedagogy and social care practitioners as social pedagogues. In the United States and Canada the term "child and youth care" is commonly used' (IASCE website, http://staffweb.itsligo.ie/gateway/asp/whatis.asp, 2005).

Camphill communities

A distinctive (in many respects a social pedagogic) approach to practice in the UK is evident in the work of the Camphill communities. The first community was established in Aberdeenshire in the North East of Scotland in the 1940s by Dr Karl Konig, an Austrian paediatrician, and a group of pioneers who together built the community over the following years. There are now over 100 Camphill communities in 20 countries across the world.

Camphill offers what it calls 'curative education' to pupils with complex special needs. Curative education simply means 'healing education'. It is based around the anthroposophical philosophy of Rudolph Steiner. Anthroposophy was developed by Steiner as an antidote to dominant natural science approaches to human nature. It emphasises the importance of the domains of body, soul and spirit, brought together within Steiner's conception of the human spirit:

> [A]... range of disciplines, such as education, care, therapy, medicine, various arts and crafts, come together and are united by the shared task of creating a holistic approach to the support of those who suffer an imbalance in the

integration of body, soul and spirit. (Hart and Monteaux, 2006, p 201)

Camphill challenges assumptions about the technical/rational nature of care and as a result can be viewed with some curiosity and suspicion by the social work establishment. There is no hierarchical management structure, and decision making is usually consensual. Workers are not paid a salary. House coordinators are given a budget for the running of their houses, including living expenses of co-workers and those of their own families. Co-workers are generally volunteers who come to live and help out in the community for a year or so although many stay for much longer. They share their life with the residents, the relationships between them characterised by mutuality and equality. Another aspect of the Camphill philosophy is that it does not expect every co-worker to perform to the same level. Each brings their own particular gifts and talents to the community. Those whose gifts are greater can expect to give more back.

BA in Curative Education (BACE)

The Camphill communities have developed their own educational programme, the BA in Curative Education (BACE), a workplace-based qualification, requiring assessment of both practice-based and academic abilities. It is a four-year degree-level programme validated by the University of Aberdeen and taught jointly by university staff and members of the Camphill community, based around the principles of curative education. In many respects it is akin to and draws explicitly on social pedagogical ideas (Jackson, R., 2006). The course attracts students from different Camphill communities, united in a common philosophical base and sharing their learning in what course staff describe as communities of practice (Lave and Wenger, 1991). BACE is recognised by the Scottish Social Services Council as suitable for registration for employment in residential child care.

Camphill offers a challenging antidote to the reductionism that characterises so much of residential child care, affirming the dignity of the 'whole person' and their potential for growth alongside others in community. It provides a lived example of how a coherent philosophy of care can be brought centre stage and owned and articulated by well-educated and creative groups of workers. Camphill evinces and lives out a moral purpose, which may not provide a template for services across the board but which undoubtedly offers much that residential care might learn from. It provides a space for those who see care more as a way of life, a vocation, rather than a job. A sense of vocation is still a motivating force in many who would work in care. It is central to such as the L'Arche communities for the learning disabled, based around the work of Jean Vanier and in pockets across Europe where adults choose to live in communities with children (Gilligan, 1996). It is perhaps to such examples of people coming together to offer care beyond the narrow municipalism of state social work that we should look in rethinking residential child care.

Conclusion

There have always been question marks over the appropriateness of social work as a professional framework within which to locate residential child care. Policy and conceptual trends are shifting in the direction of social pedagogy. A suspicion that Europe did better by its children in state care now seems to be confirmed by the research carried out by the Thomas Coram Research Unit. Social pedagogy would seem to offer better outcomes and experiences of care for both children and those who work in the field. The attraction of social pedagogy is that it provides a conceptually robust framework for children's care built around the unifying principle of upbringing fostered through relationships, which is the essence of residential child care.

ELEVEN

Conclusion: rethinking residential child care

This book has painted an ambivalent picture of residential child care. On the one hand it is hard to argue with Cameron's portrayal of the sector as one 'emptied of its potential, a dried up expression for how to manage an underclass of disadvantage' (2003, p 93). Evoking this image is not to say that residential child care is universally bad. There are many pockets of good practice and even in the worst situations there are individual carers who strive on a day-to-day basis to do their best by those they work with. The problem lies less with the individuals who work in residential child care than with the wider context in which they are expected to do their jobs. As Heron and Chakrabarti note, the 'good practice that does exist does so against a backdrop of organisational and professional failure' (2002, p 356). The corporate parents of children in state care might benefit from parenting classes.

While it is hard to ignore the current state of the sector, I hope that a positive spirit threads through the book; residential child care can be a conducive environment for children to grow up in. For this to happen, however, requires a fundamental rethink of the discourses that currently shape policy and practice. If residential care is to become a positive option in the lives of children it requires that new ways of thinking are brought to bear, based around the concept of care itself. Care is essentially a relational and moral endeavour rather than the technical/rational one it has become. Before moving on to discuss care in some more detail I will address why current attempts to manage and ostensibly improve residential child care through increasing bureaucracy and regulation are conceptually flawed. Care is emptied of its potential by the bureaucracy of solid modernity and by the neoliberal precepts of liquid modernity.

The problem with bureaucracy

Bauman (1989) offers some telling insights into the functioning and effects of bureaucracy. He likens the modern period's obsession with rationality and order to gardening. At its extreme he associates the gardening mentality, reified in the assumptions and practices of bureaucracy, as being implicated in the Holocaust.

If we think about residential child care as a garden we can imagine how bureaucracies apply a gardener's instinct to weed out the unwanted bits in an attempt to impose an order and rationality on it, a process that might be justified in the name of embedding 'best practice'. Yet concepts such as care do not lend themselves to ideas of pruning. Care is messy and ambiguous. The messy bits are those children who do silly and irrational things, disrupting the smooth running of a home. Just as often, the messy bits belong to staff whose response to anxiety can lead to behaviours every bit as irrational as those of children. They detract from the overall appearance of the garden; they threaten its tidiness, so they have to be removed. Attempts to remove the untidy bits from bureaucratic gardens, however, can only succeed by expunging the garden's potential as a medium for growth and creativity. As Bauman notes, 'For the ethical world ... ambivalence and uncertainty are its daily bread and cannot be stamped out without destroying the moral substance of responsibility' (2000, p 10). Care that is neat and tidy and conforms to bureaucratic specification is not care at all.

In practical terms what this means is that those who come into the profession 'to make a difference' to the lives of individuals and to wider society are frustrated by the proliferation of rules and procedures, which sap their moral impulse to care. This can lead to burnout or, in some cases, to social workers and carers co-opting the managerial agenda, filling out the forms and forgetting what brought them into the job in the first place. Care becomes about processing people. And this is problematic for, 'when we obscure the essential human and moral aspects of care behind ever more rules and regulations we make the daily practice of social work ever more distant from its original ethical impulse' (Bauman, 2000, p 9).

A problem with bureaucracy is that it imposes social distance. The Holocaust was made possible because the functionaries of the Nazi organisation rarely had to deal directly with those to be weeded out, the Jews, homosexuals and trades unionists. The SS guards were distanced from the objects of their work through the division of labour and extended chains of command, which acted to dissipate any responsibility they might feel for what they were doing. In the context of residential child care, Webb (2006) identifies the practice of Pindown in Staffordshire (see Chapter Three) as an example of what can happen when there is a lack of proximity in relationships and carers begin to think that the task of caring can be reduced to a set of house rules to manage behaviours. The Pindown regime did not come about because its proponents were bad or uncaring people; it came about because they began to believe and were perhaps encouraged to believe that expert systems could take the place of personal relationships in caring for children.

This notion of social distance has particular ramifications in organisational situations based around extended line management arrangements; external managers making decisions about children in social work headquarters are often distanced from the objects of these decisions by layers of other managers, rarely having to countenance directly the consequences of their decisions. On the one hand this may be argued to allow them to take decisions rationally, without the emotional dimension that proximity entails. However, a consequence of social distance, according to Bauman, is a lack of moral responsibility. Decision making is far easier when it is only a rational task rather than one with immediate human consequences. This is the problem with the idea of the corporate parent. A conception of parenting located within an amorphous bureaucratic structure cannot be parenting at all. It is all very well to suggest that corporate parenting speaks of a collective responsibility for children, but this needs to coexist with a very personalised experience of care undertaken by adults who share the lifespace with children.

The problem with neoliberalism

Problems with the bureaucracy of the modern project are compounded by the growth of neoliberalism, the precepts of which are inimical to the provision of care. Brannan and Moss identify the fundamental problem:

> … new capitalism calls for individualism, instrumental rationality, flexibility, short term engagement, deregulation and the dissolution of established relationships and practices. Caring relationships … are predicated upon an expressive rather than instrumental relationship to others. They are based upon trust, commitment over time and a degree of predictability. (2003, p 202)

Neoliberalism also valorises the two dominant discourses governing thinking about and work with children: protection and rights. Protectionism is paternalistic, viewing the child as weak, and denying them a voice. Children's rights approaches privilege the autonomous individual, and emphasise rights over relationships, and universal principles over concrete situations. Neither is sufficient in offering any rounded understanding of how to care for children.

The winds of change?

There is increasing dissatisfaction at a number of levels with how social work and social care currently operate. *Changing lives* (Scottish Executive, 2006), the Scottish review of social work, identifies a profession that is process-dominated, lacking in confidence and uncertain about its role. It claims that negative publicity around 'failures' has led to risk-averse and blame cultures and that social work has lost touch with some of its core purpose. How much more so is this apparent in residential child care?

Central policy themes of recent years, those of regulation and risk, are open to question and are largely found wanting. Regulatory regimes are costly and in many cases dysfunctional (Crerar, 2007) and like all experiments in control are perhaps destined to fail. The concept of risk, another central plank of policy discourse, is likewise appearing distinctly tenuous when subject to rigorous analysis (Barry, 2007). At a professional level dissatisfaction with technical/rational and managerial approaches to practice is increasingly identified in the social work literature (Meagher and Parton, 2004; Ruch, 2005; Ferguson, 2008). Webb develops this point arguing that social work needs to reclaim its ethical base:

> … the legitimacy of social work rests on exhortations that betray an ethical intent rather than a set of empirical or outcome based possibilities … the return to ethics should be a major theme that characterises social work in the late modern scenario. (2006, p 8)

Attempts to assert an ethical base for social work increasingly draw on the literature around an ethic of care. Meagher and Parton (2004) identify 'the capacity of the discourse of the ethics of care to offer ways of conceiving and representing the relational dimensions of social work that are obscured by the rational-technical focus of managerialism' (2004, p 11). The concept of care, oftentimes decried as being insufficiently 'professional' and encouraging of dependency, is identified as providing a way forward for social work. It is the foundation of child and youth care practice (Ricks, 1992). But what might care involve?

Putting care at the centre

The literature on care ethics can be traced back to a feminist tradition and in particular to the work of Carol Gilligan (1993). Gilligan was a student of Lawrence Kohlberg, who developed what has become the dominant schema for understanding human moral development. She challenged Kohlberg's model as reflecting predominantly male ways of thinking and acting on questions of moral reasoning. Essentially men spoke and acted from a 'justice' orientation, foregrounding qualities of objectivity, rationality and general principle; women reflected a 'care' orientation and drew on 'softer' attributes of intuition, connection and compassion in reaching moral decisions. Gilligan's work has engendered considerable debate since its publication (Larrabee, 1993), much of it revolving around the extent to which her male and female voices, the domains of justice and care respectively, are deemed to reflect essentialist characteristics of men and women or whether they merely provide a helpful framework within which to conceptualise different orientations towards moral thinking. Joan Tronto (1994) takes the debate beyond essentialising gender roles, re-conceptualising care as 'a practice, rather than a set of rules or principles.... It involves both particular acts of caring and a "general habit of mind" to care that should inform all aspects of a practitioner's moral life' (1994, pp 126-7). Sevenhuijsen (1998) states that 'an ethic of care is concerned with responsibilities and relationships rather than rules and rights; it is bound to concrete situations, rather than being formal and abstract; and it is a moral activity rather than a set of principles to be followed' (p 59). Tronto (1994) identifies care as both an activity and a disposition. It is something that we do and something that we are.

Care as an activity and a disposition

Care as something that we *do* involves a number of different elements. Tronto (1994) identifies four of these: attentiveness, responsibility, competence and responsiveness. Good intentions are themselves not enough, but they are important. Care as something that we *are* is perhaps reflected in this quote from David, a former resident in a children's home: 'There were people who really cared and that shone through; and there were people who didn't care and that also shone through' (quoted in Cree and Davis, 2007, p 87). David goes on to say, 'There was a nun, who was the head nun of our children's home who was very, very fair, and kind, but not in a "goody-goody" way – she was a just person, and she offered us protection' (p 87). This is care as a disposition, something embedded in the personal characteristics of the individual carer rather than something that can be encapsulated in the job descriptions and person specifications beloved by bureaucracies.

The idea of care as a disposition or a virtue is supported in the work of a number of philosophers from Aristotle onwards. Perhaps the foremost contemporary ethical thinker in this regard is Emmanuel Levinas. Levinas agued that human beings were called to respond to the needs of the other. We may not like the other, our relationship may be conflictual but we nevertheless have a responsibility towards them, a responsibility that is infinite and demands nothing in return. Levinas turns dominant thinking, which valorises the autonomous, free-thinking individual, on its head. For Levinas freedom only comes in relationship with others, in heteronomy (community) rather than autonomy. John Macmurray makes a similar point, claiming that 'the urge to communion ... is the basic and primary urge in human beings. Acting from the motive of care for others leads paradoxically to genuine self-realization' (Costelloe, 2002, p 327). From a residential child care perspective Austin and Halpin claim that:

> It is a truism, but nonetheless true, that children grow through being cared for and, in turn, caring. If children are not cared for, there is evidence that they cannot care for others. It is only through caring that we become human. Children in care need care. It is for this reason that care is the core of our profession, and this should not be forgotten in the search for status. We should not be ashamed to admit that we care. (Austin and Halpin, 1989)

Rethinking the theoretical base

Over the past 50 years or so residential child care has sought academic legitimacy by claiming a knowledge base rooted in the disciplines of psychology, sociology or indeed professional social work. The knowledge contained within these disciplines is limited in what it has to offer residential child care workers. It often fails to speak to or validate their experiences. When they fall back on the language of other disciplines to discuss their work, 'it requires a translation that lessens their ability to describe the impact of child and youth care work and creates an impediment to achieving professional power and capability' (Phelan, 2001c, p 1).

Despite this dissonance the move to professionalise residential child care was pursued by hitching it to the wagon of casework models of social work. A result of this is that too many workers want to counsel children or subject them to the latest risk assessment tool or cognitive behavioural programme. Too few want to get involved in the nuts and bolts issues of ensuring that socks are changed or beds made; or if they do, they see this as mere tending, not 'real' social work. By extension, it is difficult to assert that the real work of residential care is done, not in the counselling session but in the everyday 'being with' children. It is perhaps a legacy of a protestant ethic that we find it difficult to accept the value of anything that does not have an unpleasant connotation. Just 'being with' children is not enough; we need to be doing 'the work' with them. 'The work' invariably involves addressing their difficulties. We just cannot bring ourselves as a society and a profession to a place where 'the work' might actually involve playing with children and enjoying their company; the spectre of less eligibility still hovers.

This idea of 'work' with children as currently understood is misconceived. Phelan (1999) argues that the child and youth care worker is not a therapist or a counsellor in the traditional sense, but rather an 'experience arranger', someone who creates opportunities in the real world for people to experience themselves as competent and successful. The use of strategically planned and spontaneous events in the lifespace to support someone to adopt a more competent and hopeful picture of him/herself is the main tool of the profession. It is a broadly socio-educational task, a social model. In many respects it is what parents do.

Parenting

Although policy documents increasingly identify the need for the state to assume a parenting role, Cameron (2003) notes its failure to offer the same type or level of care as families. Petrie at al (2006) identify the caring task as incorporating aspects of parenting. This is conceived of as 'mind-mindedness', 'the capacity of carers to tune into and respond to their own and other peoples' mental states and processes and how these govern behaviour' (Petrie et al, 2006, p 13). Ideas of entering into the kind of shared rhythm spoken about in the child and youth care literature (Maier, 1979) come to mind. Parents are fundamentally involved in their children's upbringing.

Upbringing

The concept of 'upbringing', as identified in the previous chapter, is central to ideas of social pedagogy. In Scotland it is explicit in the

Kilbrandon Report (1964). Kilbrandon's notion of social education was conceived as being about supporting upbringing. Like parenting, upbringing was never really embraced by social work; the everyday grind of bringing children up was not deemed sufficiently 'professional'. Yet 'upbringing' is exactly what workers in residential child care are called to do. It can be a grind; there is no magic bullet that can be targeted at children to take away the messy and frustrating bits about guiding them to adulthood. In that respect it is similar to parenting. It requires constant repetition of the same message, of being on children's backs, pestering them, setting limits, saying 'No' to them when the occasion demands, sharing their stories and their hopes and fears. It is a model of social education requiring explanation, demonstration, correction and repetition. It involves keeping them in mind, not being able to walk away at the end of a shift and merely pick up where you left off the previous day. It is hard work, with no short cuts through the application of the latest worksheet.

There is an important philosophical distinction contained within this point. An Aristotelian tradition considers that human beings develop not through the Kantian notion of 'rational' prescriptivism, but rather through the patient acquisition of virtuous social habits attained through education and training. Many social work interventions proceed from the former position, placing faith in abstract principles such as rights or protection or planned interventions, all of which only achieve any meaning and perhaps any ethical substance when grounded in the everyday experience of upbringing. 'Upbringing' calls for a different way of working, one that might be encapsulated in Garfat's (1999) catchy depiction of the residential task as being about 'hanging out and hanging in'.

'Hanging out and hanging in'

'Hanging out' can confront managers of residential care facilities with a problem. It requires them to accept that they are paying staff for seeming to do nothing. Yet doing nothing but doing it well is what the best residential workers do. They hang about chatting, reading the paper, watching television, just 'being with' children as they live their lives rather than attempting to do anything *to* them. If good residential workers are adept at hanging out, they also need to be able to 'hang in' when things get tough. They need persistence and stickability and at root a belief that they can see through any difficulties with children. Again this view is at odds with ideas of caring that conceive it as a technical/rational task. It calls for carers to assume a moral responsibility for those they work with.

Rethinking the epistemological base for care

The privileging of knowledge drawn from the social sciences can lead to efforts to assess and intervene in seemingly scientific, ostensibly rational and dispassionate, ways with children. Yet Austin and Halpin claim that the caring interaction itself provides direct knowledge. What counts for knowledge needs to be located in what goes on in the relationship established between children and those working with them.

The location of knowledge in the caring relationship is given credence in Lave and Wenger's (1991) influential work on learning. As Smith notes, they suggest that:

> ... knowledge is socially constituted in the customs and practices of particular occupational groups. It is neither universal nor objective, but is identified in the social processes that exist within particular disciplines or workplaces. Knowledge is what is meaningful to workers in a particular context and learning what counts as knowledge in a particular setting is mediated through the participation of co-workers in a particular endeavour. They constitute what is termed a community of practice.... Different disciplines and indeed different settings within disciplines have their own 'insider knowledge', which new members of a team are inducted into through what Lave and Wenger (1991) term legitimate peripheral participation, a process similar to the passing on of skills in trade apprenticeships. The team nature of residential child care, the intimacy and the kind of myths and rituals that build up there make such settings crucibles of knowledge creation. They are communities of practice, but communities whose source of knowledge is rarely acknowledged or tapped. (Smith, 2005b, p 267)

Knowledge then needs to fit with and derive from what practitioners experience in the real world rather than being located in policy documents, practice standards or in the performance criteria prescribed in vocational or competency based models of training. Webb identifies the developing literature around heuristics as providing a model through which to think about the creation of knowledge in social work.

Heuristics asserts that knowledge and the decisions that follow from it are to be made through 'a process of inferential discovery based on trial and error' (2006, p 130), rather than through some more 'scientific' deductive process. To learn by trial and error practitioners need to be allowed to make mistakes and to become comfortable in working with uncertainty (Taylor and White, 2006). Striving for certainty, thinking that we know (and in current climates feeling under an expectation to know), is unsustainable. It is also undesirable. According to Ricks et al (1999, p 12), 'knowing is a learning disability'. When we think we know something, we cut ourselves off from the possibility of further learning.

Professional activism

Alternative ways of thinking of and practising residential child care require that practitioners become more assertive in determining how residential child care will look in the future. This has to happen through professional discourse rather than top-down injunction. It is a highly dysfunctional situation when those considered to be the experts in residential child care, generally those from child protection or children's rights backgrounds, rarely have any direct experience of working in the sector.

Teachers seem to be further along the road than social workers and certainly further than care workers in seeking to reclaim some of the ground from those voices that have come to dominate professional agendas in recent decades. In education Sachs (2003) calls for an activist teaching profession prepared to create the political and institutional spaces where rigorous public debate can take place and to challenge the beliefs and interests that sustain power structures. Workers in residential child care need to take charge of what is happening within or indeed to the discipline rather than seeing themselves as simple victims in the making of that history. This is work that demands professional leadership from those in the sector, encouraging practitioners to motivate and inspire one another through sharing ideas and strategies across workplaces and erstwhile boundaries (Fullan, 2003; Sachs, 2003).

This is a task that asserts a moral imperative for residential child care and those who work in it. That imperative is to help children in care access 'the good life'. Recourse to a language of rights, protection and outcomes speaks of a very limited vision for children. We need to lift our sights so that:

Joy, spontaneity, complexity, desires, richness, wonder, curiosity, care, vibrant, play, fulfilling, thinking for yourself, love, hospitality, welcome, alterity, emotion, ethics, relationships, responsibility … are part of a vocabulary which speaks about a different idea of public provision for children, one which addresses questions of the good life, including a good childhood. (Moss and Petrie, 2002, p 79)

Whether this vision can be achieved within social work as it has emerged is a moot point. In many respects the conceptual and organisational structures to support such a vision already exist on our doorstep. Social pedagogic approaches incorporate all the elements required of a coherent philosophy of care, a broadly social educational paradigm based around the concept of upbringing, an emphasis on lifespace and activity-based work, the assertion of the centrality of the personal relationship and the need for well-qualified, reflective and reflexive practitioners.

References

Abrams, L. (1998) *The orphan country*, Edinburgh: John Donald.

Ainsworth, F. (1981) 'The training of personnel for group care with children', in F. Ainsworth and L.C. Fulcher (eds) *Group care for children: Concept and issues*, London: Tavistock, pp 225-47.

Ainsworth, F. and Fulcher, L.C. (eds) (1981) *Group care for children: Concept and issues*, London: Tavistock.

Ainsworth, M.D.S., Blehar, M.C., Waters, E. and Wall, S. (1978) *Patterns of attachment: A psychological study of the strange situation*, Hillside, NJ: Erlbaum.

Anglin, J. (1999) 'The uniqueness of child and youth care: a personal perspective', *Child and Youth Care Forum*, vol 28, no 2, pp 143-50.

Anglin, J. (2002) *Pain, normality, and the struggle for congruence: Reinterpreting residential care for children and youth*, New York: The Haworth Press Inc.

Appleton, J. (2006) *Don't touch those kids!* (www.spiked-online.com/index.php?/site/article/144/, accessed 7 August 2008).

Atkinson, P. (1997) 'Narrative turn or blind alley', *Qualitative Health Research*, vol 7, no 3, pp 325-44.

Audit Scotland (2002) *Dealing with offending by young people*, Edinburgh: Audit Scotland.

Austin, D. and Halpin, W. (1988) 'The embodiment of knowledge: a phenomenological approach to child care', *Journal of Child Care*, special issue, pp 7-16 (www.cyc-net.org/cyc-online/cycol-0208-austinhalpin.html, accessed 1 August 2008).

Austin, D. and Halpin, W. (1989) 'The caring response', *Journal of Child and Youth Care*, vol 4, no 3, pp 1-7.

Bailey, R. and Brake, M. (eds) (1975) *Radical social work*, London: Edward Arnold.

Balbernie, R. (1966) *Residential work with children*, Oxford: The Pergamon Press.

Bandura, A. (1977) *Social learning theory*, New York: General Learning Press.

Barnes, M. (2006) *Caring and social justice*, Basingstoke: Palgrave Macmillan.

Barry, M. (2007) *Effective approaches to risk assessment in social work: An international literature review*, Edinburgh: Scottish Executive.

Bauman, Z. (1989) *Modernity and the holocaust*, Cambridge: Cambridge University Press.

Bauman, Z. (1993) *Postmodern ethics*, Oxford: Blackwell.

Bauman, Z (1998) *Globalisation: The human consequences*, Cambridge: Polity Press.

Bauman, Z. (2000a) *Liquid modernity*, Cambridge: Polity Press.

Bauman, Z. (2000b) Special essay: 'Am I my brother's keeper?', *European Journal of Social Work*, vol 3, no 1, pp 5-11.

Bebbington, A. and Miles, J. (1989) 'The background of children who enter local authority care', *British Journal of Social Work*, vol 19, no 1, pp 349-68.

Beck, U. (1992) *Risk society: Towards a new modernity*, London: Sage Publications.

Beckett, C. (2003) *Child protection: An introduction*, London: Sage Publications.

Bengtsson, E., Chamberlain, C., Crimmens, D. and Stanley, J. (2008) *Introducing social pedagogy into residential child care in England: An evaluation of a project commissioned by the Social Education Trust (SET) in September 2006 and managed by the National Centre for Excellence in Residential Child Care (NCERCC)*, London: Social Education Trust and NCERCC.

Berridge, D. (2007) 'Theory and explanation in child welfare: education and looked-after children', *Child and Family Social Work*, vol 12, pp 1-10.

Berridge, D. and Brodie, I. (1998) *Children's homes revisited*, London: Jessica Kingsley Publishers.

Berridge, D. and Cleaver, H. (1987) *Foster home breakdown*, Oxford: Blackwell.

Bettelheim, B. (1950) *Love is not enough: The treatment of emotionally disturbed children*, Glencoe, IL: Free Press.

Biddulph, S. (2003) *Raising boys: Why boys are different and how to help them become happy and well-balanced men*, London: Thorsons.

Bion, W.R. (1961) *Experiences in groups*, London: Tavistock.

Blackshaw, T. (2005) *Zygmunt Bauman*, London: Routledge.

Blum, L. (1994) *Moral perception and particularity*, Cambridge: Cambridge University Press.

Boddy, J., Cameron, C., Petrie, P., Simon, A. and Wigfall, V. (2006) *Working with children in care. European perspectives*, Buckingham: Open University Press.

Bowlby, J. (1951) *Child care and the growth of love*, Harmondsworth: Penguin.

Brannan, J. and Moss, P. (2003) *Rethinking children's care*, Buckingham: Open University Press.

Brearley, J. (1985) 'Anxiety in the organisational context: experiences of consultancy', *Journal of Social Work Practice*, May, pp 33-47.

Brendtro, L.K., Brokenleg, M. and Van Bockern, S. (1990) *Reclaiming youth at risk: Our hope for the future*, Bloomington, IN: National Educational Service.

Bridges, W. (1991) *Managing transitions: Making the most of change*, New York: Perseus.

Brodie, I. (2001) *Children's homes and school exclusion: Redefining the problem*, London: Jessica Kingsley Publishers.

Bronfenbrenner, U. (1977) 'Toward an experimental ecology of human development', *American Psychologist*, vol 32, pp 513-31.

Bronfenbrenner, U. (1979) *The ecology of human development*, Cambridge, MA: Harvard University Press.

Brown, K. and White, K. (2006) *Exploring the evidence base for Integrated Children's Services*, Edinburgh: Scottish Government (www.scotland. gov.uk/Publications/2006/01/24120649/0, accessed 2 September 2008).

Bullock, R., Little, M. and Millham, S. (1993) *Going home: The return of children separated from their families*, Aldershot: Dartmouth Publishing Company.

Burmeister, E. (1960) *The professional houseparent*, New York: Columbia University Press.

Burton, J. (1998) *Managing residential care*, London: Routledge.

Butler, I. and Drakeford, M. (2001) 'Which Blair project? Communitarianism, social authoritarianism and social work', *Journal of Social Work*, vol 1, no 1, pp 7-24.

Butler, I. and Drakeford, M. (2005) *Scandal, social policy and social welfare*, Bristol: BASW/The Policy Press.

Cameron, C. (2003) 'An historical perspective on changing child care policy', in J. Brannan and P. Moss (eds) *Rethinking children's care*, Buckingham: Open University Press, pp 80-95.

Cameron, C. (2004) 'Social pedagogy and care; Danish and German practice in young people's residential care', *Journal of Social Work*, vol 4, no 2, pp 133-51.

Carlebach, J. (1970) *Caring for children in trouble*, London: RKP.

Caulfield-Dow, A. (2005) 'Throughcare and aftercare', in M. Smith (ed) *Secure in the knowledge: Perspectives on practice in secure accommodation*, Glasgow: Scottish Institute for Residential Child Care, ch 4.27.

Chase, E., Simon, A. and Jackson, S. (2006) *Children and young people in and after care: A positive perspective*, London: Routledge.

Children in Scotland (2008) *Working it out: Developing the children's sector workforce*, Edinburgh: Children in Scotland

Clark, C. (2006) 'Moral character in social work', *British Journal of Social Work*, vol 36, pp 75-89.

Clark, M. (2001) 'Influencing positive behaviour change: increasing the therapeutic approach of juvenile courts', *Federal Probation*, vol 65, no 1, pp 18-28.

Clarke, J. and Newman, J. (1997) *The managerial state: Power, politics and ideology in the remaking of social welfare*, London: Sage Publications.

Clough, R., Bullock, R. and Ward, A. (2006) *What works in residential child care? A review of research evidence and the practical considerations*, London: National Children's Bureau.

Clyde, J.J. (1992) *Report of the Inquiry into the Removal of Children from Orkney in February 1991* (Clyde Report), Edinburgh: HMSO.

Collingwood, P. (2005) 'Integrating theory and practice: the three-stage theory framework', *Journal of Practice Teaching in Health and Social Work*, vol 6, no 1, pp 6-23.

Colton, M., Vanstone, M. and Walby, C. (2002) 'Victimization, care and justice: reflections on the experiences of victims/survivors involved in large-scale historical investigations of child sexual abuse in residential institutions', *British Journal of Social Work*, vol 32, pp 541-51.

Corby, B. (2000) 'The impact of public enquiries', in D. Crimmens and J. Pitts (eds) *Positive residential practice: Learning the lessons of the 1990s*, Lyme Regis: Russell House.

Corby, B. (2006) 'Book review: "*The secret of Bryn Estyn: The making of a modern witch hunt*" by R. Webster, 2005', *Child Abuse Review*, vol 15, pp 285-7.

Corby, B., Doig, A. and Roberts, V. (2001) *Public inquiries into abuse of children in residential care*, London: Jessica Kingsley Publishers.

Costelloe, J.E. (2002) *John Macmurray*, Edinburgh: Floris Books.

Coulshed, V. and Orme, J. (2006) *Social work practice: An introduction*, Basingstoke: Macmillan.

Cree, V. and Davis, A. (2007) *Social work: Voices from the inside*, Abingdon: Routledge.

Cree, V. and Wallace, S. (2005) 'Risk and protection', in R. Adams, L. Dominelli and M. Payne (eds) *Social work futures*, Basingstoke: Palgrave Macmillan.

Crimmens, D. and Milligan, I. (eds) (2005) *Facing forward: Residential child care in the 21st century*, Lyme Regis: Russell House.

Dahlberg, G. and Moss, P. (2005) *Ethics and politics in early childhood education*, London: RoutledgeFalmer.

Daniel, B., Wassell, S. and Gilligan, R. (1999) *Child development for child care and protection workers*, London: Jessica Kingsley Publishers.

Daniel, B. and Taylor, V. (2001) *Engaging with fathers: Practice issues for health and social care*, London: Jessica Kingsley Publishers.

Daniel, B., Featherstone, B., Hooper, C.-A. and Scourfield, J. (2005) 'Why gender matters for *Every Child Matters*', *British Journal of Social Work*, vol 35, no 8, pp 1343-55.

Davidson, J., McCullough, D., Steckley, L. and Warren, T. (2005) *Holding safely*, Glasgow: The Scottish Institute for Residential Child Care.

Dean, M. (1999) 'Risk: calculable and incalculable', in D. Lupton (ed) *Risk and socio-cultural theory*, Cambridge: Cambridge University Press.

de Shazer, S. (1985) *Keys to solutions in brief therapy*, New York: Norton & Co.

DfES (Department for Education and Skills) (2003) *Every Child Matters: the Green Paper*, Norwich: The Stationery Office.

DfES (2006) *Care Matters: Transforming the Lives of Children and Young People in Care*, Norwich: The Stationery Office.

DfES (2007) *Care matters: Time for change*, Norwich: The Stationery Office.

DH (Department of Health), Department of Education and Employment and The Home Office (2000) *The framework for the assessment of children in need and their families*, London: The Stationery Office.

Dixon, J. and Stein, M. (2002b) *A study of throughcare and aftercare services in Scotland*, Edinburgh: Scottish Executive.

Dockar-Drysdale, B. (1990) *The provision of primary experience*, London: Free Association Books.

Dorling, D. and Thomas, B. (2004) *People and places: A 2001 Census atlas of the UK*, Bristol: The Policy Press.

Douglas, R. and Payne, C. (1981) 'Alarm bells for the clock-on philosophy', *Social Work Today*, vol 12, no 23, pp 110-11.

du Toit, L. (2000) 'Child and youth care work in South Africa: recognition and regulation through registration – at last!', *cyc-online*, issue 12 (www.cyc-net.org/cyc-online/cycol-0100-registration.html, accessed 1 September 2008).

Easen, P., Atkins, M. and Dyson, A. (2000) 'Inter-professional collaboration and conceptualisations of practice', *Children and Society*, vol 14, pp 355-67.

Emond, R. (2000) 'Survival of the skilful: an ethnographic study of two groups of young people in residential care', Unpublished PhD thesis, University of Stirling.

Emond, R. (2004) 'Rethinking our understanding of the resident group in group care', *Child and Youth Care Forum*, vol 33, no 3, pp 93-208.

Emond, R. (2007) 'Children's voices, children's rights', in A. Kendrick (ed) *Residential child care: Prospects and challenges*, London: Jessica Kingsley Publishers, pp 183-96.

Erikson, E.H. (1995) *Childhood and society*, London:Vintage.

Ferguson, H. (2007) 'Abuse and looked-after children as "moral dirt": child abuse and institutional care in historical perspective', *Journal of Social Policy*, vol 36, no 1, pp 123-39.

Ferguson, I. (2008) *Reclaiming social work: Challenging neo-liberalism and promoting social justice*, London: Sage Publications.

Ferguson, R. and Anglin, J. (1985) 'The child care profession: a vision for the future', *Child and Youth Care Quarterly*, vol 14, no 2, pp 85-102.

Fewster, G. (1990) *Being in care: A journey into self*, New York: The Haworth Press Inc.

Fewster, G. (2000) 'Morality, empathy, and sexuality', *Journal of Child & Youth Care*, vol 14, no 4, pp 1-17.

Fewster, G. (2004) 'Making contact: personal boundaries in professional practice', *Relational Child and Youth Care Practice*, vol 17, no 4, pp 8-18.

Fewster, G. (2005) 'Just between you and me: personal boundaries in professional relationships', *Relational Child and Youth Care Practice*, vol 18, no 2, pp 7-14.

Forrest, R. (1976) 'Theories of delinquency', in F.M. Martin and K. Murray (eds), *Children's hearings*, Edinburgh: Scottish Academic Press, pp 79-98.

Francis, J. (2006) 'Could do better! Supporting the education of looked-after children', in A. Kendrick (ed) *Residential child care: Prospects and challenges*, London: Jessica Kingsley Publishers.

Freire, P. (1995) *Pedagogy of hope: Reliving pedagogy of the oppressed*, New York: Continuum.

Frost, N., Mills, S. and Stein, M. (1999) *Understanding residential child care*, Aldershot: Ashgate.

Fulcher, L.C. (1998) 'Acknowledging culture in child and youth care practice', *Social Work Education*, vol 17, no 3, pp 321-38.

Fulcher, L.C. (2001) 'Differential assessment of residential group care for children and young people', *British Journal of Social Work*, vol 31, pp 417-35.

Fulcher, L.C. (2002) 'The duty of care in child and youth care practice', *Journal of Child and Youth Care Work*, vol 17, pp 76-93.

Fulcher, L.C. (2004) 'Programmes and praxis: A review of taken-for-granted knowledge', *Scottish Journal of Residential Child Care*, vol 3, no 2, pp 33-45.

Fulcher, L.C. (2007) 'Residential child and youth care is fundamentally about team work', *Journal of Relational Child & Youth Care Practice*, vol 20, no 4, pp 30-6.

Fulcher, L.C. and Ainsworth, F. (1983) *A practice curriculum in group care*, CCETSW Paper 14.2, London: Central Council for Education & Training in Social Work.

Fulcher, L.C. and Ainsworth, F. (eds) (1985) *Group care practice with children*, London: Tavistock.

Fulcher, I.C. and Ainsworth, F. (eds) (2006) *Group care practice with children and young people revisited*, New York: The Haworth Press Inc.

Fullan, M. (2003) *The moral imperative of school leadership*, Ontario and Thousand Oaks, CA: Ontario Principals' Council/Corwin Press.

Furedi, F. (2005) *The politics of fear*, London: Continuum.

Furedi, F. (2008) *History-as-therapy*, Spiked-online, 5 March (www. spiked-online.com/index.php?/site/article/4721/, accessed 16 May).

Furnivall, J., Macquarrie, A. and Smith, M. (unpublished) 'A review of residential child care in Scotland', Glasgow: Scottish Institute for Residential Child Care.

Gabor, P. and Ing, C. (1991) 'Stop and think: the application of cognitive-behavioral approaches in work with young people', *Journal of Child and Youth Care*, vol 6, no 1, pp 43-53.

Gallagher, B. (2000) 'The extent and nature of known cases of institutional child sex abuse', *British Journal of Social Work*, vol 30, pp 795-817.

Garfat, T. (1998) 'The effective child and youth care intervention: a phenomenological inquiry', *Journal of Child and Youth Care*, special edition, vol 12, nos 1-2.

Garfat, T. (1999) 'On hanging-out (and hanging-in)', *cyc-online*, no 8, September (www.cyc-net.org/cyc-online/cycol-0999-editorial.html, accessed 12 December 2007).

Garfat, T. (2001) 'Developmental stages of child and youth care workers: an interactional perspective', *The International Child and Youth Care Network*, issue 24 (www.cyc-net.org/cyc-online/cycol-0101-garfat. html, accessed 2 October 2008).

Garfat, T. (2003a) 'Four parts magic: the anatomy of a child and youth care intervention', *cyc-online*, issue 50 (www.cyc-net.org/cyc-online/ cycol-0303-thom.html, accessed 2 March 2008).

Garfat, T. (2003b) *A child and youth care approach to working with families*, New York: The Haworth Press Inc.

Garfat, T. and McElwee, N. (2004) *Developing effective interventions with families*, Cape Town: Pretext.

Garrett, P.M. (2008) 'Social work practices: silences and elisions in the plan to "transform" the lives of children "looked after" in England', *Child & Family Social Work*, vol 13, no 3, pp 311-18.

Gerhardt, S. (2004) *Why love matters: How affection shapes a baby's brain*, London: Routledge.

Giddens, A. (1991) *The consequences of modernity*, Cambridge: Polity.

Gilligan, C. (1993) *In a different voice: Psychological theory and women's development*, Cambridge, MA: Harvard University Press.

Gilligan, R. (1996) 'A view from abroad: changes in residential child care in Ireland and Europe', in A Kendrick and A. McQuarrie (eds) *A Better Kind of Home*, Centre for Residential Child Care Practice Paper no 3, Glasgow: Centre for Residential Child Care, pp 27-41.

Gilligan, R. (2001) 'Working with social networks: key resources in helping children at risk', in M. Hill (ed) *Effective ways of working with children and their families*, London: Jessica Kingsley Publishers, pp 70-91.

Gilligan, R. (2005) 'Resilience and residential care for children and young people', in D. Crimmens and I. Milligan (eds) *Facing forward: Residential child care in the 21st century*, Lyme Regis: Russell House, pp 105-13.

Goffman, E. (1968) *Asylums*, Harmondsworth: Penguin.

Goldson, B. (2002) 'New Labour, social justice and children: political calculation and the deserving–undeserving schism', *British Journal of Social Work*, vol 32, pp 683-95.

Goldson, B. (2005) 'Differential justice? A critical introduction to youth justice policy in UK jurisdictions' in J. McGhee, M. Mellon and B. Whyte (eds) *Meeting needs, addressing deeds: Working with young people who offend*, Glasgow: NCH Scotland, pp 27-47.

Grant, C. and Gabor, P. (2006) 'An historical perspective on residential services for troubled and troubling youth in Canada revisited', *Relational Child and Youth Care Practice*, vol 19, no 4, pp 17-25.

Grant, A., Ennis, J. and Stuart, F. (2002) 'Looking after health: a joint working approach to improving the health outcomes of looked after and accommodated children and young people', *Scottish Journal of Residential Child Care*, vol 1, no 1, pp 23-30.

Hacking, I. (1992) 'World-making by kind-making: child abuse for example', in M. Douglas and D. Hull (eds) *How classification works: Nelson Goodman among the social sciences*, Edinburgh: Edinburgh University Press, pp 180-238.

Harris, J. (2002) *The social work business*, London: Routledge.

Harris, R. and Timms, N. (1993) *Secure accommodation in child care: Between hospital and prison or thereabouts?*, London: Routledge.

Hart, N. and Monteaux, A. (2006) 'The BA in curative education', in R. Jackson (ed) *Holistic special education*, Edinburgh: Floris Books, pp 199-213.

Harvey, D. (2005) *A brief history of neoliberalism*, Oxford: Oxford University Press.

Heifetz, R.A. (1994) *Leadership without easy answers*, Cambridge, MA: Belknap Press.

Heron, G. and Chakrabarti, M. (2002) 'Examining the perceptions and attitudes of staff working in community based children's homes', *Qualitative Social Work*, vol 1, no 3, pp 341-58.

Heywood, J. (1959) *Children in care*, London: Routledge and Kegan Paul, quoted in I. Butler and M. Drakeford (eds) (2005) *Scandal, social policy and social welfare*, Bristol: BASW/The Policy Press.

Hicks, L., Gibbs, I., Weatherly, H. and Byford, S. (2008) 'Management, leadership and resources in children's homes: what influences outcomes in residential child-care settings?', *British Journal of Social Work*, advanced access, published online 11 March, accessed 22 August.

Hill, M., Walker, M., Moodie, K., Wallace, B., Bannister, J., Khan, F., McIvor, G. and Kendrick, A. (2005) *Fast track children's hearings pilot: Final report of the evaluation of the pilot*, Universities of Glasgow, Stirling and Strathclyde.

Higham, P. (2001) 'Changing practice and an emerging social pedagogue paradigm in England: the role of the personal advisor', *Social Work In Europe*, vol 8, no 1, pp 21-31.

Home Affairs Committee (2002) *The conduct of investigations into past cases of abuse in children's homes* (www.publications.parliament. uk/pa/cm200102/cmselect/cmhaff/836/83603.htm#a1, accessed 7 June 2008).

Horwath, J. (2000) 'Childcare with gloves on: protecting children and young people in residential care', *British Journal of Social Work*, vol 30, pp 179-91.

Humphrey, J.C. (2003) 'New Labour and the regulatory reform of social care', *Critical Social Policy*, vol 23, no 1, pp 5-24.

Infed (2007) *Johann Heinrich Pestalozzi* (www.infed.org/thinkers/et-pest.htm, accessed 22 August 2008).

Jack, G. (2001) 'Ecological perspectives in assessing children and families', in J. Horwath (ed) *The child's world: Assessing children in need*, London: Jessica Kingsley Publishers.

Jackson, P. (2004) 'Rights and representation in the Scottish children's hearings system', in J. McGhee, M. Mellon and B. Whyte, *Meeting needs, addressing deeds: Working with young people who offend*, Glasgow: NCH, pp 71-9.

Jackson, R. (2006) 'The role of social pedagogy in the training of residential child care workers', *Journal of Intellectual Disabilities*, vol 10, no 1, pp 61–73.

Jackson, S. (2006) 'Looking after children away from home: past and present', in E. Chase, A. Simon and S. Jackson (eds) *In care and after: A positive perspective*, London: Routledge, pp 9–25.

Jackson, S. and Martin, P.Y. (1998) 'Surviving the care system: education and resilience', *Journal of Adolescence*, vol 21, no 5, pp 569–83.

Jackson, S., Ajayi, S. and Quigley, M. (2005) *Going to university from care: Final report of the By Degrees project*, London: Institute of Education.

Jones, A. and Waul, D. (2005) 'Residential care for Black children', in D. Crimmens and I. Milligan (eds) *Facing forward: Residential care in the 21st century*, Lyme Regis: Russell House.

Jones, C. (1983) *State social work and the working class*, London: Macmillan.

Jones, C. and Novak, T. (1999) *Poverty, welfare and the disciplinary state*, London: Routledge.

Jones, K. and Fowles, A.J. (1984) *Ideas on institutions: Analysing the literature on long-term care and custody*, London: Routledge and Kegan Paul.

Joseph Rowntree Foundation (2006) *Monitoring poverty and social exclusion in the UK 2006* (www.jrf.org.uk/knowledge/findings/socialpolicy/1979.asp, accessed 2 October 2008).

Joseph Rowntree Foundation (2008) *A minimum income standard for Britain: What people think* (www.jrf.org.uk/knowledge/findings/socialpolicy/2244.asp, accessed 14 August 2008).

Kahan, B. (1994) *Growing up in groups*, London: HMSO.

Kahan, B. (1995) *Highlight: An introduction to residential child care: Part 1*, London: National Children's Bureau.

Keenan, C. (2002) 'Working Within the Life-Space' in J. Lishman (ed) *Handbook of theory for practice teachers in social work*, London: Jessica Kingsley Publishers, pp 220–32.

Kellmer-Pringle, M.K. (1975) *The needs of children*, London: Hutchinson.

Kelly, G. (1998) 'The influence of research on child care policy and practice: the case of "children who wait" and the development of the permanence movement in the United Kingdom', in D. Iwaniec and J. Pinkerton (eds) *Making research work: Promoting child care policy and practice*, Chichester: Wiley, pp 47–58.

Kemshall, H. (2002) *Risk, Social Policy and Welfare*, Buckingham: Open University Press.

Kendrick, A. (1998) *Abuse of children in residential and foster care: A brief review*, Scottish Institute for Residential Child Care (SIRCC) (www.sircc.strath.ac.uk/research/kendrick.html, accessed 9 September 2008).

Kendrick, A. and Fraser, A. (1992) 'Summary of the literature review', in *Another kind of home: A review of residential child care*, Edinburgh: HMSO.

Kent, R. (1997) *Children's safeguards review*, Edinburgh: Stationery Office.

Kilbrandon, Lord (1964) *The Kilbrandon Report: Children and Young Persons Scotland*, Edinburgh: HMSO.

Kohlberg, L. (1984) *The psychology of moral development: The nature and validity of moral stages*, San Francisco, CA: Harper & Row.

Krueger, M. (1991) 'Central themes in child and youth care', *Journal of Child and Youth Care*, vol 5, no 1, pp 77-87.

Kubler-Ross, E. (1973) *On death and dying*, London: Routledge.

La Fontaine, J. (1994) *Extent and nature of organized ritual abuse*, London: Department of Health.

La Fontaine, J. (1998) *Speak of the devil: Tales of satanic abuse in contemporary England*, Cambridge: Cambridge University Press.

Lamb, M.E. (2004) *The role of the father in child development* (4th edn), Hoboken, NJ: Wiley.

Lane, D. (2001) *The Radisson Report*, Manchester: The Social Education Trust.

Larrabee, M.J. (ed) (1993) *An ethic of care: Feminist and interdisciplinary perspectives*, New York: Routledge.

Lave, J. and Wenger, E. (1991) *Situated learning: Legitimate peripheral participation*, Cambridge: Cambridge University Press.

Lee, P. and Pithers, D. (1980) 'Radical residential child care: Trojan horse or non-runner', in M. Brake and R. Bailey, *Radical social work and practice*, London: Edward Arnold, pp 86-123.

Levitas, R. (1998) *The inclusive society? Social exclusion and New Labour*, Basingstoke: Macmillan.

Levy, A. and Kahan, B. (1991) *The Pindown experience and the protection of children: The Report of the Staffordshire Child Care Inquiry*, Staffordshire County Council.

Lister, R. (2003) 'Investing in the citizen-workers of the future: transformations in citizenship and the state under New Labour', *Social Policy & Administration*, vol 37, no 5, pp 427-43.

Lister, R. (2004) *Poverty*, Cambridge: Polity Press.

Lynch, K. (2007) 'Love labour as a distinct and non-commodifiable form of care labour', *Sociological Review*, vol 55, no 3, pp 550-70.

Lyotard, J.-F. (1984) *The postmodern condition*, Manchester: Manchester University Press.

McBeath, G. and Webb, S. (2002) 'Virtue ethics and social work: being lucky, realistic, and not doing one's duty', *British Journal of Social Work*, vol 32, pp 1015-36.

McCluskey, S., Greaves, E. and Kean, C. (2004) 'Scottish Health Network: promoting the health and well-being of children and young people in and leaving care', *Scottish Journal of Residential Child Care*, vol 3, no 2, pp 55-8.

McGhee, J. and Waterhouse, L. (1998) 'Justice and welfare: has the Children (Scotland) Act 1995 shifted the balance?', *Journal of Social Welfare and Family Law*, vol 20, no 1, pp 49-63.

McGuire, J. (ed) (1995) *What works – Reducing reoffending: Guidelines from research and practice*, Chichester: Wiley.

Macintyre, A. (1984) *After virtue*, Notre Dame, IN: University of Notre Dame Press.

McKenzie, R. (1996) *The home: A memoir of growing up in an orphanage*, New York: Basic Books.

McLaughlin, K. (2007) 'Regulation and risk in social work: the General Social Care Council and the Social Care Register in context', *British Journal of Social Work*, vol 37, no 7, pp 1263-77.

McNeill, F., Batchelor, S., Burnett, R. and Knox, J. (2005) *21st century social work: Reducing re-offending: Key practice skills*, Edinburgh: Scottish Government.

McPheat, G. (2007) 'Evaluation of City of Edinburgh Residential Child Care Recruitment and Development Centre', unpublished MSc thesis, University of Strathclyde.

McWilliam, E. (1999) *Pedagogical pleasures*, New York: Peter Lang.

McWilliam, E. and Jones, A. (2005) 'An unprotected species? On teachers as risky subjects', *British Educational Research Journal*, vol 31, no 1, pp 109-21.

Magnuson, D. (2003) 'Preface', in T. Garfat (ed) *A child and youth care approach to working with families*, New York: The Haworth Press Inc.

Maier, H.W. (1979) 'The core of care: essential ingredients for the development of children at home and away from home', *Child Care Quarterly*, vol 8, no 4, pp 161-73.

Maier, H.W. (1981) 'Essential components in care and treatment environments for children', in F. Ainsworth and L.C. Fulcher (eds) *Group care for children: Concepts and issues*, London: Tavistock, pp 19-70.

Maier, H.W. (1982) 'The space we create controls us', *Residential Group Care and Treatment*, vol 1, no 1, pp 51-9.

Maier, H.W. (1985) 'Primary care in secondary settings: inherent strains', in L.C. Fulcher and F. Ainsworth (eds) *Group care practice with children*, London: Tavistock, pp 21–47.

Maier, H.W. (1987) *Developmental group care of children and youth: Concepts and practice*, New York: Haworth.

Maier, H.W. (2002) 'Hugging and physical touch', *cyc-online*, issue 36, January (www.cyc-net.org/cyc-online/cycol-0102-maier.html, accessed 12 August 2008).

Mandell, D. (2003) *Deadbeat dads: Subjectivity and social construction*, Toronto: University of Toronto Press.

Marris, P. (1974) *Loss and change*, London: Routledge & Kegan Paul.

Marshall, K. and Parvis, P. (2004) *Honouring children: The human rights of the child in Christian perspective*, Edinburgh: St Andrew's Press.

Martin, F.M. and Murray, K. (eds) (1976) *Children's hearings*, Edinburgh: Scottish Academic Press.

Martin, F.M. and Murray, K. (eds) (1982) *The Scottish juvenile justice system*, Edinburgh: Scottish Academic Press.

Mattingly, M. (2006) 'Managing occupational stress for group care personnel', in L.C. Fulcher and F. Ainsworth (eds) *Group care practice with children and young people revisited*, New York: The Haworth Press Inc.

Meagher, G. and Parton, N. (2004) 'Modernising social work and the ethics of care', *Social Work and Society* (www.socwork.net/2004/1/articles/426/meagher-Parton2004.pdf, accessed 2 October 2008).

Meltzer, H. (2000) *The mental health of children and adolescents in Great Britain*, London: Office of National Statistics.

Menzies Lyth, I.E.P. (1970) 'The functioning of social systems as a defence against anxiety', *Human Relations*, vol 13, pp 95–121.

Menzies Lyth, I.E.P. (1979) 'Staff support systems: task and anti-task in adolescent institutions', in R.D. Hinshelwood and M. Manning (eds) *Therapeutic communities: Reflections and progress*, London: Routledge and Kegan Paul.

Millham, S., Bullock, R. and Hosie, K. (1978) *Locking up children: Secure provision within the child-care system*, Farnborough: Saxon House.

Millham, S., Bullock, R., Hosie, K. and Haak, M. (1981) *Issues of control in residential child care*, London: HMSO.

Milligan, I. (1998) 'Residential care is not social work', *Social Work Education*, vol 17, no 3, pp 275–86.

Milner, J. and O'Byrne, P. (2002) *Assessment in social work*, Basingstoke: Palgrave Macmillan.

Milligan, I. and Stevens, I. (2006) *Residential child care: Collaborative practice*, London: Sage.

Morgan, R. (2006) 'Teachers "have lost courage to tackle bad behaviour"', *The Times*, 21 August (www.timesonline.co.uk/tol/news/uk/article614678.ece, accessed 19 June 2008).

Moss, P. and Petrie, P. (2002) *From children's services to children's spaces*, London: RoutledgeFalmer.

Munro, E. (1999) 'Common errors of reasoning in child protection', *Child Abuse and Neglect*, vol 23, no 8, pp 745-58.

Murphy, E. (2001) *The solution focused residential unit: A whole-team approach: Helping children and young people to thrive in care*, London: Eileen Murphy Consultants.

Myers, C.L. (2000) 'Dilemmas of children's welfare policies and practices: a critical and discursive perspective' (www.well.com/user/clmyers/children, accessed 20 August 2008).

NCERCC (National Centre for Excellence in Residential Child Care) (2007) *Social pedagogy seminars: Building a pedagogic workforce in residential child care*, Cheadle: NCERCC and National Children's Bureau.

NEF (New Economics Foundation) (2007) *Unintended consequences: How the efficiency agenda erodes local public services and a new public benefit model to restore them* (www.neweconomics.org/gen/z_sys_PublicationDetail.aspx?pid=248, accessed 20 February 2008).

Neil, A.S. (1966) *Summerhill*, Harmondsworth: Penguin.

Nicholson, D. and Artz, S. (2003) 'Preventing youthful offending: where do we go from here?', *Relational Child and Youth Care Practice*, vol 16, no 4, pp 32-46.

Noddings, N. (1996a) 'The cared for', in S. Gordon, P. Benner and N. Noddings (eds) *Caregiving: Readings in knowledge, practice, ethics and politics*, Philadelphia, PA: University of Pennsylvania Press.

Noddings, N. (1996b) 'The caring professional', in S. Gordon, P. Benner and N. Noddings (eds) *Caregiving: Readings in knowledge, practice, ethics and politics*, Philadelphia, PA: University of Pennsylvania Press.

Oliver, C. (2003) 'The care of the illegitimate child: the Coram experience 1900–45', in J. Brannan and P. Moss (eds) *Rethinking children's care*, Buckingham: Open University Press, pp 44-60.

Orme, J. (2001) 'Regulation or fragmentation? Directions for social work under New Labour', *British Journal of Social Work*, vol 31, pp 611-24.

Parton, N. (1985) *The politics of child abuse*, Basingstoke: Macmillan.

Parton, N. (1991) *Governing the family*, Basingstoke: Macmillan.

Parton, N. (1999) 'Reconfiguring child welfare practices: risk, advanced liberalism and the governance of freedom', in A.S. Chambon, A. Irving and L. Epstein (eds) *Reading Foucault for social work*, New York: Columbia University Press.

Parton, N. (2002) 'Postmodern and constructionist approaches to social work', in L. Dominelli, R. Adams and M. Payne (eds) *Social work: Themes, issues and critical debates*, Basingstoke: Palgrave.

Parton, N. (2006) *Safeguarding childhood: Early intervention and surveillance in a late-modern society*, Basingstoke: Palgrave.

Petrie, P. (2001) 'The potential of pedagogy/education for work in the children's sector in the UK', *Social Work in Europe*, vol 8, no 3, pp 23-6.

Petrie, P. (2004) 'Pedagogy – a holistic, personal approach to work with children and young people across services: European models for practice, training and qualification', Unpublished paper, London: Thomas Coram Research Unit, Institute of Education, University of London.

Petrie, P., Boddy, J., Cameron, C., Wigfall, V. and Simon, A. (2006) *Working with children in care: European perspectives*, Maidenhead: Open University Press.

Petrie, P., Boddy, J., Cameron, C., Heptinstall, E., McQuail, S., Simon, A. and Wigfall, V. (2008) *Pedagogy – a holistic, personal approach to work with children and young people, across services: European models for practice, training, education and qualification*, London: Thomas Coram Research Unit, Institute of Education, University of London Briefing Paper, Update 2008.

Phelan, J. (1990) 'Child care supervision: the neglected skill of evaluation', in J.P. Anglin, C.J. Denholm, R.V. Ferguson and A.R. Pence (eds) *Perspectives in professional child and youth care*, New York: Haworth.

Phelan, J. (1999) 'Experiments with experience', *Journal of Child and Youth Care Work*, vol 14, pp 25-8.

Phelan, J. (2001a) 'Another look at activities', *Journal of Child and Youth Care*, vol 14, no 2, pp 1-7.

Phelan, J. (2001b) 'Experiential counselling and the CYC practitioner', *Journal of Child and Youth Care Work*, vols 15 and 16, special edition, pp 256-63.

Phelan, J. (2001c) 'Notes on using plain language in child and youth care work' (www.cyc-net.org/cyc-online/cycol-1101-phelan.html, accessed 1 September 2008).

Phelan, J. (2006) 'Articulating treatment dynamics in residential care', *Relational Child and Youth Care Practice*, vol 19, no 4, pp 27-31.

Piaget, J. (1971) *The child's conception of the world*, London: Routledge and Kegan Paul.

Piper, H. and Smith, H. (2003) '"Touch" in educational and child care settings: dilemmas and responses', *British Educational Research Journal*, vol 29, no 6, pp 879–94.

Piper, H., Powell, J. and Smith, H. (2006) 'Parents, professionals and paranoia: the touching of children in a culture of fear', *Journal of Social Work*, vol 6, no 2, pp 151–67.

Pitts, J. (2001) 'Youth justice', *Community Care Research Matters*, vol 11, pp 38–42.

Pitts, J. (2005) 'The dismal fate of the secure estate', in D. Crimmens and I. Milligan (eds) *Facing forward: Residential child care in the 21st century*, Lyme Regis: Russell House, pp 186–97.

Pollitt, C. (1990) *Managerialism and the public services*, Oxford: Blackwell.

Polsky, H.W. (1962) *Cottage six*, New York: Russell Sage Foundation.

Ramsden, I. (1997) 'Cultural safety: implementing the concept. The social force of nursing and midwifery', in P. Te Whaiti, M. McCarthy and A. Durie (eds) *Mai I Rangiatea: Maori wellbeing and development*, Auckland: Auckland University Press, pp 113–25.

Rayner, E. (1978) *Human development: An introduction to the psychodynamics of growth, maturity and ageing*, London: Allen & Unwin.

Redl, F. and Wineman, D. (1951) *Children who hate*, Glencoe, IL: The Free Press.

Redl, F. and Wineman, D. (1957) *Controls from within: Techniques for treatment of the aggressive child*, New York: Free Press.

Ricks, F. (1992) 'A feminist's view of caring', *Journal of Child and Youth Care*, vol 7, no 2, pp 49–57 (available at www.cyc-net.org/features/ft-ricks-fem.html, accessed 21 September 2008).

Ricks, F. (2001) 'Without the self there is no other', *cyc-online*, issue 27, April (www.cyc-net.org/cyc-online/cycol-0401-ricks.html, accessed 21 November 2008).

Ricks, F. and Bellefeuille, G. (2003) 'Knowing: the critical error of ethics in family work', in T. Garfat (ed) *A child and youth care approach to working with families*, New York: The Haworth Press Inc.

Ricks, F., Charlesworth, J., Bellefeuille, G. and Field, A. (1999) *All together now: Creating a social capital mosaic*, Ontario: Vanier Institute of the Family.

Rowe, J. and Lambert, L. (1973) *Children who wait: A study of children needing substitute families*, London: British Association for Adoption and Fostering.

Ruch, G. (2005) 'Relationship-based practice and reflective practice: holistic approaches to contemporary child care social work', *Child and Family Social Work*, vol 10, pp 111–23.

Sachs, J. (2003) 'Teacher activism: mobilising the profession', Plenary Address to British Educational Research Association Conference, Heriot Watt University, Edinburgh, September.

Sachs, J. and Mellor, L. (2005) 'Risk anxiety, child panic and child protection: a critical examination of policies from Queensland and New South Wales', *Journal of Education Policy*, vol 20, no 2, pp 131-46.

Saleebey, D. (ed) (1997) *The strengths perspective in social work practice* (2nd edn), New York: Longman.

Scott, K. (1999) 'Connecting kids with their world', *Child & Youth Care*, vol 17, no 2, pp 3-4.

Scottish Executive (2005a) Letter from Peter Peacock, Minister for Children and Young People, to Michael McMahon MSP, 25 August.

Scottish Executive (2005b) *Getting It Right For Every Child: Proposals For Action*, Edinburgh: Scottish Executive.

Scottish Executive (2006) *Changing lives: 21st century social work review*, Edinburgh: Scottish Executive.

Scottish Government (2007a) *Looked After Children and Young People: We Can and Must Do Better* (www.scotland.gov.uk/Publications/2007/01/15084446/0, accessed 20 February 2008).

Scottish Government (2007b) *The Crerar Review: The Report of the Independent Review of Regulation, Audit, Inspection and Complaints Handling of Public Services in Scotland* (www.scotland.gov.uk/Publications/2007/09/25120506/0, accessed 2 October 2008).

Scottish Office (1992) *Another Kind of Home: A Review of Residential Child Care,* (The Skinner Report) Edinburgh: HMSO.

Scourfield, P. (2007) 'Are there reasons to be worried about the "cartelisation" of residential care?', *Critical Social Policy*, vol 27, no 2, pp 155-81.

Search Institute (1997, 2007) '40 developmental assets for adolescents (ages 12-18)' (www.search-institute.org/content/40-developmental-assets-adolescents-ages-12-18, accessed 1 September 2008).

Seed, P. (1974) 'Should any child be placed in care? The forgotten great debate 1841–74', *British Journal of Social Work*, vol 3, no 3, pp 321-30.

Sen, R., Kendrick, A., Milligan, I. and Hawthorn, M. (2007) 'Historical abuse in residential child care in Scotland 1950–1995: A literature review', in T. Shaw, *Historical abuse systemic review*, Edinburgh: Scottish Government, App 2.

Sevenhuijsen, S. (1998) *Citizenship and the ethics of care. Feminist considerations on justice, morality and politics*, Abingdon: Routledge.

Sewpal, V. (2005) 'Global standards: promise and pitfalls for re-inscribing social work into civil society', *International Journal of Social Welfare*, vol 14, pp 210-17.

Shaw, T. (2007) *Historical abuse systemic review: Residential schools and children's homes in Scotland 1950 to 1995*, Edinburgh: Scottish Government (www.scotland.gov.uk/Publications/2007/11/20104729/0, accessed 21 February 2008).

Short Report (1984) *Second Report from the Social Services Committee: Children in Care*, vol 1, London: HMSO.

Singh, S. (2005) 'Thinking beyond "diversity": Black and minority ethnic children in Scotland', in D. Crimmens and I. Milligan (eds) *Facing forward: Residential child care in the 21st century*, Lyme Regis: Russell House, pp 45-56.

Skinner, A. (1992) *Another kind of home: A review of residential child care*, Edinburgh: The Scottish Office.

Skinner, B.F. (1938) *The behavior of organisms: An experimental analysis*, Upper Saddle River, NJ: Prentice Hall.

Smart, M. (2006) 'Making more sense of transitions', *Relational Child and Youth Care Practice*, vol 19, no 4, pp 33-43.

Smith, M. (2003a) 'Towards a professional identity: is residential child care still social work?', *Journal of Social Work*, vol 3, no 2, pp 235-52.

Smith, M. (2003b) 'Boys to men: exploring masculinity in child and youth care', *Relational Child and Youth Care Practice*, vol 16, no 4, pp 12-21.

Smith, M. (2005a) 'Rethinking residential child care: a child and youth care approach', in D. Crimmens and I. Milligan (eds) *Facing forward: Residential child care in the 21st century*, Lyme Regis: Russell House, pp 115-26.

Smith, M. (2005b) 'Applying ideas from learning and teaching in higher education to develop professional identity: the case of the MSc in Advanced Residential Child Care', *Child and Youth Care Forum*, vol 34, no 4, pp 261-76.

Smith, M. with Forrest, B., Garland, P. and Hunter, L. (2005) *Secure in the knowledge: Perspectives on practice in secure accommodation*, Glasgow: Scottish Institute for Residential Child Care.

Smith, M. (2008) 'Historical abuse in residential child care: an alternative view', *Practice*, vol 20, no 1, pp 29-41.

Smith, M. and Milligan, I. (2005) 'The expansion of secure care places in Scotland: in the best interests of the child?', *Youth Justice*, vol 4, no 3, pp 178-91.

Smith, M. and Whyte, B. (2008) 'Social education and social pedagogy: reclaiming a Scottish tradition in social work', *European Journal of Social Work*, vol 11, no 1, pp 15-28.

Smith, M., McKay, E. and Chakrabarti, M. (2004) 'What works for us – boys' views of their experience in a former List D school', *British Journal of Special Education*, vol 31, no 2, pp 89-93.

Spalek, B. (2006) *Crime victims: Theory, policy and practice*, Basingstoke: Palgrave Macmillan.

Statham, J. and Mooney, A. (2006) 'Location, location, location: the importance of place in care work with children', in J. Boddy, C. Cameron and P. Moss (eds) *Care work: Present and future*, Abingdon: Routledge.

Steckley, L. (2005a) 'Just a game? The therapeutic potential of football', in D. Crimmens and I. Milligan (eds) *Facing forward: Residential child care in the 21st century*, Lyme Regis: Russell House, pp 137-48.

Steckley, L. (2005b) 'Activities', in M. Smith (ed) *Secure in the knowledge: Perspectives on practice in secure accommodation*, Glasgow: Scottish Institute for Residential Child Care, ch 4.08.

Steckley, L. and Kendrick, A. (2007) 'Young people's experiences of physical restraint in residential care: subtlety and complexity in policy and practice', in M. Nunno, L. Bullard and D.M. Day (eds) *For our own safety: Examining the safety of high-risk interventions for children and young people*, Washington, DC: Child Welfare League of America.

Steckley, L. and Kendrick, A. (forthcoming) 'Physical restraint in residential child care: the experiences of young people and residential workers', *Childhood* (accepted for publication).

Stein, M. (2006) 'Missing years of abuse in children's homes', *Child and Family Social Work*, vol 11, no 1, pp 11-21.

Stevens, I. (2004) 'Cognitive-behavioural interventions for adolescents in residential child care in Scotland: an examination of practice and lessons from research', *Child and Family Social Work*, vol 9, no 3, pp 237-46.

Stewart, G. and Tutt, N. (1987) *Children in custody*, Aldershot: Avebury.

Summit, R. (1983) 'The child abuse accommodation syndrome', *Child Abuse & Neglect*, vol 7, pp 177-93.

Taylor, C. and White, S. (2006) 'Knowledge and reasoning in social work: educating for humane judgement', *British Journal of Social Work*, vol 36, no 6, pp 937-54.

Taylor, L. (2005) 'Theoretical perspectives', in M. Smith (ed) *Secure in the knowledge: Perspectives on practice in secure accommodation*, Glasgow: Scottish Institute of Residential Child Care, ch 3.

Thomas, N. (2005) *Social work with young people in care*, Basingstoke: Macmillan.

Trieschman, A., Whittaker, J.K. and Brendtro, L.K. (1969) *The other 23 hours: Child-care work with emotionally disturbed children in a therapeutic milieu*, New York: Aldine De Gruiter.

Triseliotis, J. (1988) 'Residential care from a historical perspective', in J.E. Wilkinson and G. O'Hara (eds) *Our children: Residential and community care*, London: National Children's Bureau.

Tronto, J. (1994) *Moral boundaries: A political argument for an ethic of care*, New York: Routledge, Chapman and Hall Inc.

Trotter, C. (1999) *Working with involuntary clients: A guide to practice*, London: Sage Publications.

UNICEF (2007) *The state of the world's children* (www.unicef.org/sowc07, accessed 20 February 2008).

Utting, W. (1991) *Children in the public care: A review of residential child care*, London: HMSO.

Utting, W. (1997) *People like us: The report of the review of the safeguards for children living away from home*, London: The Stationery Office.

van Beinum, M., Martin, A. and Bonnett, C. (2002) 'Catching children as they fall: mental health promotion in residential child care in East Dunbartonshire', *Scottish Journal of Residential Child Care*, vol 1, no 1, pp 14–22.

Vander Ven, K. (1985) 'Activity programming: its developmental and therapeutic role in group care', in L.C. Fulcher and F. Ainsworth (eds) *Group care practice with children*, London: Tavistock, pp 155–86.

Visser, J.G. (2002) 'Eternal verities: the strongest links', *Emotional and Behavioural Difficulties*, vol 7, no 2, pp 68–84.

Vorrath, H.H. and Brendtro, L.K. (2000) *Positive peer culture*, New York: Aldine de Gruyter.

Vygotsky, L.S. (1962) *Thought and language*, Cambridge, MA: The MIT Press.

Wade, J. (2008) 'The ties that bind: support from birth families and substitute families for young people leaving care', *British Journal of Social Work*, vol 38, no 1, pp 39–54.

Wagner, G. (1988) *Residential care: A positive choice: Report of the Independent Review of Residential Care*, London: HMSO/National Institute for Social Work.

Walker, M., Barclay, A., Hunter, L., Kendrick, A., Malloch, M., Hill, M. and McIvor, G. (2006) *Secure accommodation in Scotland: Its role and relationship with 'alternative services'* (www.scottishexecutive.gov.uk/Publications/2006/09/01153312/0, accessed 21 February 2008).

Ward, A. (1993) *Working in group care: Social work in residential and day care settings*, Birmingham: Venture Press.

Ward, A. (2000) 'Opportunity led work', Paper given to Scottish Institute of Residential Child Care Conference, Glasgow, 28 September.

Ward, A. (2006) 'Towards a theory of the everyday: the ordinary and the special in daily living in residential care: international perspectives on rethinking residential care', *Child and Youth Care Forum*, vol 33, no 3, pp 209-25.

Warner, N. (1992) *Choosing with care: Report of the Committee of Inquiry into the Selection, Development and Management of Staff in Children's Homes*, London: HMSO.

Waterhouse, R. (2000) *Report of the Tribunal of Inquiry into the Abuse of Children in Care in the Former County Council Areas of Gwynedd and Clwyd since 1974: Lost in care*, London: The Stationery Office.

Webb, S. (2006) *Social work in a risk society: Social and political perspectives*, Basingstoke: Palgrave.

Webster, R. (1994) *The politics of the body and the body politic* (www.richardwebster.net/thepoliticsofthebody.html, accessed 21 August 2008).

Webster, R. (2005) *The secret of Bryn Estyn*, Oxford: Orwell Press.

Whitaker, J. (1981) 'Major approaches to residential treatment', in F. Ainsworth and L.C. Fulcher (eds) *Group care for children: Concept and issues*, London: Tavistock, pp 89-127.

White, K. (2008) *The growth of love: Understanding the five essential elements of child development*, Wiltshire: Barnabas.

Wilkinson, R.G. and Pickett, K.E. (2007) 'The problems of relative deprivation: why some societies do better than others?', *Social Science and Medicine*, vol 65, pp 1965-78.

Wilks, T. (2005) 'Social work and narrative ethics', *British Journal of Social Work*, vol 35, pp 1249-64.

Winnicott, D.W. (1971) *Playing and reality*, Routledge: London.

Young, C. (2001) 'Where the boys are', *cyc-net*, 21 February (www.cyc-net.org/today2001/today010221.html, accessed 18 July 2008).

Index

P

parenthood after care 140
parenting 171
  see also corporate parenting
Parton, N. 4, 10-11, 13, 50, 59, 103, 107, 136, 168
Payne, C. 29, 98
peer group 89-90
People like us (Utting) 10, 40, 42, 58
permanency movement 28
permanency theory 28, 29
personal–professional relationship 119-21
  boundary management 133-5
  building through activities 116
  in care settings 121-2
  complexity 136
  contact boundary 122, 123, 135
  love 123-5
  power 96-7
  restraint 128-33
  sexuality 125-6
  in social pedagogy 155
  staff qualities 122-3
  touch 127-8
personal safety, staff concerns 47-8
Petrie, P. 65, 70, 107, 112, 152-3, 158, 171, 175
Phelan, J. 70, 85, 93, 115, 116, 117, 120, 170, 171
Philanthropic Society 22
physical abuse 40
  see also child abuse
physical activity 116-17
physical environment 97-102
  activity 99
  developmental interaction 101-2
  rhythm 99-101
  rituals 101
  space, use of 98
  time, use of 98-9
physical restraint 37, 48, 128-33
Piaget, J. 75
Pickett, K.E. 65
Pindown Inquiry 39
Pindown regime 39, 48, 69, 166-7
Piper, H. 128, 133, 134

Pithers, D. 45
Pitts, J. 56, 91, 114
placement 53-4
  family placement 27-8, 29
  foster care 27-8, 46-7, 54, 154, 155
  residential care as positive choice 39, 46, 103, 154, 155
placement plans 112
play 115
play fighting 128
policy directions
  achievement of children in care 59
  care standards 58-9
  outcomes focus 63-4
  Quality Protects initiative 58
  universal policy framework 59
Pollitt, C. 7
Poor Laws 20-2
positive choice of residential care 39, 46, 103, 154, 155
A positive choice (Wagner) 39
post-modernity 4
Pound, John 22
poverty 7, 13, 20-1, 64-6
pre-Reformation church 20
privacy 37
private space 98
problem families 13, 29
professional activism 174-5
professional–personal relationship
  see personal–professional relationship
professional qualifications 47, 157, 160
  BA in Curative Education (BACE) 162-3
  Certificate of Social Service (CSS) 30
professionalisation 29, 136, 158
  child and youth care 26-7, 160-1
professionalism 7, 28, 29, 136
programme abuse 35
programmes 113-14, 118
protectionism 15, 32, 167
  see also child protection
psycho-social development 75-6
psychodynamic theory 71-2

Y

young offenders institutions (YOIs)
57
youth crime 57

Z

zone of proximal development
(ZPD) 81